Budgeting à la Carte

Budgeting à la Carte

Essential Tools for Harried Business Managers

John A. Tracy, Ph.D., CPA

Author of the national bestseller
How to Read a Financial Report, Fourth Edition

JOHN WILEY & SONS, INC.
New York • Chichester • Brisbane • Toronto • Singapore

Library of Congress Cataloging-in-the Publication Data:

Tracy, John A.
    Budgeting à la carte : essential tools for harried
business managers / John A. Tracy.
    p.   cm.
    Includes index.
    ISBN 0-471-10929-0 (cloth : alk. paper).—ISBN 0-471-10928-2
(pbk. : alk. paper)
    1. Budget in business.   2. Corporations—Finance.   I. Title.
HG4028.B8T73   1996
658.15′4—dc20   96-22265

Printed in the United States of America

10 9 8 7 6 5 4 3 2 1

For my two sons,

John and Tage,

and my three daughters,

Mary, Chris, and Jackie

PREFACE

To be honest, I nearly abandoned this book idea. John Wiley & Sons asked me some time ago to do a book on budgeting, and in a weak moment I agreed. Then I had serious second thoughts. Why write another book on budgeting when there are already many budgeting books on the market? Could I really offer anything new and different? Could I build a better mousetrap?

Then there was a change of editors at Wiley. I met with Myles Thompson, my new executive editor. Lee Thompson, vice president of marketing, also attended the meeting. For our meeting I prepared a sample chapter, which evolved into what is now Chapter 1, "So, Why Budget?"

In thinking about this chapter I came to see that other budgeting books take the "whole nine yards approach." They treat budgeting as a *system*. Their premise is that you have to buy the whole system, not just parts of it. Of course, many business organizations have adopted a budgeting system. They have put into place comprehensive and formal policies and procedures for management planning, authorization, and control. But budgeting does not have to be bought as a system, or as a whole meal from appetizers through dessert. From this book's title, you can plainly see that I take a different approach. Like walking through a cafeteria line, business managers should select only what they really need and can put to their best use.

At our meeting I presented the sample chapter for my new executive editor and the marketing vice president. They liked it. The more we talked, the more enthused I got about doing the book. Also, I got a real bonus in the deal. Bari Zahn, Esq., became my editor and worked closely with me in developing the book. The book is immensely better for her keen insights and suggestions. She's one hell of a line editor; no sloppy sentences get by her beady eyes.

Budgeting à la Carte is written mainly for business managers. Other business professionals may find much useful information in the book—especially how a business makes profit, what determines cash flow from profit, and the capital needed to support profit-making operations. In it I break down budgeting into its separate parts and different analysis tools. Although short, this book includes quite a few chapters. I chose this format to keep the explanation of each topic brief and to the point, so you can learn quickly what advantages it offers and how to use it.

This book explains the purposes, advantages, essential steps, and analysis tools of budgeting for businesses in all stages of their life cycles. However, I do not discuss implementation practices and issues, such as the Budget Director's role, the budget calendar, and the communication problems of budgeting in larger organizations.

Budgeting à la Carte will help managers in accomplishing the three financial objectives of every business:

- To make profit
- To plan and control the capital invested in net operating assets needed for making profit
- To generate cash flow from profit

For each of these three business financial imperatives there is a corresponding financial statement: the profit report (Income Statement); the financial condition report (Balance Sheet); and the cash flow report (Cash Flow Statement). These three financial statements form the essential framework of budgeting. You can't get too far into explaining budgeting without demonstrating what you mean with financial statements.

Early in this book I review these three primary financial statements from the *manager's* point of view, in contrast to external financial reporting. External financial statements are prepared in accordance with generally accepted accounting principles (GAAP), which in actual practice have become minimum accounting and disclosure standards that very few external financial reports go beyond. For decision making and control, managers need more information than what is found in external financial statements. In fact, much management information is very confidential and would never be included in an external financial report open to public view.

Budgeting is an integrative process; different pieces of the financial puzzle have to be fitted together. Of particular importance are the relative sizes between revenue and expenses of a business and the operating assets and liabilities needed to carry on its profit-making operations. For instance, if annual sales revenue is $10 million how much should accounts receivable be? *Operating ratios* are the measures of these interconnections between the assets and liabilities reported in the balance sheet and the revenue and expenses reported in the income statement. The balance sheet and income statement are fitted together tongue-in-groove with operating ratios. Operating ratios are the absolute starting point for budgeting. Hence, this book discusses operating ratios in some detail—an essential topic that is not explained in other budgeting books.

Budgeting à la Carte then moves through additional budgeting topics and tools of analysis. The chapters rest on a decision-making foundation. The focus never strays from the key profit and cash flow factors that managers must make decisions about and must control. The final two chapters deal with capital investment analysis and shy away from the wrong-headed mathematical and equation-ladened approach of other books.

Again, I thank Myles and Lee for their encouragement and ideas. I'm especially indebted to Bari for her excellent editing on the book. Last, I would like to remember my father who died more than a decade ago. He never finished high school during the Depression, but he ran a business for many years. He taught me much about business. He was looking over my shoulder while I was writing this book.

JOHN A. TRACY

Boulder, Colorado
June 1996

CONTENTS

Budgeting à la Carte

1

SO, WHY BUDGET?

To the Busy Business Manager

The last thing you need is a sermon on budgeting, so I'll skip the usual exhortations about the purposes and advantages of budgeting. And I won't treat you as a sinner if you don't do any budgeting. You may have the right approach to budgeting already. Then again, you may not. Which is what this book is all about.

Chapter 1 presents an overview of budgeting for the busy business manager. I will not try to sell you on the idea of budgeting as a system. Not every business needs a complete, full-blown, formal budget system typical in the large business organization.

Even a large corporation should be frugal in doing budgeting. The budget should be budgeted. Any budget system worth its name should be put to a ruthless cost-versus-benefits test. The large corporation may do too much budgeting–going through rituals that have little management value. Other businesses may do too little budgeting and fail to take advantage of one or more budgeting techniques that would have a high payoff.

I know your time is scarce. But I also know that you want to keep your business profitable and solvent. The key question facing the busy business manager is how much budgeting to do—to identify and make efficient use of those particular techniques that can improve profit, cash flow, and financial condition.

The System Versus the Parts

Most books and articles discuss budgeting as a system. The presumption is that you have to adopt and implement a whole budgeting system or none at all. However, this is nonsense. You shouldn't look at budgeting as a monolithic system that you have to buy into on an all-or-nothing basis. The word *budgeting* is an umbrella term covering a diversity of separate elements and distinct techniques. A business has to be fairly large—I'd guess perhaps $100 million or so in annual sales revenue—to justify the cost of implementing budgeting as a truly comprehensive and coordinated system throughout the organization.

In the smaller business the owner-manager is the "system." The owner-manager doesn't have to put all the budgeting pieces together into a system. Even in fairly large organizations, it may be best to focus on the pieces of budgeting rather than looking at budgeting as a system.

So, let's think of budgeting as a toolbox—one stocked with a wide variety of tools. Few of us use all the tools a professional mechanic needs, but we often use screwdrivers, pliers, hammers, and wrenches. Business managers may think they don't have the time or can't afford to use any budgeting tools, but some tools in the budgeting cabinet can be very helpful and well worth the cost. For example, using just one or two budgeting tools may have a high payoff to the small business, even if it does not have a budget system.

To sum up: I am not advocating a seven-course dinner budgeting system. Rather, I am offering budgeting à la carte, in which you, the busy business manager, can select from the items offered to suit your particular business situation, in an effort to protect and improve financial performance and position.

Business Budgeting Versus Individual and Government Budgeting

Please don't confuse *business* budgeting with the budgeting done by individuals and households or with the budgeting done by government. Budgeting by individuals, households, and by government agencies is driven primarily by the need to allocate scarce resources among excessive demands and to stay within these allocated amounts once the budget is adopted.

Given their limited incomes and existing debts, individuals find it helpful to rank order and prioritize their needs and preferences. Some items may have to be removed from their shopping list. Budgeting also draws attention to the cost of each item, which may lead to cost-saving tactics.

Cost savings are as good as additional income, even better as a matter of fact. Cost savings are not taxable to individuals, whereas additional income is taxable. Three dollars of cost savings provide three additional dollars of spending power. On the other hand, receiving three dollars of additional income generally increases taxable income by the same amount, thus generating about one dollar of additional income tax and leaving only two dollars for additional spending. (A technical note: this assumes the costs savings are in nondeductible expenditures.)

Governments, from the federal level to the local school district, have only so much revenue available, and they have to make difficult choices regarding how to spend their limited tax revenue. In fact, formal budgeting is legally required for almost all government entities. Furthermore, once money is appropriated and the budgets are adopted the budget imposes rather strict spending limits.

Certainly there are some common features between business budgeting and budgeting by individuals and governments, but the differences are more important. A business doesn't have limited or constrained revenue as such; its revenue depends on making sales.

The allocation of scarce resources is not the main driving force behind business budgeting. Sales revenue brings with it certain costs and expenses necessary to generate the sales revenue. The goal in business is to make the "optimal matchup" of its revenue on the one side with its costs and expenses on the other side. This does not necessarily mean minimizing expenses.

Budgeting for Better Management or for Better Profit?

The dominant and overriding purpose of budgeting is to protect and improve financial performance and position. Financial performance means both the *profit* earned by the business and the *cash flow* of the business. Financial position refers to the efficient use of *capital* by the business (found on the asset side of its balance sheet) and the *liquidity* and *solvency* of the business, which means its ability to meet the obligations found on the other side of its balance sheet (in the several liability and owners' equity accounts).

I want to make this very clear at the start because, surprisingly, the large majority of discussions on budgeting do not stress the bottom line or financial purposes of budgeting. Instead emphasis is placed on the "best management practices" reasons for budgeting. The underlying theme is, "you want to be a good manager, don't you?"

Of course good management should lead to good profit, good cash flow, and a good financial condition. Who could argue with this? But more to the point, I assume that as a business manager your eye never strays very far from the financial bottom lines of the business—profit, cash flow, and financial condition. So I approach budgeting from this viewpoint.

Budgeting Up Close

Budgeting consists of separate elements, procedures, techniques, and purposes. Each has its own management function and value. In this section we take a brief look at each of these budgeting "pieces." The more comprehensive the budget and the larger the business organization, the more critical it is to put the budgeting pieces together into an integrated and coordinated system. On the other hand, any business can profitably use just one or two of the pieces without using the entire system.

Accounting Reports to Managers

The typical accounting system is designed mainly with two things in mind: (1) the preparation of tax returns and (2) the preparation of the financial statements included in the external financial reports of the business. Budgeting puts additional demands on the typical accounting system. The company's accounting system may have to be modified to improve the format and content of accounting reports to managers.

Accounting reports to managers should *not* be facsimiles of the company's external financial statements. True, management accounting reports contain more detail about the expenses of the business not reported in the external financial statements (income statement). But otherwise the classification of expenses tends to be the same. This won't do for budgeting.

External financial reports go to the creditors and outside investors in the business. Managers should understand them, of course. Managers are responsible for their financial statements and the other disclosures in the external financial reports. But external financial reports are not adequate for management use. One demand of budgeting is that the internal accounting reports be reexamined and redesigned for better management analysis.

Vision, Strategy, and Goals

It is surprising how many businesses—and I'm sure your business is the exception of course—suffer from not having a clear mission statement or a clearly stated strategy and do not have definite and explicit goals to serve as benchmarks to measure achievement and progress toward their objectives. The business manager may have all this information in his or her mind, but it may not be made explicit or written down.

The foundation of budgeting is the articulation of the fundamental concept and "story" of the business, including its general strategy for success and the quantification of its goals in observable numbers. This provides the basic anchoring for the budgeting process and for the comparison of actual outcomes against the budgeted objectives.

Planning

Planning means getting down to brass tacks—putting together an action plan on paper that spells out in detail how objectives and goals will be achieved, when things will be done, who will do them, what products will produce how much profit, how much cash flow will be generated from profit, how present problems will be corrected and not repeated in the future, and so on.

In the minds of many, budgeting is almost synonymous with planning. Planning, however, refers more specifically to following through on all the details that have to be incorporated in the budget once the basic vision, strategy, and goals have been adopted.

The busy manager may not take the time to do enough planning. However, budgeting is a strong incentive to set aside enough time to prepare a plan in sufficient detail to serve as a good road map for the business.

Change Analysis

All business managers should take time to focus on changes that will affect the business—to anticipate changes in time to prepare for them, rather than waiting for the changes to happen. One element of budgeting is to examine and analyze what will happen to the business as a result of such anticipated changes and to think out how the business plans to handle the changes.

Business managers are aware of the multitude of changes buffeting the business this way and that. It's one thing to be generally aware of changes; it's quite another matter to analyze in sufficient detail the effects that will be caused by the changes. Budgeting, from this viewpoint, is the technique to analyze the effects of changes and how to deal with them.

Forecasting

Forecasting may be used in planning and change analysis, but technically it is a separate activity. Forecasting uses certain "scientific" tools and techniques, such as statistical trend analysis and business cycle analysis. Many larger businesses make use of very sophisticated econometric models of the entire economy and the major segments of the economy having the most impact on their markets.

Inflation rates, unemployment rates, the prime interest rate, and hundreds or thousands of other economic variables are thrown into the computer model. The primary purpose is to take output from the forecast model to determine the impact on demand for the company's products, its costs of operations, and its other business variables.

Forecasting can be very expensive. Designing, developing, and constantly updating a large-scale, computer-based forecasting model is quite expensive. Even some very large corporations do not do all their own forecasting in-house. They buy the forecasts and analysis reports from economic consultants and universities. On the other hand, much forecasting type information and many opinions are found "free" in the financial press in articles and editorials that project the broad trends in the economy. Trade associations also publish more specific types of forecast information that even small businesses may find useful.

Modeling Profit, Cash Flow, and Financial Condition

To do budgeting you need a fairly good analytical grip on the business. In other words, a good budget is based on a good analytical model or set of financial specifications of the business. The model should capture the causes and effects of profit, cash flow, and financial condition of the business.

The basic factors that propel profit, that drive cash flow, and that determine financial condition should be connected with one another. The relationships among the key factors need to be identified and put into definite measures called *operating ratios*. This sort of financial model of the business is a very useful management analysis tool.

Motivation of Managers and Employees

Although there is no small amount of debate and disagreement on this point, the consensus is that budgets have a good motivational impact on employees and managers and serve as strong incentives to managers to strive for and achieve the goals and objectives of the business. The main point is that budgets can both reward good results and punish bad results.

One key assumption behind this line of reasoning is that the budgeting process is done well, which usually means there is a fair amount of participation by everyone who is accountable under the budget and that the goals of the budget are realistic without being too easy. The behavioral premise is that managers need to know the game plan of the business to know what's expected of them, and they need clear-cut feedback regarding whether they are performing at satisfactory levels.

Business Plan

To raise capital the new or emerging business usually has to put together a convincing business plan. Since these businesses have little or no history, the business plan must show that the manager(s) have thought out all major aspects of the business with a clear strategy—including marketing its products, manufacturing or purchasing its products, the labor force of the business, and the competition. It must be a persuasive document to convince bankers to make loans and venture capital firms to invest in the business.

One essential component of the business plan is the pro forma financial statements of the business for the next year and beyond. These projected financials must be as convincing as the marketing plan. Raising too little capital to survive and to grow is one of the chief reasons the majority of start-up businesses fail. There are many reasons for the failure of start-up business ventures, but the lack of adequate capital planning is always in the top five or ten reasons.

The tools and procedures of budgeting are very helpful for putting together sound and realistic financial statements for business plans. In fact, if the start-up business makes clear in its business plan that it has used budgeting procedures this in itself probably will add credibility to the plan.

Cost and Expense Control

One element of budgeting has been deliberately delayed to this point in the discussion. The reason may be obvious, but maybe not. Keep in mind that this book is directed to business budgeting, not individual or government budgeting. Individuals and governments use budgets for cost control, because their primary purpose for budgeting is the allocation of limited revenue. The allocated amounts for each item become spending limits.

The financial goal of business, on the other hand, is not primarily to keep its expenses and costs within preset limits but rather to optimize its profit performance, which depends on *profit margins*. The best profit margin is not necessarily the situation with the lowest cost and expense. Profit margin is the spread between sales price less cost and expenses. A better profit margin may require a higher level of costs and expenses that is offset by an even higher sales price.

On the other hand, certain costs and expenses of a business are not directly in the profit margin equation. These are called *fixed* costs and expenses. Establishing control limits for these may not be a bad idea. If a budgeted control limit is hit, the preset amount acts like a circuit breaker that prevents any further expenditure until management reviews the situation and authorizes an additional amount.

Communication

Budgets are generally touted as a good means of communication of the goals and expectations of the business organization. It's not always clear what exactly the term *communication* really means, however. Once adopted, a budget certainly must be made clear to all those responsible for meeting the goals and objectives of the budget. The budget could hardly be kept a secret.

Often the implication is that the budgeting process improves the communication throughout the different units, departments, locations, and divisions of the organization. Keep in mind that business organizations make use of many means of communication. The budget is just one of many means. The communication reasons for budgeting depend very much on the size and culture of the business organization. The very small business probably would not use budgeting for communication purposes.

Performance Evaluation

The functions and roles of business executives and managers are defined and redefined endlessly—as leaders, motivators, innovators, change agents, peak coordinators, problem solvers, consensus builders, negotiators, conflict resolvers, and so on. Clearly business executives and managers perform many different functions. Personally I have observed that one key function of business managers gets second billing. Managers are *performance evaluators*.

Managers, among their wide variety of functions, have to take a hard look at what's going on and ask: How are we doing? Should we be doing better? Managers are professional evaluators, as it were. I suspect the reason this dimension of management gets short shrift is that it sounds negative and fault finding.

In developing objectives, goals, and targets, budgeting should help the performance evaluation function. Budgets lay out standards of performance in advance. The persons being evaluated should feel that they are being evaluated more fairly and not at the whims of higher level managers.

Compensation of Managers

Setting salaries for managers and deciding on incentive-based management compensation arrangements are no easy matters. Budgeting provides objective goals and standards of performance on which to base bonuses and salary increases. Many large and midcap corporations use a "make or beat the budget" approach for compensating managers.

For the small business, budgets can help the owner-manager decide on his or her salary takeout from the business, as well as the salaries of other key managers. The profit plan (budget) for the year can be used to award year-end bonuses according to whether designated goals are achieved.

Problem Identification and Solving

In setting financial goals—the key step in budgeting—managers often discover that the business should be doing better. Budgeting helps the manager identify problems that may otherwise go overlooked. Budgeting takes a hard look at the present level of performance and the present position of the business and asks: Is this good enough?

Nothing focuses attention on an issue so much as having to put a number on it. Take dieting. Are you overweight? Putting a number on what you should weigh is more likely to force you to go on a diet. Although certainly not the whole enchilada, it is important to manage a business by the numbers. Budgeting is clearly a big help in this regard. Budgeting is a tonic against creeping complacency with the present performance and position of the business.

Looking at Your Future Financial Statements

The business manager may find one aspect of budgeting rather intriguing and that is to look at your *future* financial statements today. The projected financial statements of the business for next year are the centerpiece of the budgeting process. There is a lot of value in looking ahead to where you are likely to be a year from now.

In this regard, business budgeting is like following out a savings/investment plan into the future to see if you will have enough money to send your children to college or to retire. Budgeting plots the financial trajectory of the business and takes a look at the future landing site, which might not look all that good or might be a pleasant surprise. But you don't know until you do it.

Costs and Pitfalls of Budgeting

Budgeting does not always go smoothly and in fact can lead to counterproductive results. And then there are the costs of budgeting.

I should mention as an aside that "no budgeting" doesn't necessarily mean no control. By management control, I don't mean the preventive aspects of control. Rather, I mean achieving the financial goals and objectives of the business. The emphasis is on the positive of accomplishment, not the negative of cost and expense control. Budgeting is helpful but not essential for management control. Many businesses don't do any budgeting, yet they make a good profit and remain solvent and financially healthy.

They depend on management accounting reports that track their actual profit performance, financial position, and cash flow. But they have no explicit budget goals or standards against which to compare actual results. More than likely they use last year as the reference for comparison.

The larger the organization, the more likely you'll find a formal and comprehensive financial budgeting process in place. The budget provides the benchmarks for evaluating performance of managers at all levels. Actual is compared against budget and significant variances are highlighted, which are investigated and reported up the line. Managers are rewarded for meeting or exceeding the budget, and they are held accountable for unfavorable variances.

But even large corporations admit that budgeting has its down side. Budgeting is costly and may lead to a lot of game playing and dysfunctional behavior. Managers have been known to manipulate the budget or sometimes resort to out-and-out fraud, massaging the numbers and cooking the books to make their "actual" numbers look good relative to the budget.

The most important cost of budgeting is the time it takes the manager to do his or her part of the budgeting process, as well as the time of other managers. I needn't tell you that your time is a very scarce commodity. You only have so much time, energy, and attention, which must be carefully apportioned among many competing demands.

Some of the mechanical procedures of budgeting—assembling the budgeted financial statements for example—can be done by your accountant or an outside CPA. But, make no bones about it—budgeting takes time. So it makes sense to select just those budgeting techniques with the highest payoff.

This book is based on this premise. In other words, we do not explore budgeting as a big business organization system and all that would entail. Instead, focus on those specific budgeting techniques that, in my opinion, have the most value—the best return on your time investment. You can get a good idea of these techniques by referring to the Contents for the remainder of the book.

Where We're Headed

We focus on the following budgeting issues and financial analysis matters in the remainder of the book:

- *Modifying the internal management financial statements* to make them more useful for decision-making analysis, for budgeting, and for control. Your income statement probably is in most need of a makeover. It's probably too much like your external income statement instead of being a well-designed report for management use.
- *Rearranging your balance sheet* and to a lesser extent your cash flow statement. (You do get a regular cash flow accounting report, don't you?) By portraying a better analytical working model of your business, the reconstituted financial statements will help you understand your business better.
- Explaining and demonstrating the central and unifying importance of *operating ratios,* the backbone of budgeting. Operating ratios are the vital links of revenue and expenses with assets and liabilities. You may be surprised to learn that cash flow from profit depends very heavily on these operating ratios.

- Identifying and developing the *basic financial ratios* for evaluating the performance and position of business. These budgeting yardsticks and targets should be very clearly understood by managers. These are the key ratios applied to the business by banks, other sources of credit capital, and stockholders.
- Demonstrating how to put together the *capital needs budget* to support the growth of the business. Again, operating ratios play a key role in determining how much additional capital will be needed to grow the business.
- Analyzing the *key management variables* of the business, starting with sales volume changes, and then taking a close look at changes in sales prices and costs that change profit margins. Having a good budget or analytical financial model of the business is virtually indispensable for good management decision making.

Other topics that are discussed focus on specific issues and problems, such as sales mix analysis, manufacturing cost accounting, and budgeting the future cash returns needed on capital investments.

2

INTERNAL VERSUS EXTERNAL ACCOUNTING

Overview of Accounting Systems

This book is very financial statements-oriented. Why? Because financial statements are the source of information about the three primary financial imperatives of every business—profit, cash flow, and financial condition. Whether or not a business does budgeting, it prepares financial statements at the end of each period. Quite simply every business has to know how it's doing and where it stands financially. Financial statements are the source of this vital information.

Financial statements are no better than the accounting system from which they are prepared. If the accounting system of the business has errors, its financial statements will have errors. One reason for an audit by an outside CPA firm is to examine whether the accounting information and database of the business is complete, accurate, and up-to-date, which depends on the internal controls built into the accounting system.

Very often the auditor finds errors and unrecorded developments that require "adjusting" entries at year-end to correct the accounts for preparation of the financial statements. These adjusting entries may be evidence that the accounting system needs serious corrections and improvements.

Exhibit 2.1 presents an accounting system overview of the main functions of and user demands on the system. Some aspects may not be all that familiar, so the exhibit deserves your close study at this point.

Accounting systems are schizophrenic to some extent. The different demands on the system are not completely congruent and may pull in opposite directions. For example, on the one hand, managers may want to minimize taxable income but, on the other hand, they will also need to know "actual" or "true" profit for internal and external financial reports. Obviously, accountants have to wear different hats.

External Functions of Accounting

Let's begin with the two basic external functions of accounting. Accountants prepare the financial statements included in the business's external financial reports, and they also prepare its many different tax returns, in particular the business's federal income tax returns. See Exhibit 2.1.

Accountants have to stay abreast of changes in authoritative financial reporting standards and accounting pronouncements in order to prepare financial statements that conform with generally accepted accounting principles (GAAP)—the ground rules for financial reports. State and federal income taxes, payroll taxes, property taxes, and sales taxes are governed by exceedingly complex and constantly changing laws and rules. Accountants have their hands full just keeping up with tax regulations.

Accountants are the professional profit measurers of the business world. This is their speciality and their raison d'être. They are the profit referees in the game of business. We live in the age of experts and accountants are the experts in measuring profit. Of course, this is not their whole function, but it is at the center of what they do. Rightly or wrongly, managers may override how accountants prefer to measure profit; more on this later.

Allow me here to comment on one general misconception about profit accounting. Contrary to what seems to be a popular misconception, companies do *not* keep two sets of books. Profit is measured and recorded by one set of accounting methods, which are the same for both internal and external financial statements.

Managers may ask their accounting staff to prepare an analysis of what profit would be if alternative accounting methods had been used, such as a different inventory/cost of goods sold expense method or a different depreciation expense method. But only one set of numbers is recorded and booked. There is not a "true" or "real" or "better" profit figure secreted away someplace that only managers know.

Do you have at least a nodding acquaintance with financial statements as found in external financial reports? I assume so. Although there are many detail-level differences from company to company, the basic format and classification of these public view financial statements are very much the same from company to company.

Internal Functions of Accounting

Now we shift attention to the two basic internal functions of accounting. The accounting system is the source of data and information and documents for the enormous volume of daily-weekly-monthly operations of every business. This includes preparing payroll checks on time and collecting withholdings that have to be remitted over to several agencies, keeping track of all the inventory stock, tracking the cash balance of the business, paying its bills on time, sending out statements to its customers, and so on.

No business can keep going very long if these operational details are not attended to. This basic function requires many forms and procedures: Nitty gritty details for sure, but it must be done and done well. This particular function of accounting is known as accounting systems and data processing. It is not explored any further in this book.

The second basic internal function of the accounting system is to support the overall management process of the business, starting with the strategy phase through the control phase. See Exhibit 2.1 again. At a minimum this function requires that internal financial statements and other accounting reports are prepared for managers. Profit, cash flow, and financial condition are indispensable information to managers.

Internal management financial statements should be designed specifically to help managers in their decision-making analysis. Simply reporting more detail than in the external statements is not enough. Rather, a different classification and presentation of information is required. But, all too often in actual practice the "extra management" design step is not done. This gap is a major concern of this book.

A business that does budgeting also prepares budgeted, projected financial statements and supporting schedules. Management control depends on accounting reports that are very detailed and that highlight exceptions to the plan and out-of-control areas. Last, notice in Exhibit 2.1 that, as the occasion demands, accountants prepare specific focus reports to help managers deal with unexpected problems and developments.

EXHIBIT 2.1   ACCOUNTING SYSTEM OVERVIEW

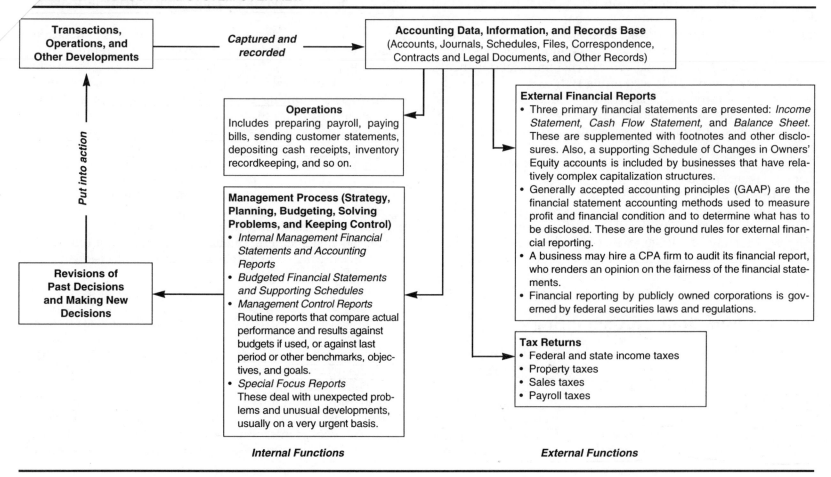

Transactions, Operations, and Other Developments

Captured and recorded →

Accounting Data, Information, and Records Base
(Accounts, Journals, Schedules, Files, Correspondence, Contracts and Legal Documents, and Other Records)

Put into action

Revisions of Past Decisions and Making New Decisions

Operations
Includes preparing payroll, paying bills, sending customer statements, depositing cash receipts, inventory recordkeeping, and so on.

Management Process (Strategy, Planning, Budgeting, Solving Problems, and Keeping Control)
- *Internal Management Financial Statements and Accounting Reports*
- *Budgeted Financial Statements and Supporting Schedules*
- *Management Control Reports*
  Routine reports that compare actual performance and results against budgets if used, or against last period or other benchmarks, objectives, and goals.
- *Special Focus Reports*
  These deal with unexpected problems and unusual developments, usually on a very urgent basis.

External Financial Reports
- Three primary financial statements are presented: *Income Statement, Cash Flow Statement,* and *Balance Sheet.* These are supplemented with footnotes and other disclosures. Also, a supporting Schedule of Changes in Owners' Equity accounts is included by businesses that have relatively complex capitalization structures.
- Generally accepted accounting principles (GAAP) are the financial statement accounting methods used to measure profit and financial condition and to determine what has to be disclosed. These are the ground rules for external financial reporting.
- A business may hire a CPA firm to audit its financial report, who renders an opinion on the fairness of the financial statements.
- Financial reporting by publicly owned corporations is governed by federal securities laws and regulations.

Tax Returns
- Federal and state income taxes
- Property taxes
- Sales taxes
- Payroll taxes

Internal Functions

External Functions

External Income Statement: The Point of Departure

Let's talk profit here. The principal financial motive of business is to make a profit—fairly, honestly, and legally I would emphasize. So the income statement naturally occupies center stage. It reports the profit performance of the business for the latest period; it's the core of management analysis.

Exhibit 2.2 presents a typical example of an externally reported income statement. Other than interest and income tax, notice that only two basic expense groupings are reported in this very realistic example. Some businesses break out one or two additional types of expenses, but by and large, the disclosure of expenses is parsimonious. The theory is that competitors should not know too much about each other's expenses.

We don't spend any more time on the external income statement here because it's not relevant for management decision making. For instance, consider the following situation. Suppose you have done some market research and are of the opinion that if you were to reduce sales prices 5% then sales volume would increase 20%. Would this be a good move? Of course the prediction of a 20% sales volume increase is critical. This large jump in sales volume may or may not materialize.

The main limitation of the standard-issue income statement found in external financial reports is that it does not report information regarding how expenses would react to the 20% sales revenue increase. Expense behavior is the rock bottom type of information that managers must analyze before moving ahead with such a major decision.

EXHIBIT 2.2   EXTERNAL INCOME STATEMENT

Sales Revenue	$10,000,000
Cost of Goods Sold Expense	(6,000,000)
Gross Profit	4,000,000
Selling, General & Administration Expenses	(2,920,000)
Earnings Before Interest and Income Tax	1,080,000
Interest Expense	(160,000)
Earnings Before Income Tax	920,000
Income Tax	(312,800)
Net Income	$ 607,200

Moreover, managers should look beyond the profit dimension; they should carefully identify the changes such a decision would cause in the financial condition and cash flow of the business, or in that segment of the business for which they have management responsibility.* For all they know there might be

---

* Many departments and other organizational units have no direct profit responsibility, although they may have either revenue responsibility, such as a sales territory, or cost responsibility, such as the purchasing or the data processing department. Accordingly, only revenue is reported to a revenue center and only costs are reported to a cost center.

The discussion in this chapter refers to a manager who has profit responsibility for an autonomous segment (division, subsidiary, etc.) of the business or for the entire business. In some organizations profit centers are isolated from any further financial responsibility. The discussion in later chapters takes the broader view, which includes financial condition and cash flow. Clearly, someone in the organization has to be responsible for these financial issues; profit is not the whole picture.

dire consequences on cash flow or financial condition, even if profit should increase. Cash flow and financial condition are the stuff of Chapters 4 and 5.

Summary

A company's accounting system serves four basic purposes: Operations and management information are the two internal demands on the system; public financial reports and tax returns are the two external demands on the system. Different output for different purposes should be the guiding principle in serving the four basic functions of the accounting system.

In Chapter 3 we turn to the design of the most important management financial statement—the internal profit report, or management income statement. The manager as a decision maker needs a sure-handed analytical grip on the profit formula of the business. Don't expect to see too much resemblance to the external income statement.

3

REMAKING THE
INCOME STATEMENT

Introducing the Management Income Statement

Exhibit 3.1 presents the internal profit report, or management income statement, for the example company discussed in Chapter 2. This example company is used throughout the book for continuity. Although hypothetical, this example has been carefully constructed based on actual business cases and is realistic for a very broad range of businesses that sell products.

The internal profit report, or management income statement, is classified quite differently from the externally reported income statement and presents new and very important information, which you can see by comparing Exhibit 2.2 (the external income statement) and Exhibit 3.1 (the internal profit report). Thus the title of the chapter—Remaking the Income Statement.

Exhibit 3.1 includes several balloons or callouts to provide a legend for explaining key items in the profit report. I hope you find these helpful to answer questions you might have and to clarify aspects about the item you may not be entirely certain about. Internal management financial reports do not usually include such explanatory notes; the assumption is that the users (managers) know all this material. Legends or captions such as the balloons in the exhibit are not unheard of however. Some businesses employ them to remind managers of the official definitions and classifications adopted by the company. However, this is not too common in my experience.

Note the four different profit lines in the management income statement. Profit is a four-step management process:

1. The business has to earn an adequate *contribution profit margin*. All variable expenses are deducted from sales revenue to measure this first line of profit, which is the essential starting point in the profit equation.
2. Fixed operating expenses are deducted, which yields *operating earnings*. This profit line is also called earnings before interest and income tax (sometimes abbreviated EBIT).
3. Interest expense is deducted to arrive at *earnings before income tax*.
4. Income tax expense is deducted to arrive at the bottom-line *net income*.

Perhaps you think profit is simply revenue less expenses. Well, not so fast. Managers have to work on each profit line. As its balloon says, the first profit line (contribution profit margin) is the key starting point. If this profit is not enough the rest of the story is not pretty. When managers talk about their "profit margins," this line is the one they refer to most often. But, keep in mind that this profit is before a big chunk of fixed expenses are deducted. You could make good contribution profit margin but blow it on fixed expenses that are too high for the sales volume of the business.

Managers have to keep on top of an unending stream of changes in today's business environment. Few factors remain constant very long. Managers need to quickly assess the profit (and other financial impacts) of changes. Deciding the best response to changes is never easy, but one thing is clear. As pointed out in Chapter 1, one advantage of budgeting is that it forces the manager's attention on change analysis. A properly designed internal profit report is extraordinarily helpful.

EXHIBIT 3.1   INTERNAL PROFIT REPORT (MANAGEMENT INCOME STATEMENT)

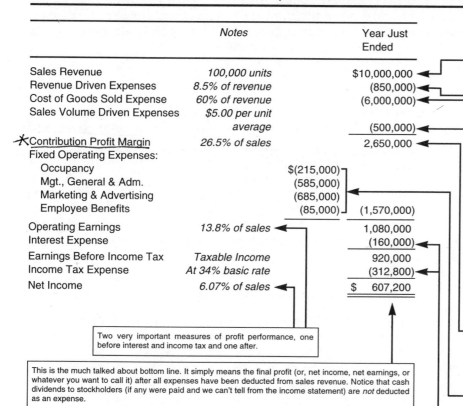

	Notes	Year Just Ended
Sales Revenue	100,000 units	$10,000,000
Revenue Driven Expenses	8.5% of revenue	(850,000)
Cost of Goods Sold Expense	60% of revenue	(6,000,000)
Sales Volume Driven Expenses	$5.00 per unit average	(500,000)
✳Contribution Profit Margin	26.5% of sales	2,650,000
Fixed Operating Expenses:		
Occupancy	$(215,000)	
Mgt., General & Adm.	(585,000)	
Marketing & Advertising	(685,000)	
Employee Benefits	(85,000)	(1,570,000)
Operating Earnings	13.8% of sales	1,080,000
Interest Expense		(160,000)
Earnings Before Income Tax	Taxable Income	920,000
Income Tax Expense	At 34% basic rate	(312,800)
Net Income	6.07% of sales	$ 607,200

Equals total sales volume times final net sales prices of all products sold during the period, one year in this example. Final net sales prices are list prices minus all deductions from list prices, such as prompt payment discounts, quantity discounts, rebates, coupons, adjustments after the point of sale, special allowances, and so on.

These operating expenses are driven by and depend primarily on sales revenue, i.e., the total dollar amount of sales revenue. Common examples are sales commissions, bonuses based on sales revenue quotas, credit card discounts paid by the business, franchise fees based on total sales revenue, and so on.

This total amount equals sales quantities times the unit costs of all the individual products sold during the period. Unit cost should be full cost, including incoming freight charges and other handling costs. The accounting system may not include these additional costs in unit costs, but they should be included in the total cost of goods sold expense for the period. The cost of inventory shrinkage caused by shoplifting and by inventory damage, aging, and obsolescence should also be included here. Be warned: Unit product costs change over time, so the business has to decide between the first-in, first-out (FIFO) sequence of moving costs out of inventory into this expense account, or the last-in, first-out (LIFO) method.

These operating expenses are driven by and depend primarily on sales volume, i.e., the total quantities or number of units sold, which is 100,000 units in this example. Common examples are transportation costs, packaging costs, and storage space costs. If sales volume were to increase then these expenses would increase in direct proportion.

Two very important measures of profit performance, one before interest and income tax and one after.

This management line is the most important in the income statement, keeping in mind that you have to make sales to make profit and that the ultimate objective of the business is to make a good bottom-line profit. But, the key is the profit margin, which must be adequate to cover fixed expenses, pay interest and income tax, and leave enough bottom-line profit.

This is the much talked about bottom line. It simply means the final profit (or, net income, net earnings, or whatever you want to call it) after all expenses have been deducted from sales revenue. Notice that cash dividends to stockholders (if any were paid and we can't tell from the income statement) are *not* deducted as an expense.

These operating expenses are relatively fixed and nonvariable over the period. These costs would be more or less the same whether sales volume had been substantially higher or lower, within limits of course. Fixed operating costs should be broken down into major categories, such as the one you see in this example. Each category or "bucket" is important in its own right in making decisions and exercising control.

The company in this example had $2,000,000 interest-bearing debt borrowed during the year. The average annual interest rate was 8% for total interest of $160,000. Like other expenses, interest is deductible for income tax, a key point discussed in Chapter 7. Currently the corporate income tax rate is 34% which is used in this example. The company's accounting methods are the same for both tax and financial reporting, which is typical.

Please take a few minutes to walk your way through this profit report and to read the balloons attached to each item. Also notice the Notes column in the profit report, which includes vital information to managers that can't be put in the financial columns. The remainder of this chapter offers brief explanations of the items in the internal profit report. Generally, I won't repeat the comments in the balloons.

The Internal Profit Report

Sales Revenue

Sales revenue accounting is fairly straightforward, although there can be some problems. The major decision is when to book a sale as sales revenue. The general answer is at the time when the goods and services are sold and delivered. For some businesses this is not clear-cut. Automobile manufacturers, for example, sell their products to their franchised dealers not to final consumers. You can argue that a sale to company-controlled dealers is too early for recording final sales revenue.

In the example the company's sales revenue is correctly recorded, which means that the sales are final and the products will not be returned by customers. But managers should keep in the back of their minds that there is always a residual possibility of sales returns by a few customers.

I would emphasize one key point in the sales revenue balloon (see Exhibit 3.1). Sales revenue in the management income statement is reported *net* after deducting any sales price reductions, such as rebates, coupons, discounts, and so on. These sales price offsets are quite common, as you probably know. More detailed information on these sales price reductions should be reported in a separate supporting schedule. This information would clutter the main profit report with too much detail.

Sales Revenue-Driven Expenses

Several expenses vary directly with the dollar amount of sales revenue. Two examples are sales commissions and credit card discounts charged to the business by the bank credit card issuer. Salespersons may be paid a 5% sales commission for example. Or a customer's credit card sales slip for $100.00 is sent to the bank, which credits the business with 98% of the amount, or a 2% discount. Another example of an expense that depends on the dollar amount of sales revenue is bad debts expense. This expense consists of those customers accounts receivable from credit sales that cannot be collected and have to be written off in part or in full.

Sales revenue-driven expenses come right off the top; revenue is reduced immediately by these expenses. Thus they are a logical first line expense deduction against sales revenue. The manager may prefer that this particular expense be put on a later line in the internal profit report. Managers call the shots here. Accountants should design the internal profit reports as the managers prefer.

Cost of Goods Sold Expense

Next is the cost of goods sold expense, the largest single expense line in the management income statement. Cost of goods sold expense, as its title suggests, is the cost of the products sold to customers. Sales revenue less this particular expense is called *gross margin* or *gross profit*. From Exhibit 3.1 we see that the company's cost of goods sold expense is 60% of sales revenue; thus, its gross profit is 40%.

Cost of goods sold usually is the largest expense of companies that sell products, typically 50-60% or more of sales revenue (and is as much as 80-85% for some high volume retailers). Thus, it's not too often that you see gross margins at a level of more than 40–50%. However, there are some interesting exceptions. The cosmetics industry has high gross profit margins. Coca-Cola's gross profit margin recently has been over 60%. A full-service restaurant, as a rough rule of thumb, should keep its food costs at one-third of its sales revenue, leaving a two-thirds gross margin. Apple Computer earned high gross margins until it adopted a more aggressive sales pricing strategy on its personal computers in its attempt to get a larger market share. This cut deeply into its traditional high profit margins.

A rule of thumb is this: The lower the gross margin percent, the higher the *inventory turnover*. The interval of time from acquisition of the product to the sale of the product is one inventory turnover. High turnover is five or more turns a year, or maybe six or seven turns a year depending on who you talk with.

Food supermarkets, for example, have very high inventory turnover—their products do not stay on the shelves very long. Even taking into account the holding period in their warehouses before the products reach their retail store shelves, their inventory turnover is very high. Thus, supermarkets can work on fairly thin gross margin percents of 20%, give or take a little. In contrast, a retail furniture store may hold an item in inventory for more than six months on average before it is sold, so it needs fairly high gross margin percents.

Cost of goods sold is the major sales volume-driven variable expense. It moves in lockstep with changes in sales volume. If sales volume were to increase by 10%, then this expense should increase by 10%, assuming unit product costs remained constant over time. But unit product costs—whether the company is a retailer who purchases the products it sells or the business is a producer who manufactures the products it sells—do not remain constant very long. Unit product costs may drift steadily upward over time with inflation. Or, because of competitive pressures or technological improvements, unit product costs can take sharp nosedives.

Unit product cost changes cause one rather irksome accounting problem. The accountant has to choose the sequence to charge out unit costs to cost of goods sold expense. Intuitively it would seem the proper accounting method is the chronological sequence. In other words, the first items in unit costs should be the items first out to expense. This sequence is called the first-in, first-out method, or FIFO.

More than 50 years ago Congress changed the federal income tax law to permit businesses to use the reverse chronological order method. This reverse order approach is called the last-in, first-out method, or LIFO. The most recent, or last-in costs are charged to cost of goods sold expense first and so on backward along the time line. During periods of cost inflation the more recent costs are the higher costs, so cost of goods sold expense is higher and taxable income is lower.

However, older costs are left in inventory with the result that after several years the company's inventory asset account may carry a balance that is considerably less than the current replacement cost of the inventory. The current replacement cost should be reported in a footnote to the balance sheet if the difference is material. Our example uses FIFO, in case you're wondering.

Sales Volume-Driven Expenses

In addition to the sales volume-driven cost of goods sold expense, most businesses have other operating costs that also vary with sales volume—not with sales dollars mind you, but with the *quantities* of products sold. Delivery costs, for one example, vary with sales volume or the quantities sold and shipped. Storage costs as well as packaging and crating costs vary with the number of units, not the sales value of the goods. Also, inventory shrinkage may depend on sales volume. These additional sales volume-driven costs are significant and thus are reported on a separate expense line in the internal profit report.

Contribution Profit Margin

Deduct the three variable expenses from sales revenue to determine the first profit line in the management income statement—*contribution profit margin* (see Exhibit 3.1). *Contribution* comes from the idea that this preliminary amount of profit contributes or helps to cover fixed operating expenses. *Margin* emphasizes that it is the difference remaining after deducting cost of goods

sold expense and other variable operating expenses from sales revenue.

Contribution margin should be large enough to cover the company's fixed operating expenses, its interest expense, and its income tax expense and still provide a residual amount of final profit (net income). In short, there are a lot of further demands on this first-step measure of profit. Even if a business earns a good total contribution margin (sales revenue less all variable expenses), it isn't necessarily out of the woods.

Interestingly enough it's difficult to find any standard benchmarks for this key profit ratio. The reason is that the main source of information is external income statements, but variable expenses are not separated from fixed expenses in these external financial reports. Very few companies divulge this information in their external financial reports. In this example the company's contribution profit margin ratio is 26.5% of sales revenue (see Exhibit 3.1: $2,650,000 ÷ $10,000,000 = 26.5% contribution profit margin).

Suppose that sales revenue had been $100,000 more than it was. The company's contribution profit margin should have been $26,500 higher, equal to 26.5% of the sales revenue increase.* In summary, the contribution profit margin is an important line of demarcation between the variable profit factors above the line and the fixed expenses below the line.

---

* It makes a difference whether the sales revenue increase is caused by sales volume increases or sales price increases, a key point explored in Chapters 11 and 12.

Fixed Operating Expenses

All businesses have *fixed* operating expenses. From Exhibit 3.1 notice that the company's total fixed operating expenses were $1,570,000 for the year just ended. *Fixed* means that, for most practical purposes, these operating costs would have remained the same over a broad range of sales activity. Sales volume could have been, say, 20–30% higher or lower and these fixed costs would have been the same. Sometimes fixed costs are called the "nut" of the business, a shell of costs that are hard to crack.

Examples of fixed costs include employee salaries, office rent, retail store rent (unless it is pegged to annual sales revenue, in which case it is a sales revenue-driven expense), annual real estate taxes, most types of insurance, the CPA audit fee, and many other expenses too numerous to mention. Most advertising—billboards, newsprint ads, direct mailings—are fixed costs, the exceptions being rebates and coupons that vary with sales revenue. Actually rebates and coupons are often viewed as sales promotion costs distinct from advertising. Most fixed costs are committed in advance and cannot be changed over the short run. For example, a five-year lease contract is signed for warehouse space or a key manager is given a three-year compensation contract. In dire circumstances, fixed costs can be reduced but at a price. For instance, persons on fixed salaries can be laid off but they may be entitled severance pay. Leases can be broken but require a penalty payment. Over time, managers have to "adjust" the company's fixed costs to fit the sales level activity of the company—a very important task.

The fixed operating costs examples just discussed are identified by their *object of expenditure*. In contrast, Exhibit 3.1 presents fixed costs by *functional classification*. In other words, the costs are reported not by what you are paying for (salary, property tax, audit), but rather what you are getting for the cost. For instance, real estate taxes, building insurance, salaries of maintenance and security employees, gas and electricity, and other costs are all grouped together into the Occupancy expense category in the management profit report.

Depreciation is also a fixed operating expense, although quite different from other fixed operating expenses. The annual depreciation expense amount depends on which method of depreciation is selected—either the level straight-line method or the quicker accelerated method. Other fixed operating expenses are not so heavily dependent on the choice of accounting methods as compared with depreciation.

Depreciation is a write-down of the book (recorded) value of long-term, fixed operating assets. (The cost of land is not depreciable, as it generally cannot be used up or become obsolete.) For this reason, depreciation sometimes is referred to as "only a book entry." This description is misleading however. Fixed operating assets do wear out over time and are eventually put on the junk heap. A Boeing 727 might fly 25 or even 35 years, but sooner or later the aircraft will be retired. Personal computers are replaced every two, three, or four years in contrast.

In Exhibit 3.1, fixed operating expenses, including depreciation, are reported by functional classification. So, depreciation on the office building and the data processing equipment are placed in the Management, General & Administration class, whereas depreciation on the autos used by the outside sales force are in the Marketing & Advertising account. Depreciation for the year is also reported as a separate item in the cash flow statement because it is a noncash outlay expense, as discussed in Chapter 5.

Nondepreciable assets (other than fixed assets) are occasionally written off. An entry is made to record an expense or loss and the asset's book value is decreased by the same amount. For example, inventory may have to be marked down, or "knocked down" if the products cannot be sold or will have to be sold below cost. Inventory is also written off to record shrinkage due to shoplifting and employee theft. Accounts receivable may have to be written off if they are not fully collectible, which causes bad debts expense.

Managers definitely should know where such write-offs are being reported in their internal profit reports. For instance are inventory knock-downs included in the cost of goods sold expense? Normal recurring write-offs are classified in the normal expenses you see in the management profit report (Exhibit 3.1). On the other hand, unusual nonrecurring losses and gains are reported on separate lines. The example shown in Exhibit 3.1 does not have any of these extraordinary gains or losses.

Operating Earnings, Interest, Income Tax, and Bottom-Line Net Income

Deducting fixed operating expenses takes us down to the profit line labeled Operating Earnings. This is also referred to as earnings before interest and tax (EBIT). Interest expense is shown as one item in the internal profit report (see Exhibit 3.1 again). Alternatively, interest on short-term debt could be separated from interest on long-term debt. Perhaps interest rates differ substantially between the two and management might be considering a restructuring of the company's debt. Interest expense should include loan origination fees and points paid by the business.

The last expense shown in the internal management income statement is income tax. Only one total amount is reported, although the state income tax amount generally should be separated from the federal amount. Only federal income tax is included in this example. Income tax is complicated by many factors. In the examples throughout the book, a flat income tax rate based on the present tax law is used, which is fairly realistic.

Net income, the celebrated bottom-line, is $607,200 which is only 6.07% of sales revenue (the top line). Like most businesses the company in the example has a fairly thin margin of profit. Many persons think the typical business makes a huge profit, maybe 20–30% or more of sales revenue. Few businesses can squeeze out more than a 10% profit ratio on sales revenue, although there are some interesting exceptions.

Summary

The main focus of the chapter has been the internal management profit report that separates expenses between those that are variable and those that are fixed. Variable expenses are further separated between those that vary with sales volume and those that vary with sales revenue dollars. The central importance of the internal profit report cannot be overstated.

Sales revenue and expenses, which are summarized in the income statement, not only determine profit, but these profit-making transactions are the primary determinants of the assets and liabilities reported in the balance sheet. The assets and liabilities determine the cash flow of the business. These important topics are examined in Chapters 4 and 5.

"Homework"

Compare your most recent internal income statement with Exhibit 3.1. You'll probably see many differences. Remake your internal income statement according to the format and expense classifications shown in Exhibit 3.1. Your own business is the best example in which to apply the lessons of the chapters.

4

MANAGEMENT
BALANCE SHEET

Balance Sheet for Managers

Exhibit 4.1 presents the *management* balance sheet for the example company introduced in Chapter 2 and discussed throughout the book. This internal financial statement is arranged for management analysis. The layout is not all that different from the typical format found in external financial reports. This management layout would be acceptable, and in my opinion, wouldn't violate generally accepted accounting principles (GAAP) for external financial statement reporting. However, the accounting report you see in Exhibit 4.1 rearranges the balance sheet information for more useful management analysis.

The company's externally reported balance sheet discloses most of this information (in a somewhat different format). Actually only two additional items of information are included in Exhibit 4.1 that are not disclosed in the external balance sheet. In sharp contrast the internal management profit report (see Exhibit 3.1) does divulge additional information about expenses that is never reported in external income statements.

At this time, please take a moment to read down the explanatory balloons attached to the main items in the balance sheet (see Exhibit 4.1). You can also use these call-outs as a convenient reference later in the chapter and throughout the book.

The management balance sheet format in Exhibit 4.1 is organized as follows:

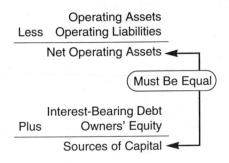

The company's operating assets are listed first and its operating liabilities are deducted to get a very important figure—*net operating assets*.

To make sales of $10,000,000 and earn net income of $607,200 (these top and bottom lines are from the Exhibit 3.1 income statement), the business needed over $4 million in net operating assets ($5,301,888 total operating assets less $1,120,639 operating liabilities = $4,181,249 net operating assets). The company had to raise this much capital from debt and owners' equity sources. For now, however, our concern is why the business needs more than $4 million in net operating assets.

What Determines the Balance Sheet?

You probably know that the income statement reports the sales revenue and expenses of the business. However, you might not know that these profit-making operations, to a very large extent, determine the balance sheet of the business. This point

EXHIBIT 4.1   INTERNAL MANAGEMENT BALANCE SHEET

| | At End Of | | |
	This Year	Last Year	Changes
Operating Assets			
Cash	$ 603,212	$ 346,725	$256,487
Accounts Receivable	961,538	826,345	135,193
Inventory	1,384,615	1,187,645	196,970
Prepaid Expenses	200,385	168,955	31,430
Property, Plant & Equipment	2,810,463	2,318,775	491,688
Accumulated Depreciation	(658,325)	(343,325)	(315,000)
Total Operating Assets	$5,301,888	$4,505,120	
Operating Liabilities			
Accounts Payable–Inventory	$ 461,538	$ 436,575	24,963
Accounts Payable–Operating Expenses	250,481	218,445	32,036
Accrued Expenses–Operating Expenses	350,673	398,675	(48,002)
Accrued Expenses–Interest Expense	26,667	24,330	2,337
Income Tax Payable	31,280	26,440	4,840
Total Operating Liabilities	$1,120,639	$1,104,465	
Net Operating Assets	$4,181,249	$3,400,655	
Sources of Capital			
Short-Term Notes Payable	$ 600,000	$ 500,000	100,000
Long-Term Bonds Payable	1,400,000	1,300,000	100,000
Total Debt	$2,000,000	$1,800,000	
Capital Stock	$ 750,000	$ 700,000	50,000
Retained Earnings	1,431,249	900,655	530,594
Total Stockholders' Equity	$2,181,249	$1,600,655	
Total Debt & Owners' Equity	$4,181,249	$3,400,655	

The changes lead directly into the cash flow statement. See Exhibit 5.1.

Annotation boxes (left side):

Cash is usually in checking accounts; however, some coin and currency is held by many retailers. Cash equivalents such as highly marketable, short-term securities may be included in the cash amount.

These are the three basic short-term operating assets whose turnover is generally between one month to three months or perhaps five or six months for some businesses.

These are long-term operating assets whose useful lives range from three to five years all the way to 30 or more years for buildings. Their cost (except land) is depreciated over their useful life estimates according to accelerated or straight-line methods.

This is the cumulative portion of the original cost of the assets that has been charged to depreciation expense since the date of acquisition.

These are noninterest-bearing, short-term liabilities that arise from two operating sources: (1) the purchase of inventory on credit, and (2) the acquisition of services and other items charged to expense that are not paid for immediately. In short, these are unpaid bills.

These are expenses that have been recorded, not from a purchase as such, but rather to match all expenses for the period against sales revenue to measure profit for the period. A primary example is accrued vacation and sick pay and other employee fringe benefits that haven't been paid by the year-end.

Usually not all the income tax for the year has been paid by year-end. This is the unpaid portion, usually due within two or three months.

These are interest-bearing liabilities from borrowing. Short-term means one year or less; long-term can be from one to 20 or more years. Footnotes disclose maturity dates for the long-term notes or bonds issued by the company.

Owners' equity arises from two sources: (1) capital invested by the owners for which they receive shares of stock (if the business is a corporation); and (2) profit earned but not paid out as a dividend, which is retained in the business.

is made clearer when we examine the financial nature and effects of sales revenue and expenses:

Income Statement	Balance Sheet
Sales Revenue ⟶	+ Asset, or − Liability
Expense ⟶	− Asset, or + Liability

Sales revenue either increases an asset or decreases a liability. A cash sale increases cash immediately; a credit sale increases the asset accounts receivable, which is converted into cash when collected at a later date. Although not too common, some companies, such as magazine publishers, collect cash *before* delivering their products. As the product is delivered they decrease the liability that was recorded previously for the advance payments from customers. In other words, they do not record sales revenue until they deliver the product even though the cash was received before this time.

Expenses either decrease an asset or increase a liability. An expense can decrease cash, such as employee salaries. The cost of goods sold expense decreases the inventory asset account; when products are sold, their cost is removed from the asset account and charged to expense. Many expenses are recorded by first increasing the accounts payable liability, which is paid at a later date. More expenses than you might imagine are recorded by increasing liabilities. Depreciation expense is unusual; it decreases the recorded amount, or book value, of the long-term (fixed) operating assets of the business.

In the process of making a profit, a business generates certain short-term, noninterest-bearing liabilities that are part of carrying out its profit-making transactions. A good example is when the business buys inventory on credit. This purchase causes an accounts payable liability, which will be paid in a month or so, perhaps even sooner. These purchases are sometimes called "spontaneous" liabilities because they are caused by transactions that are not designed to borrow money or to raise capital.

Accounts payable are called *trade credit*; these sources of credit do not charge interest (unless the business is very late in paying the bill). The business does not borrow money from its suppliers like it does from a bank. The business convinces its suppliers to sell products to the business on the strength of its credit reputation and good name. The business has the use of the inventory for the month or so before the accounts payable liability has to be paid. Holding inventory beyond this time, which is typical, means that the business has to secure capital from its longer-term debt or equity sources.*

---

* Keep in mind that in *external* financial statements the short-term notes payable liability account (as well as the short-term, i.e., one year or less portion of long-term liabilities) is included with the company's short-term operating liabilities to determine a subtotal called *Current Liabilities*. Total current liabilities is compared with the company's total short-term operating assets, labeled *Current Assets*, as a rough measure of the company's short-term solvency or debt-paying ability. However, in Exhibit 4.1 all interest-bearing debt, both short-term and long-term, is included under Sources of Capital, which is a more useful management analysis layout.

The relationships and interconnections of revenue and expenses with their corresponding assets and liabilities are measured by *operating ratios*. This very important tool of analysis is explained in Chapter 6.

Summing up briefly at this point: The balance sheet is mainly determined by the revenue and expenses of the business, that is, the profit-making operations of the business that are reported in its income statement. The balance sheet is prepared at the close of business on the last day of the profit measurement period. The revenue and expenses drive the operating assets and operating liabilities of the business. We now turn our attention to where the business gets the capital needed for its net operating assets.

Sources of Capital
(to Finance Net Operating Assets)

The business must raise capital to finance the investment in its net operating assets. This capital comes from two main sources—debt and equity. Managers must convince lenders to loan money to the company and must convince sources of equity capital, such as shareholders, to invest their money in the company. The several basic differences between debt and equity are discussed briefly at this point.

Both debt and equity sources of capital demand to be compensated for the use of their capital. Interest is paid on debt and reported in the income statement as expense (see Exhibits 2.2 and 3.1 to review this fundamental point). In contrast, no "charge" or "expense" of equity capital is reported in the income statement.

Bottom-line profit is the return or earnings on equity capital. Net income in and of itself is the "payment" as it were to the owners of the business. The business is this much better off from earning the profit and, presumably, the worth of the business increases by the amount of net income. Shareholders may or may not be paid part of net income as a cash dividend. Dividends, if any, are reported in the cash flow statement as discussed in Chapter 5. (Dividends are also reported in the separate schedule of changes in owners' equity accounts, if this schedule is prepared.)

At the most recent year-end, the example company has over $4 million invested in its net operating assets to carry on its profit-making operations. Where did this capital come from? The company tapped two basic sources, each divided into two parts (see Exhibit 4.1 for the following numbers):

1a. Short-term debt of $600,000; and,
1b. Long-term debt of $1,400,000 for total debt of $2,000,000; and,
2a. Paid-in capital from stockholders of $750,000; and,
2b. Retained earnings of $1,431,249 for total owners' (stockholders') capital of $2,181,249.

Collectively these capital sources are referred to as the *capitalization* or *capital structure* of the business.

We could ask at this point whether the company is using the optimal or best capital structure. Perhaps the company should have carried more debt. Maybe the company could have gotten by on a smaller cash balance, say $100,000 less, which means that $100,000 less debt or owners' equity capital would have been needed. Perhaps the business should have kept its accounts receivable and inventory balances lower, which would have reduced the need for capital.

This basic question comes down to a few fundamental choices that include: debt versus equity; issuing capital stock versus retained earnings; and, a lean versus a larger working cash balance. The analysis tools explained in this book are very helpful for deciding these questions. Let us review the essential features of and differences between debt and equity.

Debt may be very short term, usually meaning six months or less, or very long term, which means 20 years or more. (A recent *New York Times* article commented on the increasing trend of debt issues with 50-year maturities and mentioned one issue with a 999-year maturity date.) The term *debt* means *interest-bearing* in almost all cases. Interest rates can be fixed over the life of the debt contract or can be subject to change usually at the lender's option.

A key feature is whether the debt must be *amortized* . When applied to debt, amortization refers to reducing the amount borrowed, which is called the *principal*. In addition to paying interest the business (who is the borrower, or debtor) may have to make payments to reduce the principal balance of the debt, instead of waiting until the final maturity date to pay off all the principal amount at one time.

For example, a business loan may call for equal quarterly amounts over five years. Each quarterly payment amount is fixed to pay interest and to pay down part of the principal balance so that at the end of the five years the loan principal will be paid off. Alternatively, the business may negotiate a *term* loan. Nothing is paid on the principal during the life of a term loan; the entire amount borrowed (the principal) is paid at the maturity date of the loan.

Debt may be secured with collateral or not. Debt instruments, such as bonds, may have very restrictive covenants (conditions), or may be quite liberal and nonbinding on the business. Some debt is convertible into equity stock shares, although generally this feature is limited to publicly held corporations whose stock shares are actively traded. The debt of a business may be a private loan, or debt securities that are actively traded on a bond market may be issued.

Equity capital may be supplied by just one person who operates the business as a sole proprietor (the business is not organized as a separate legal entity). Or, the business may be legally organized as a partnership of two or more persons, which is a separate entity. Many businesses, including even relatively small ones, are organized as corporations, which are legal entities separate from their owners. Corporations are a legal type of entity that limit the liability of the owners (the stockholders). The corporate form is a practical way to organize equity ownership over a large number of investors.

There are literally millions of corporations in the American economy. Other countries around the globe have the equivalent of corporations, although the names of these organizations as well as their legal and political features differ somewhat from country to country. Corporations issue stock shares, which are the units of equity ownership in the corporation. A corporation may issue only one class of stock shares, called *common stock* or *capital stock.* Or, a corporation may issue both preferred and common stock shares. A corporation may issue both voting and nonvoting classes of stock shares.

Equity capital, unlike debt instruments, does not bear an explicit and legally contracted rate of interest.* Nevertheless, equity capital has an imputed or implicit cost. Management must earn a satisfactory rate of earnings on the equity capital of the business to justify the use of this capital. Failure to do so reduces the value of the equity and makes it more difficult to attract additional equity capital (if and when needed).

Equity capital assumes the risk of business failure and poor performance. On the optimistic side, equity has no limits on its participation in the success of the business. Continued growth can lead to continued growth in cash dividends. The market value of the equity shares have no theoretical upper limit. The lower limit is zero (the shares become worthless), although shares could be *assessable*, which means the corporation has the right to assess shareholders and make them contribute additional capital into the organization. Almost all corporate stock shares are issued as nonassessable shares, although one can't be too careful about this.

Operating Assets and Liabilities

Several different operating assets are needed to carry on the profit-making operations of a business. And, several different

---

* Preferred stock shares carry a stated rate of cash dividend per period; but, the actual payment of the dividend is contingent on the corporation earning enough net income and having enough cash on hand to pay the dividend.

kinds of operating liabilities are generated as a normal part of its profit-making transactions. Certain assets have to be in place before sales and expense transactions can be carried on. For example, inventory has to be purchased or manufactured before it can be offered for sale to customers. Several expenses have to be prepaid, such as insurance premiums and office supplies.

Other operating assets and liabilities are the end result of sales revenue and expense transactions. For example, accounts receivable are the result of making sales on credit. Accounts payable are the result of buying inventory on credit and not paying expenses until sometime after they are recorded as expenses.

In Exhibit 4.1, notice that the Accounts Payable section is separated into two parts: the amount from inventory purchases on credit and the amount from operating expenses bought on credit. Both are due in the short run, usually not much longer than a month, give or take a week or so. Accrued expenses are also separated into two parts: the amount from operating expenses and unpaid interest.

These separations are needed to explain the analysis tools discussed in Chapter 6, which are called operating ratios. Also, from the management point of view each separate liability balance is the result of different decisions and policies.

Operating assets don't earn interest income and operating liabilities don't require interest expense, although there are minor exceptions. For example, temporary excess cash balances may be invested for short periods in highly liquid and very safe securities (such as U.S. government issues) to earn some interest income on surplus cash instead of letting it lie fallow. Customers who don't pay their receivables on time may be penalized with an interest charge if they delay too long beyond the normal credit period.

Likewise, if the business delays too long beyond the credit period extended by its vendors and suppliers before paying its accounts payable, the company may be charged an interest penalty for late payment. Putting aside these minor exceptions, operating assets don't earn interest income and operating liabilities don't bear interest expense.

Managers should know which particular operating assets and liabilities are needed. They should also know how large each operating asset and liability should be relative to sales revenue and the expenses of the business. For instance, managers should know how large the accounts receivable balance should be relative to total credit sales for the period, given the normal credit terms of the business and the history of its customers regarding late payment.*

Certain operating assets, such as accounts receivable and inventory, have relatively short investment lives; they are converted back into cash in a few weeks or months. In contrast, certain operating assets, such as buildings, equipment, and vehicles, have long investment lives; they are not converted back into cash for 3, 10, or more years. Investments in these long-term, or fixed, assets are called *capital expenditures* to emphasize the capital commitments in these long-term economic resources.

---

* The analysis tool for this comparison is called an operating ratio; Chapter 6 explains operating ratios.

In overview, a business needs a "portfolio" of operating assets and liabilities that are essential for making profit. To carry on its sales revenue and expense activities, the company in this example uses $5,301,888 total operating assets—consisting of Cash, Accounts Receivable, Inventory, Prepaid Expenses, and long-term depreciable fixed assets (Property, Plant & Equipment)—at the end of its most recent year.

The company's total operating liabilities are $1,120,639, consisting of Accounts Payable, Accrued Expenses, and Income Tax Payable (see Exhibit 4.1). Its total net operating assets are $4,181,249, which is financed by $2,000,000 debt and $2,181,249 owners' (stockholders') equity. Believe it or not, we will have a lot of fun with these numbers in later chapters.

Summary

Several different operating assets are needed to make a profit, and the sales and expense transactions also generate certain operating liabilities. Subtracting the operating liabilities from the operating assets gives the amount of net operating assets, which is the amount of capital the business has to raise from debt and equity sources.

Each asset, liability, and owners' equity reported in the balance sheet is like a piece in a puzzle; putting the pieces together gives a good picture of the financial health and position of the business at a particular moment in time. This financial statement is a "freeze frame" from the video tape of the company's operations that are in constant motion.

In broad overview the balance sheet results from three basic types of transactions:

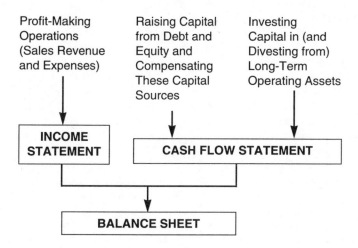

The second and third types of transactions are not reported in the income statement because they are not sales revenue and expenses. These financing and investing transactions are reported in the cash flow statement—the third primary financial statement. Chapter 5 explains the cash flow statement.

5

CASH FLOW STATEMENT

Cash Flow Statement
for Managers

Exhibit 5.1 presents the internal management cash flow statement for the example company. At this time, you can read the explanatory balloons attached to the main items in the cash flow statement, or you can use them for convenient reference later. Of course, this report is for the same year as the income statement discussed previously (see Exhibit 3.1). Also recall that the balance sheet is prepared at the end of the year, that is, on the last day of the year for which the income and cash flow statements are prepared.

The cash flow statement is the new kid on the block; it was not required until 1987. Until the 1900s only a balance sheet was reported. Then the income statement became a required financial statement. Despite calls from security analysts starting soon after World War II for a cash flow statement, the accounting profession did not make it a required statement for external financial reports until 1987. (A much inferior type of funds flow statement was required earlier.) Today it is a mandatory statement.

The cash flow statement is in three parts, because there are three main types of "cash flows" through a business.

The first section of the cash flow statement discloses how much cash flow *from profit* the business generated during the year. Profit is not cash flow, which business managers absolutely have to understand. In a given situation a business could earn a nice profit and yet have a negative cash flow result, which means cash outflows for expenses exceeded cash inflows from revenue.

Conversely, a business could suffer a loss for the year and yet have a positive cash flow result, which means cash inflow from revenue exceeded cash outflow for expenses. How can this happen? More generally, why does the cash throw-off from profit not equal the profit earned for the year? These questions are answered in the first section of the cash flow statement, if you understand how to read it.

The second section of the report presents the cash inflows and outflows from the business's *investing activities* (transactions) during the year. In Exhibit 5.1 there is only one investing activity—the $491,688 total cash outlays for purchases of fixed assets, for example, the property, plant, and equipment. These business investments are called *capital expenditures*.

The term *capital* here means long-term; these investments are for more than one year. In comparison, investments in inventories are for short-term periods and are not called capital expenditures. In Exhibit 5.1 there were no disinvestments or sales of fixed assets. However, if there had been, this section would have reported the receipts from the disposals as cash inflows.

The third section of the report presents the cash inflows and outflows from the *financing* activities of the business. As you can see in Exhibit 5.1, this section summarizes the changes in the sources of capital to the business during the year. The company in this example increased both its short-term and long-term interest-bearing liabilities and also issued some new stock shares. This section also reports that the corporation paid $76,606 in cash dividends to its stockholders during the year.

EXHIBIT 5.1   INTERNAL MANAGEMENT CASH FLOW STATEMENT

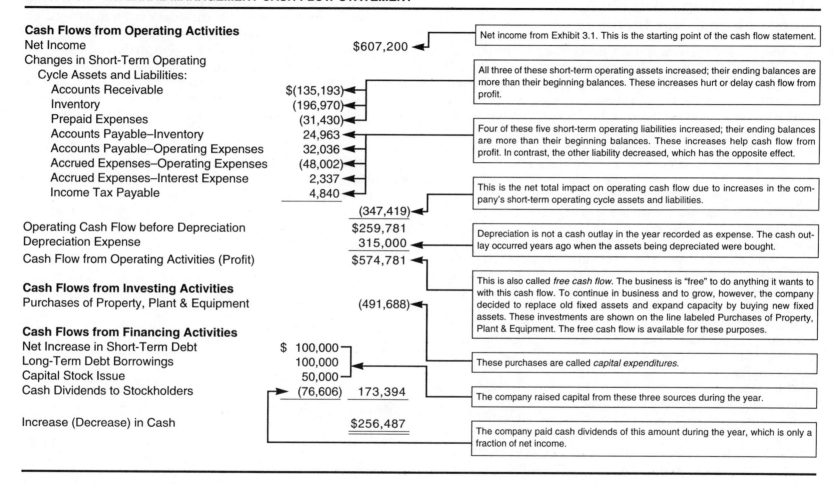

Cash Flows from Operating Activities

Net Income $607,200

Net income from Exhibit 3.1. This is the starting point of the cash flow statement.

Changes in Short-Term Operating
Cycle Assets and Liabilities:

Accounts Receivable	$(135,193)
Inventory	(196,970)
Prepaid Expenses	(31,430)
Accounts Payable–Inventory	24,963
Accounts Payable–Operating Expenses	32,036
Accrued Expenses–Operating Expenses	(48,002)
Accrued Expenses–Interest Expense	2,337
Income Tax Payable	4,840
	(347,419)

All three of these short-term operating assets increased; their ending balances are more than their beginning balances. These increases hurt or delay cash flow from profit.

Four of these five short-term operating liabilities increased; their ending balances are more than their beginning balances. These increases help cash flow from profit. In contrast, the other liability decreased, which has the opposite effect.

This is the net total impact on operating cash flow due to increases in the company's short-term operating cycle assets and liabilities.

Operating Cash Flow before Depreciation	$259,781
Depreciation Expense	315,000
Cash Flow from Operating Activities (Profit)	$574,781

Depreciation is not a cash outlay in the year recorded as expense. The cash outlay occurred years ago when the assets being depreciated were bought.

Cash Flows from Investing Activities

Purchases of Property, Plant & Equipment ..... (491,688)

This is also called *free cash flow*. The business is "free" to do anything it wants to with this cash flow. To continue in business and to grow, however, the company decided to replace old fixed assets and expand capacity by buying new fixed assets. These investments are shown on the line labeled Purchases of Property, Plant & Equipment. The free cash flow is available for these purposes.

Cash Flows from Financing Activities

Net Increase in Short-Term Debt	$ 100,000	
Long-Term Debt Borrowings	100,000	
Capital Stock Issue	50,000	
Cash Dividends to Stockholders	(76,606)	173,394

These purchases are called *capital expenditures*.

The company raised capital from these three sources during the year.

Increase (Decrease) in Cash $256,487

The company paid cash dividends of this amount during the year, which is only a fraction of net income.

Why Operating Cash Flow Doesn't Equal Net Income

Net income for the year almost never equals operating cash flow for the period. But, as my youngest son Tage, the CPA, asks: "If we're in the black, where's the green?" The answer is a little involved, although relatively straightforward.

We live in a credit economy. A business extends credit to its customers and credit is extended to it by its suppliers and vendors. A business must record its accounts receivable and accounts payable; it cannot keep its books on a simple cash basis. Accounts receivable are uncollected sales revenue–cash not yet received by year-end. But all sales revenue is recorded for profit measurement. Accounts payable are unpaid expenses—cash not yet paid out by year-end. But all expenses are recorded for profit measurement.

As you know, a business invests in inventory and fixed assets. These are cash outlays today that are not recorded as expenses for profit measurement until sold (inventory) or used (fixed asset depreciation). Surely these prepaid costs should not be charged off to expense at the time of purchase. The cost of inventory should be matched up with sales revenue when, and not until, the products are sold. The cost of fixed assets should not be expensed until the assets contribute to the operations of the business year after year, which is accomplished by recording depreciation expense to each year.

In short, sales revenue and expenses are recorded on the *accrual accounting basis*. "Accrual" simply means that sales revenue is recorded before cash is received and some expenses are recorded before cash is paid out. Also, accrual means that cash outlays for prepaid costs (mainly inventory and fixed assets) are not recorded as expenses until the assets are sold or used up. Cash flow marches to the beat of a different drummer than accrual-based accounting revenue and expenses.

Let's go through a very simple example to illustrate the accrual basis of accounting versus cash flow from profit. Consider a new business that makes $1,000,000 in sales for its first year. The top line in its income statement is $1,000,000 sales revenue for the year.

The company sells all of its products on credit. At the end of the year it has $120,000 in accounts receivable, which are uncollected. Now suppose the company had no expenses (which is done only to illustrate the point here). Suppose also that the company had no operating assets other than cash and accounts receivable. The company's financial statements in a very abbreviated form would be as follows:

Income Statement

Sales Revenue	$1,000,000
Expenses	none
Net Income	$1,000,000

Balance Sheet

Cash	$ 880,000
Accounts Receivable	120,000
Total Assets	$1,000,000
Total Liabilities & Owners' Equity	$1,000,000

Cash Flow Statement

Net Income	$1,000,000
Accounts Receivable	(120,000)
Cash Flow from Profit	$ 880,000

The company earned $1,000,000 profit (or, net income), but only $880,000 was converted into cash by year-end because accounts receivable increased from zero at the start of the year to $120,000 at the end of the year.

Rules for Determining Operating Cash Flow from Profit

Although the simple example just examined is not very realistic, it does set the stage for the basic rules for determining cash flow from net income (profit), which are summarized as follows:

Start with Net Income, then adjust Net
Income as follows:

+ Operating Asset   = − Cash Flow
− Operating Asset   = + Cash Flow
+ Operating Liability = + Cash Flow
− Operating Liability = − Cash Flow

In brief, operating cash flow moves opposite to changes in operating assets and moves in the same direction as changes in operating liabilities.

The beginning balances of accounts receivable, inventory, and prepaid expenses are compared with their ending balances. In our company example, all three increase as you can see from Exhibit 4.1 (the company's internal balance sheet). Likewise, we do start-of-year versus end-of-year comparisons for the five short-term operating liabilities. Four of these liabilities increase as you can see in Exhibit 4.1. But one liability, namely the accrued expenses–operating expenses liability, decreased during the year.

The net effect of all these changes in the company's short-term operating cycle assets and liabilities is to decrease its cash flow from profit $347,419 (see Exhibit 5.1). This is very serious. More than half of the company's net income was lost to cash flow. Net income generated only $259,781 in cash flow before depreciation is taken into account. These changes may be very smart business decisions, but the company's managers should understand that they take away $347,419 from operating cash flow. We could say that this much of the net income was shifted out of cash flow and into the short-term operating assets and liabilities of the business.

In later chapters we see how changes in short-term operating cycle assets and liabilities can have dramatic impacts on operating cash flow. As we move through the chapters in this book, you will become more and more comfortable with cash flow analysis. Remember, like learning to enjoy the taste of olives, cash flow analysis is an acquired taste that takes some getting used to.

Summing up to this point, as shown in Exhibit 5.1, the amount of operating cash flow before depreciation expense is $259,781. As just mentioned, this is less than half of the

$607,200 net income for the year, which probably explains why the company didn't pay out much in cash dividends to its stockholders during the year. But we're getting ahead of ourselves here. The next step is to consider depreciation.

Depreciation and Cash Flow

If one thing causes confusion, it's depreciation and cash flow. So let's walk carefully through this verbal minefield. The final step in the first section of the cash flow statement adds depreciation to the $259,781 operating cash flow after taking into account the changes in the short-term operating cycle assets and liabilities of the business.

Depreciation for the year, which is included in the fixed operating expenses of the company, is $315,000. Adding depreciation to $259,781 gives the final line of the first section—cash flow from operating activities, or, more simply, operating cash flow. As you can see in Exhibit 5.1, this key number is $574,781 for the year. Why is depreciation an "add-back" or a positive cash flow factor?

When depreciable assets are bought or constructed, the business invests cash in these long-lived operating assets, called Property, Plant & Equipment in the balance sheet or *fixed assets* for short. As a business uses its fixed assets, of course, it does not have to pay for them again. If you paid cash for a new car, you don't have to pay for the car again as you drive it. The cost of a company's fixed assets can be thought of as a long-term prepaid expense that is gradually used up over the assets' useful economic lives.

The depreciation expense for the year is a real expense, but it is unique because it was paid for in previous years—going back many years for some fixed assets. To repeat: Depreciation expense is not a cash outlay in the year it's recorded. The cash outlay occurred years earlier. If, on the other hand, the company had rented its assets instead of buying them, the rent expense is a cash outlay in the period the expense is recorded.

The rules given above to determine cash flow from profit apply to depreciation of fixed assets as well. Recall that a decrease in an operating asset is an increase in cash flow. The difference is that fixed assets are long-term operating assets, whereas accounts receivable, inventory, and prepaid expenses are short-term operating assets.

A company may invest in long-term *intangible* operating assets, such as patents, that have several years of useful life to the business. The cost of intangibles is amortized, which means charged off over the predicted economic useful life of the asset. Amortization is just like depreciation, although the income tax amortization schedules and methods are different than those used for depreciation. In any case, if the business had recorded any amortization expense for the year it would have been treated the same as depreciation in the cash flow statement. (By the way, don't confuse the amortization of an intangible asset's cost with the amortization of a loan, which refers to the payoff schedule of the debt's principal.)

There is another reason to give depreciation expense special attention in the cash flow statement. Suppose you tell me that your business made a profit (bottom-line net income) for the year. I assume that you mean that you made net income after deducting all expenses, including depreciation. Correct? Yes, I'm sure you mean this.

Suppose your accountant recorded $100,000 depreciation expense to the year. Therefore, your sales prices were set high enough to recoup part of the capital invested in your fixed assets. It's like a taxicab owner setting fares high enough to recover the cost of the cab. Every time the taxi driver collects a fare it's as if a small time-share in the cab is sold to the passenger. This same analogy is applicable to your business. In other words, if your business collects $100,000 in revenues from customers, it's as if your business sold off $100,000 of your fixed assets to these customers. You converted this much of the original cost of the fixed assets back into cash during the year.

Free Cash Flow

At this time, please refer to the cash flow statement (Exhibit 5.1). Notice that after adding back depreciation the company's cash flow from profit is $574,781. More and more often this figure has come to be known as *free cash flow*. Well, nothing is free as you know. This term means that this much cash is available for management use. But there are always competing demands on the cash. Generally speaking, free cash flow is allocated among four basic alternative uses (in no particular order):

1. To replace and/or expand fixed assets
2. To add to the working cash balance
3. To pay cash dividends from net income, and
4. To reduce debt and/or equity

The remainder of the cash flow report addresses what the business did with its free cash flow, or to be a little more formal, with its operating cash flow, or to use the more technical accounting term, with its cash flow from operating activities.

Free Cash Flow and the Investing and Financing Activities of the Business

The remainder of the cash flow statement reports what management did with its free cash flow. It also shows the other sources and uses of cash. This information is divided into two sections: investing activities and financing activities.

Investing means long-term commitments of capital by the business. The main examples are replacement and expansion of fixed assets and the acquisition of intangible assets, which generally are called capital expenditures. Businesses also make other types of long-term investments, such as purchases of other corporations' stock shares as part of joint ventures and strategic alliances. Or, a business may purchase real estate for long-term periods, or may hold marketable securities for long times. The second section of the cash flow report also includes disinvestments, such as selling fixed assets and liquidating joint ventures (there are none in this example).

Financing refers to the sources of business capital. Financing activities are mainly the raising of capital from debt and equity sources, and the return of capital to these sources. It also includes cash dividends paid to the stockholders of the business because this distribution goes to one of its main capital sources—the shareholders of the corporation.

If a corporation were to buy back some of its outstanding stock shares this purchase would be included in the third section of the cash flow report. In this example, the business did not buy back any of its stock shares. Just the opposite; it issued additional stock shares to raise additional capital from its stockholders.

In the investing activities section we see that the company used most of its free cash flow to purchase new fixed assets (see Exhibit 5.1). The business spent $491,688 on fixed assets leaving $83,093 from its free cash flow:

$574,781	Operating Cash Flow
− $491,688	Capital Expenditures
$ 83,093	Remaining Free Cash Flow

This remainder provides enough for the cash dividends, which are $76,606 for the year. If the business had not raised any other capital, its cash would have increased a small amount:

$83,093	Remaining Free Cash Flow
− $76,606	Cash Dividends
$ 6,487	Cash Increase

But, to build up its cash balance, the business increased its debt by $200,000 (half from short-term and half from long-term debt) and also issued additional stock shares for $50,000. Together these capital additions raised $250,000, which means that the company's cash balance after including the $6,487 left over after cash dividends increased by $256,487. As you can see, this figure is the bottom line of the cash flow statement.

Is the company's year-end $603,212 cash balance an adequate amount for its working cash balance; or, is this amount too much? We shall return to these questions in later chapters.

Summary

This chapter presents a short guided tour through the cash flow statement, the financial report that summarizes the cash inflows and cash outflows for the period. The cash flow statement begins with determination of cash flow from profit, which is also called operating cash flow or free cash flow. This is the *internal* and self-generated cash flow of the business.

Other sources of cash are *external*, or from outside the business. When a business goes outside for its capital, it is always subject to the willingness of the capital sources to put more money in the business. The internal versus the external sources of cash can be compared in the statement. The uses of cash reported in this statement reflect very important decisions made by managers of the business, in particular whether the business is building for the future, holding to the status quo, or downsizing. The business example shows evidence of sizing up for growth.

6

OPERATING RATIOS: THE BACKBONE OF BUDGETING

Vital Connections between Income Statement and Balance Sheet

Exhibit 6.1 extracts sales revenue and expenses from the company's management income statement and it extracts operating assets and operating liabilities from its management balance sheet. Operating assets and liabilities depend on sales revenue and expenses; these lines of dependence are shown in the exhibit. Each line shows the *operating ratio*, which is the measure of the operating asset or liability relative to its "driver," or the sales revenue or expense that determines the size of the asset or liability.

Exhibit 6.1 is unusual. It does *not* show any totals, subtotals, or differences that are reported in regular financial statements. For instance, net income—the residual difference after subtracting all expenses from sales revenue—is not given at the bottom of the income statement in Exhibit 6.1. (We have previously seen that net income is $607,200.) Likewise, total operating assets and total operating liabilities are not given in the balance sheet. And the difference—net operating assets—is not given. Only bare essentials are shown.

Exhibit 6.1 displays the vital links between making profit, the particular assets and liabilities needed, and the result of making profit. The basic point is that the profit-making operations of a business, in other words, its sales revenue and expenses, determine its operating assets and liabilities.

The company's interest-bearing liabilities and its owners' equity accounts are not shown in Exhibit 6.1; these are not directly driven by the profit-making operations of the business. We know, of course, that the business has to raise capital from these two basic sources to finance its net operating assets.

The business has over $4 million invested in its net operating assets, as shown in Exhibit 4.1, the management balance sheet. Total net operating assets at year-end is $4,181,249. Debt sources supply $2,000,000 of this capital and stockholders' equity provides the other $2,181,249. Both capital sources have a cost, which Chapter 7 discusses. This chapter examines why the business needs over $4 million to earn its profit.

Operating Ratios

This chapter presents a compact but reasonably comprehensive summary of the operating ratios that determine the hard core of a company's balance sheet—the amounts of its operating assets and liabilities. The operating ratios presented in Exhibit 6.1 are based on the nature of the business, its history, and its policies. The example is typical of a broad range of companies, but, of course, different businesses have different operating ratios.

For instance, a company that makes all cash sales and no credit sales does not have the accounts receivable operating asset. A company that leases or rents every one of its fixed assets does not have the property, plant, and equipment account nor the accumulated depreciation account. This company makes sales on credit and owns most of its fixed assets.

We do not start with cash, which you might think is the logical place to begin. Cash is an operational asset to be sure. But cash is affected by everything; it is a master clearing account for profit-making activities, as well as financing and investing

EXHIBIT 6.1 OPERATING RATIOS

Revenues and Expenses
(From Income Statement; see Exhibit 3.1)

Operating Assets and Liabilities
(From Balance Sheet; see Exhibit 4.1)

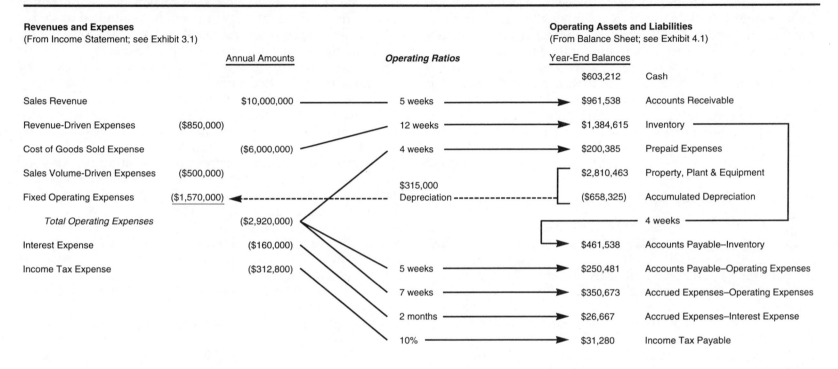

	Annual Amounts	*Operating Ratios*	Year-End Balances	
			$603,212	Cash
Sales Revenue	$10,000,000	5 weeks	$961,538	Accounts Receivable
Revenue-Driven Expenses	($850,000)	12 weeks	$1,384,615	Inventory
Cost of Goods Sold Expense	($6,000,000)	4 weeks	$200,385	Prepaid Expenses
Sales Volume-Driven Expenses	($500,000)		$2,810,463	Property, Plant & Equipment
Fixed Operating Expenses	($1,570,000)	$315,000 Depreciation	($658,325)	Accumulated Depreciation
Total Operating Expenses	($2,920,000)	4 weeks		
Interest Expense	($160,000)		$461,538	Accounts Payable–Inventory
Income Tax Expense	($312,800)	5 weeks	$250,481	Accounts Payable–Operating Expenses
		7 weeks	$350,673	Accrued Expenses–Operating Expenses
		2 months	$26,667	Accrued Expenses–Interest Expense
		10%	$31,280	Income Tax Payable

Note: No profit lines from the income statement are shown above, so, net income is not presented.

Note: Total operating assets and total operating liabilities are not shown above and neither is net operating assets. And, the debt and equity sources of capital that finance the investment in net operating assets are not shown.

activities. Cash is a buffer or slack variable for which there is no basic operating ratio as such. Remember that the cash flow statement reports how much cash is generated from profit and the financing and investing activities of the business.

More than any other operating asset, cash depends heavily on management's policies and attitudes, as well as the financial stresses and strains on the business at any moment in time. Cash is discussed later, once we have gone through all other operating assets and liabilities. We start with the operating connection between accounts receivable and sales revenue.

Receivables/Revenue Operating Ratio

$$\$10,000,000 \text{ annual Sales Revenue} \times (5/52)$$
$$= \$961,538 \text{ ending Accounts Receivable}$$

In this example company, all sales are made on credit; the company sells to other businesses that demand credit. The accounts receivable balance is the amount of uncollected sales revenue at year-end—sales made on credit that have not yet been turned into cash receipts, but will be early next year. The time it takes to collect receivables depends on the credit terms offered to customers. This company's actual average collection period is five weeks, even though its normal credit term is one month.

Thus, the last five weeks of annual sales revenue is not collected yet at year-end. The ending balance of accounts receivable equals the last five weeks of sales revenue. In this example company, sales are uniform during the year. Any five weeks during the year have the same sales revenue as any other five weeks. Thus, annual sales revenue can be multiplied by (5/52) to determine the accounts receivable balance, as shown above.

For many businesses, sales volume fluctuates month to month or quarter to quarter. For example, sales during the Christmas season may be much higher than at other times during the year. In this situation the final five weeks of sales revenue should be used. Sales would be at their seasonal peak at the end of the calendar year, so the ending balance of accounts receivable would also be at its peak.

The five weeks receivables/revenue operating ratio is supplied in this example and is a key parameter of the business. Managers should know this ratio and whether the company is in fact controlling the ratio and keeping it at five weeks. In passing, I should mention that this operating ratio can be expressed in days instead of weeks. We could use 35 days for the ratio. For showing computations, however, using weeks is much more convenient.

Instead of presenting the receivables/revenue operating ratio as five weeks I could have said that annual sales revenue is 10.4 times the ending accounts receivable balance:

$$\$10,000,000 / \$961,538 = 10.4$$

The 10.4 is called the *accounts receivable turnover ratio*. (Notice that 52 weeks ÷ 10.4 = 5 weeks, which is the receivables/revenue operating ratio we started with.) The accounts receivable turnover ratio is one of the basic ratios published by business financial statement data collection and reporting agencies such as Dun & Bradstreet, Standard & Poor's, and Moody's.

However, for budgeting and management analysis it is preferable to focus on how many weeks of sales are in ending accounts receivable. My experience is that business managers think in terms of weeks (or days) of receivables from sales, not in terms turnover ratios.

Inventory/Cost of Goods Sold Operating Ratio

$6,000,000 annual Cost of Goods Sold × (12/52)
= $1,384,615 ending Inventory

This example company sells products, which is what you probably expected. Virtually every company that sells products has to carry an inventory, or a stock of products, for a period of time before the products are sold and delivered to customers. Of course, the holding period depends on the particular business. For example, supermarkets have short holding periods, whereas retail furniture stores have fairly long holding periods.

In this example the inventory level equals twelve weeks of annual cost of goods sold expense, as you can see above. This operating ratio is a *cost to cost* ratio. (In contrast, both numbers in the receivables/revenue operating ratio are in terms of sales prices.) Inventory is carried at cost, and then charged to the cost of goods sold expense when sold. This operating ratio is based on the company's holding periods averaged across all products.

Generally speaking, inventory should not be held longer than necessary. Holding inventory is subject to several risks and requires several costs. Products may become obsolete, or may

be stolen, or may be damaged, or even misplaced. Products have to be stored, usually have to be insured, and may have to be guarded. These costs should be classified in the sales volume driven expense class in the management income statement, because the higher the sales volume then the higher the quantity of inventory and the higher are these costs.

Instead of presenting the inventory/cost of goods sold operating ratio, I could have told you that annual cost of goods sold is 4.33 times the ending inventory:

$$\frac{\$6,000,000}{\$1,384,615} = 4.33$$

The 4.33 is called the *inventory turnover ratio* (52 weeks ÷ 4.33 = 12 weeks, the inventory/cost of goods sold operating ratio we started with). The inventory turnover ratio is another of the basic ratios published by business financial statement data collection and reporting agencies.

As previously mentioned, this key operating ratio is stated in the number of weeks that inventory bears to cost of goods sold. For budgeting purposes and decision-making analysis, managers think in terms of how many weeks inventory has to be held rather than in turnover ratios.

Accounts receivable and inventory are the big two short-term operating assets of a business, or, to be more precise, of a business that sells products on credit. Accountants classify these two assets in the *current* asset section of the externally reported balance sheet. "Current" means the assets will be converted into cash in the normal flow of operations in one operating cycle, or one year maximum.

Before moving on to the next current (short-term) operating asset, which is prepaid expenses, let's leapfrog over it and first discuss depreciation. Depreciation is driven by the fixed, or long-term operating assets of the business.

Depreciation and Fixed Assets

$2,810,463 Property, Plant & Equipment cost
× depreciation method percents for year
= $315,000 Depreciation expense for year

The cost of fixed assets, except for land, are charged to an annual depreciation expense over their useful life estimates according to a fixed allocation method. Both factors are heavily influenced by what is allowed for federal income tax purposes. Congress establishes the basic schedules of depreciable lives for different types of fixed assets and the allocation methods permitted for federal income tax purposes.

Currently the scheme for depreciation in the federal income tax code is titled the modified accelerated cost recovery system (or MACRS). The title ought to tell you something. Depreciation methods are front-loaded; more depreciation can be taken in early years than in later years. Although longer straight-line methods can be used, most businesses opt for shorter accelerated depreciation methods. So, depreciation is generally recorded too fast, which causes net income to be recorded too slow, at least as far as this expense is concerned.

The annual depreciation expense is not deducted from the cost of fixed assets, which might seem logical. Instead, the annual depreciation expense amount is added to the accumulated depreciation contra account, the balance of which is deducted from the cost of fixed assets. "Book value" refers to the undepreciated cost of fixed assets, which is accumulated depreciation subtracted from the cost of fixed assets. Recall that no differences are reported in Exhibit 6.1, so the fixed assets' book value is not shown.

In this example company, total depreciation expense for the year is more than 10% of the fixed assets' cost. The company owns its building, which is being depreciated by the straight-line method over 39 years, or only about 2.5% of cost per year. But its other fixed assets have three to ten years useful life estimates and are depreciated by accelerated (front-loaded) allocation methods. Given the mix of its fixed assets the depreciation expense recorded for this particular year is 11.2% of cost. Managers have to cast a wary eye on this expense because it is based on rather arbitrary choices of useful life estimates and allocation methods.

There is no operating ratio as such for the annual depreciation expense, although clearly it depends on the cost of the company's fixed assets. Depreciation depends on where the business is on its depreciation curve, as well as the composition of its fixed assets. You'll notice that only the amount of depreciation expense is given in Exhibit 6.1, with a broken-line over to fixed operating expenses in the income statement to indicate that depreciation is included in this total expense amount.

Recall that depreciation is not reported on a separate expense line in the management income statement; it's included in fixed operating expenses (you can refer back to Exhibit 3.1 to check this point). Also, depreciation is not a cash outlay in the year it's recorded as an expense. The cash outlay happened when the fixed assets were purchased several years ago. Thus, depreciation has to be removed from the total fixed operating expenses amount in the following operating ratios.

Prepaid Expenses/Operating Expenses Ratio

$$\$2,605,000^* \text{ annual Operating Expenses} \times (4/52)$$
$$= \$200,385 \text{ ending Prepaid Expenses}$$

Every business prepays several expenses. For example fire insurance must be prepaid for six months or more, and several weeks of office supplies or shipping materials are bought. These costs are not charged to expense until the items are used or the costs are allocated over the period of benefit. Such paid-in-advance costs are recorded in the prepaid expenses asset account, and they stay in this account until the time that it is reduced and an expense account is charged for the cost of the items used.

The ending balance of the company's prepaid expenses equals four weeks of its total operating expenses excluding depreciation. This balance is the average of the different types of prepaid costs the business has to make. Notice in Exhibit 6.1 that the company's three different operating expenses are added into one total of $2,920,000. Deducting the $315,000

---

* This figure is net of depreciation expense: $2,920,000 total operating expenses − $315,000 depreciation expense = $2,605,000.

depreciation expense gives the $2,605,000 basis for this and certain other operating ratios.

All businesses have prepaid costs, although the relative size of their prepaid expenses to total operating expenses varies from industry to industry. Seldom would total prepaid expenses be very large compared with accounts receivable and inventory. But prepaids cannot be ignored; the business has over $200,000 "invested" in these prepaid costs, which is no small amount. It should be noted that inventory can be thought of as a "prepaid" cost of goods sold expense, keeping in mind of course that inventory and prepaid expenses are two entirely different assets.

Accounts Payable–Inventory/Inventory Operating Ratio

$$\$1,384,615 \text{ Inventory} \times (4/12)$$
$$= \$461,538 \text{ ending Accounts Payable–Inventory}$$

Most businesses buy their inventory on credit (or, if it is a manufacturer, the business buys its raw materials on credit). At any one time not all of its inventory purchases have been paid for; there is still a balance owing to the suppliers of its products. As you probably know, trade credit terms vary from industry to industry. In this example company, the year-end balance of accounts payable from inventory purchases equals four weeks of ending inventory cost; so, the accounts payable–inventory/inventory operating ratio is 4/12. This operating ratio is based on the normal credit terms offered by the suppliers and the company's actual payment experience and practices.

We have just seen that inventory is held 12 weeks. So the first eight weeks of ending inventory is paid for by year-end, but the last four weeks of inventory is still unpaid at year-end. The unpaid balance is recorded in the accounts payable–inventory account, which is separated from the second accounts payable account discussed next.

Accounts Payable–Operating Expenses/Operating Expenses Ratio

$2,605,000* annual Operating Expenses × (5/52)
= $250,481 ending Accounts Payable–Operating Expenses

Many services and items charged to expense are bought on credit, such as professional fees paid to lawyers and CPAs. Telephone and other utility services are billed on credit. These "unpaid" expenses are recorded in the accounts payable liability account. These items are quite different from inventory purchases, so they are put in a separate account for better management attention and focus.

In this example company the ending balance of accounts payable from operating expenses equals five weeks of annual total operating expenses, excluding depreciation. This operating ratio is based on the average credit terms offered by the vendors of these expenses. A business with any history can determine this key operating ratio.

---

* This figure is net of depreciation expense: $2,920,000 total operating expenses – $315,000 depreciation expense = $2,605,000.

Accrued Expenses–Operating Expenses/Operating Expenses Ratio

$2,605,000* annual Operating Expenses × (7/52)
= $350,673 ending Accrued Expenses–Operating Expenses

In my experience, managers and business professionals do not appreciate the rather large size of accruals for various operating expenses. Many operating expenses are not on a pay-as-you-go basis. For example, accumulated vacation and sick leave benefits are not paid until the employees actually take their vacations and sick days. At year-end the company calculates profit-sharing bonuses and other profit-sharing amounts, which are recorded as expense in the period just ended, even though they will not be paid until some time later.

Product warranty and guarantee costs should be accrued and charged to expense so that these follow-up costs are recognized in the same year that sales revenue is recorded—to get a correct matching of sales revenue and expenses to measure profit. In summary, a surprising number of expense accruals are recorded.

Accruals are quite different than accounts payable. For one thing, an account payable is based on an actual invoice received by the vendor, whereas accruals have no such hard copy that serve as evidence of the liability. Accruals depend much more on good faith estimates of the accountants and others making these calculations. So, the accrued expenses from operating

---

* This figure is net of depreciation expense: $2,920,000 total operating expenses – $315,000 depreciation expense = $2,605,000.

expenses are shown as a separate liability line item in the balance sheet (see Exhibit 4.1).

In this example company, the ending balance of this accrued liability equals seven weeks of annual total operating expenses excluding depreciation expense. This operating ratio is based on the types of accruals that the company records, such as accrued vacation and sick pay for employees, accrued property taxes, accrued warranty and guarantee costs on products, and so on. It takes into account the average time between when each expense is recorded and when it is eventually paid in cash, which can be quite a long time for some items but rather short for others.

Accrued Expenses–Interest/Interest Expense Operating Ratio

$160,000 annual Interest Expense × (2/12)
= $26,667 ending Accrued Expenses–Interest

Interest expense grows, or as accountants say *accrues*, day by day but is paid at the end of periodic intervals. At the end of each accounting year, the accountant records any unpaid interest in this liability account, so that the full amount of the interest for the year is recognized as an expense for the year. In this example two months, or one-sixth of its annual interest expense is unpaid at year-end, so this operating ratio is 2/12. There is no standard or rule of thumb for this operating ratio; it varies from company to company. A lot depends on the particular due dates for interest payments.

Income Tax Payable/Income Tax Expense Operating Ratio

$312,800 annual Income Tax Expense × (10%)
= $31,280 ending Income Tax Payable

The federal corporate tax law requires, assuming the code is strictly observed, that virtually all of the estimated income tax for the year has been paid by the end of the year.

In this example, however, 10% is unpaid at year-end which is not unrealistic. Although a 10% unpaid income tax operating ratio would not be unusual, there are many technical reasons why the year-end unpaid income tax might be more than 10%, or perhaps less. It would be unusual for this liability to be a large percent of the annual income tax expense, although sometimes a business can be in an unusual tax situation.

Other Operating Relationships

Eight basic operating ratios have been discussed so far, as well as the depreciation expense, which is not a ratio as such. These operating ratios are fairly "tight" for a particular business. Once the company has gotten its sea legs and settled on its strategy and policies, these operating ratios should not vary too much from period to period, unless the company makes major changes or is affected by major changes in its environment.

Other operating relationships between sales revenue and certain assets of the business should also be discussed here briefly. I call them *relationships* instead of ratios because the connection is there but they cannot really be reduced to a definite number, such as depreciation. Whereas the eight operating ratios discussed above are fairly tight, the following relationships are fairly loose.

Sales Revenue/Fixed Assets Operating Relationship

$$\$10,000,000 \text{ annual Sales Revenue} \div \$2,810,463 \text{ Property, Plant \& Equipment} = 3.6 \text{ times}$$

Property, Plant & Equipment is the broad asset account title that includes land, buildings, real estate improvements, machinery, manufacturing and other operating equipment, tools, furniture, shelving, vehicles, computers and data processing equipment, and so on. These assets provide *capacity* to carry on the activities of the business—so many square feet of space, so many employee hours, and so on.

The size of these so-called fixed assets relative to annual sales revenue depends on whether the industry is capital intensive or, in other words, whether it requires many such assets or not. Generally speaking manufacturers need a lot more fixed assets than retailers. The average production line worker may use $500,000, $1,000,000, or more of machinery and equipment, to say nothing of the building space needed. A supermarket employee would not need so much.

No general rule of thumb can be applied across industries; even within the same line of business, the relative size of these long-term operating assets varies depending on when the business acquired its fixed assets. These assets are recorded at original cost and are not written up in value even though replacement costs for similar assets may be much higher. The older the assets, the older the cost. Current replacement cost estimates are not reported in the balance sheet.

In this example company, the original cost of these fixed assets is $2.8 million (rounded). Annual sales are $10 million, or 3.6 times the original cost of its fixed operating assets. These long-term operating assets are depreciated, so the book value of the assets (original cost less accumulated depreciation) is considerably less than original cost of the assets. Sales revenue divided by book value would be 4.7. However, in my experience I'm not quite sure what the value of this ratio is in terms of its practical use.

Sales Revenue/Cash Operating Relationship

$$\$10,000,000 \text{ annual Sales Revenue} \div \$603,212 \text{ ending Cash balance} = 16.6 \text{ times, or 3+ weeks}$$

In light of our previous discussions, it's now time to return to the cash account. In this example the company's year-end cash balance is a little more than three weeks of annual sales revenue (see above). There's no doubt that every business needs to keep enough cash in its checking account (or on hand in currency and coin for cash-based businesses such as grocery stores and gambling casinos), but precisely how much? Every business manager would worry if cash were too low to meet the next payroll. Some liabilities can be put off for days or even weeks, but employees have to be paid on time.

Beyond a minimal, rock bottom amount of working cash balance to meet the payroll and to provide at least a bare bones margin of safety, it is not clear how much additional cash balance a business should carry. It's somewhat like your friends: some may walk around with only $5.00 to $10.00, but others could reach in their billfold or purse and pull out $500.00.

Of course, excess cash balances should be avoided. For one thing, capital has a cost and excess cash is an unproductive asset that doesn't pay its way toward meeting the company's cost of capital. For another thing, excess cash balances can cause managers to get lax in controlling expenses. If the money is there in the bank, waiting only for a check to be written, it is more of an incentive to make unnecessary expenditures and not to scrutinize expenditures as closely as needed. Also, excess cash balances can lead to greater opportunities for fraud and embezzlement.

Yet, having a large cash balance is a tremendous advantage in some situations. The business may be able to drive a hard bargain with a major vendor by paying cash up front rather than asking for the normal credit terms. There are many such reasons for holding a cash balance over and above what's really needed to meet payroll and to provide for a safety buffer for the normal lags and leads in the company's cash receipts and disbursements. Quite frankly, if this were my business, I think I would want more than three weeks of cash balance. But, three weeks of cash is probably workable.

The company may be able to go to its external sources of capital, such as debt and owners' equity, for additional money. Or, maybe not. The company may be already borrowed up to its limit, and its stockholders may not be willing or able to put any more money in the business. Keep in mind that I wanted to use an example with enough (but not too much) cash because this situation should heighten your attention in the cash flow analysis discussed in later chapters.

An executive of a leading company said he kept the company's cash balance "lean and mean" to keep its managers on their toes. There's probably a lot of value to this theory. But, if too much time and effort goes into managing day-to-day cash flow, then the more important strategic factors may not be well managed.

Sales Revenue/Total Assets Operating Relationship

$10,000,000 annual Sales Revenue
÷ $4,181,249 year-end Net Operating Assets = 2.4 times

I don't know if I can get away with calling this formula a relationship because in actual business practice this computation is called the *asset turnover ratio*. It's a very gross ratio; it's a macro level or composite average of the several more specific operating ratios and relationships that have been discussed in this chapter. For decision making and control, however, managers have to focus on the specific operating ratios. One particular ratio may be out of control, but the other operating ratios may be satisfactory.

Also I should point out that this ratio is often based on total assets, not net operating assets as shown above. In any case, the idea of the ratio is to compare how much in assets is needed to generate sales revenue. This company generates $2.40 sales revenue of every $1.00 of assets it uses (net operating assets).

Summary and Cautions

The operating assets and liabilities discussed in this chapter are fundamental for a large range of businesses across many different industries. However, some industries are unique; nonproduct, service-based businesses are quite different. Commercial banks and other financial institutions do not fit the example company used in this chapter. For one thing they do not have inventory, so the inventory/cost of goods sold operating ratio does not apply.

Nevertheless, every business, whether product-based or service-based, regulated or nonregulated, small or large, privately held or publicly owned, should develop operating ratios for its revenue and expenses that connect with its corresponding operating assets and liabilities. Without these essential benchmark ratios, it is very difficult to analyze the profit performance, financial condition, and cash flow effects of decisions. Managers would be without vital reference points for planning and control.

7

EVALUATING PROFIT AND INVESTMENT PERFORMANCE

From Last Chapter to This Chapter

Chapter 6 explains the fundamental ratios that determine the operating assets and liabilities of a business. We found that the example company uses over $4 million total net operating assets to carry on its profit-making operations. The business had to raise this much capital from its debt and equity sources of capital.

This chapter crosses over from the operating side to the financial side of the business and focuses on whether the company is making good use of its capital. We examine how well the business is performing as an investor, or capital user. The basic concern is whether the business has made enough profit on its capital investment.

Exhibit 7.1 presents an overview analysis of the profit and investment performance of the business. Data is from the earlier exhibits that present the management financial statements for the company, which, by now, should be fairly familiar to you. In the exhibit, notice that operating earnings are distributed among the three basic "claims" on this profit. The $1,080,000 operating earnings for the year is divided accordingly: $160,000 to debt capital, $312,800 to income tax, and $607,200 to stockholders' (owners' equity).

The exhibit highlights certain profit and return on investment ratios. Every business is under pressure to meet minimum benchmark performance ratios for profit and return on capital (investment). If the business falls short in making these numbers, it will be penalized in capital markets, and its stockholders may search for better uses of their money.

Profit Ratios

Three basic profit ratios are shown down the left side of Exhibit 7.1. First, notice that the company's *contribution profit margin ratio* is 26.5% of sales revenue. This ratio is the key starting point for the profit success of any business. If this ratio is not high enough, then the business won't be able to cover its fixed costs and generate enough operating profit to cover its costs of capital.

In passing, let me mention one profit ratio *not* shown in Exhibit 7.1—the *gross profit ratio*. Gross profit equals sales revenue less only cost of goods sold expense, which is $4 million in this example or 40% of sales revenue. Let me quickly point out that every business has variable expenses driven by sales revenue or sales volume. So, the gross profit ratio is not the end of the story. Quite clearly, if the gross profit ratio is too low, then the contribution profit margin will be too low.

The second profit ratio in Exhibit 7.1 is the *operating earnings ratio*—10.8% of sales revenue. This figure is the percent of profit remaining from sales revenue after cost of goods sold and all operating expenses (variable and fixed) are deducted, but before interest expense (cost of debt) and income tax expense (cost of government) are deducted. Operating earnings is the line of separation between the *inside* expenses of the business (its product costs and operating expenses) and its *outside* expenses (costs of capital and income tax).

The third and final profit ratio in Exhibit 7.1 is the bottom-line profit ratio, or *net income ratio*, which is 6.07% of sales rev-

EXHIBIT 7.1   EVALUATING BUSINESS PROFIT AND INVESTMENT PERFORMANCE

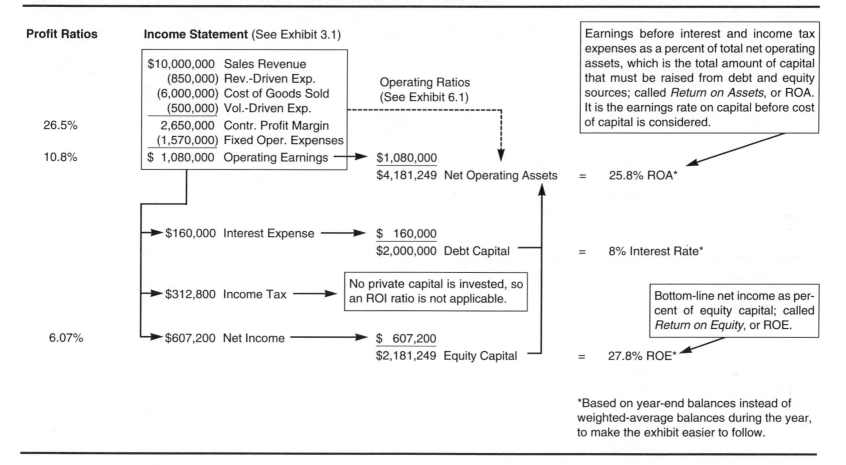

Profit Ratios

Income Statement (See Exhibit 3.1)

$10,000,000	Sales Revenue
(850,000)	Rev.-Driven Exp.
(6,000,000)	Cost of Goods Sold
(500,000)	Vol.-Driven Exp.
2,650,000	Contr. Profit Margin
(1,570,000)	Fixed Oper. Expenses
$ 1,080,000	Operating Earnings

26.5%

10.8%

Operating Ratios
(See Exhibit 6.1)

$1,080,000
$4,181,249 Net Operating Assets   =   25.8% ROA*

Earnings before interest and income tax expenses as a percent of total net operating assets, which is the total amount of capital that must be raised from debt and equity sources; called *Return on Assets*, or ROA. It is the earnings rate on capital before cost of capital is considered.

$160,000 Interest Expense
$ 160,000
$2,000,000 Debt Capital   =   8% Interest Rate*

No private capital is invested, so an ROI ratio is not applicable.

$312,800 Income Tax

Bottom-line net income as percent of equity capital; called *Return on Equity*, or ROE.

6.07%

$607,200 Net Income
$ 607,200
$2,181,249 Equity Capital   =   27.8% ROE*

*Based on year-end balances instead of weighted-average balances during the year, to make the exhibit easier to follow.

enue. As mentioned previously, a popular misconception is that most businesses rip off the public because they keep 20, 30, or more percent of sales revenue as profit. Few businesses can make more than a 10% bottom-line profit on sales. The 6.07% net income ratio in this example is quite respectable.

Profit on Capital, or Return on Investment

The basic measure for evaluating capital investment performance is the *return on investment* (ROI) ratio. The amount of profit, or earnings returned on the amount of capital investment, is expressed as the following percent:

$$\text{Return} \div \text{Investment} = \%$$

ROI is always for a period of time, one year unless stated otherwise. "Return" can mean different things—earnings, or income, or profit, or gain, or appreciation in value. "Investment" means the amount of capital used during the period to generate the return. The ratio of the two is called *return on investment*.

For instance, if ROI is 10% for the year, the earnings (or profit, or income, or gain) equals 10% of the amount of capital invested to produce the earnings. ROI is the percent of capital value growth or the improvement in wealth expressed as a percent of the amount of capital started with.

ROI does not indicate or imply what was done with the earnings. The earnings may have been spent on consumption.

Or, the earnings may have been saved and added to the capital base of the investor. We don't know just from the ROI ratio. We need to know more about the investment to answer these questions.

Business capital investment performance evaluation uses two fundamental ROI ratios: (1) *return on assets* (ROA); and, (2) *return on equity* (ROE). Both are needed, as we shall see. Return on assets (ROA) is calculated as follows (see Exhibit 7.1 for data):

$$\text{ROA} = \text{Operating Earnings} \div \text{Net Operating Assets}$$
$$25.8\% = \$1,080,000 \div \$4,181,249^*$$

ROA is the before-cost-of-capital rate of return on investment for the business. It's the percent the company made on the total capital invested in its net operating assets before the cost of interest on debt capital and before the "cost" of equity capital is taken into account.

Return on equity takes a more restrictive point of view—that of the equity owners in the business, who supply only part of the total capital used by the business. This investment performance ratio excludes debt capital (which is included in the

---

* The year-end amount of net operating assets is used to compute ROA. The theoretically more correct amount is the weighted average for the year. However, the ending balance is a clearer trail to follow and usually is good enough for this type of analysis.

ROA) and looks only at the equity sources of capital. ROE is computed as follows (see Exhibit 7.1 for data):

$$ROE = \text{Net Income} \div \text{Owners' Equity}$$
$$27.8\% = \$607,200 \div \$2,181,249^*$$

To achieve a satisfactory ROE, the business must start with a satisfactory ROA; this is why both ratios are important to understand. But you should notice right here that ROE is higher than ROA! How is this possible? We'll answer this question shortly.

Pivotal Role of Income Tax

In a world without income taxes, operating earnings would be simply divided between the two capital sources—interest on debt and the residual net income for the equity owners (stockholders). But in the real world, income tax takes out a good chunk of operating earnings (see Exhibit 7.1).

We are talking about return on capital investment, so the following question might be asked. Is income tax a return on

government capital investment? The federal government does not invest private capital in business, of course. In a broader sense, however, government provides what could be called *public capital*. Government provides public use facilities (highways, schools, etc.), the political stability, the monetary system, the legal structure, and police protection. In short, government provides the infrastructure for carrying on business activity and collects for this through the income tax (as well as through other taxes of course).

Under our federal income tax law (the U.S. Internal Revenue Code) interest paid by business is *deductible* to determine annual taxable income. Cash dividends paid to stockholders—even though these payments for use of equity capital can be viewed as the equity equivalent of interest payments for use of debt capital—are *not* deductible to determine taxable income. This basic differentiation in the tax law has significant impact on the amount of operating profit that has to be earned to cover the company's cost of capital.

To pay one dollar of interest, a business has to earn just one dollar of operating earnings. One dollar of operating earnings used to pay one dollar of interest results in zero taxable income. In contrast, to earn one dollar of *after-tax* net income a business has to earn before-tax operating earnings equal to: $1.00 net income $\div$ (1 – 34% income tax rate), or ($1.00 $\div$ .64), which equals $1.52 operating earnings. Income tax would be $.52 on the $1.52 operating earnings, leaving only $1.00 net income after income tax.

Let's apply this point to the concrete facts of the example company (refer to Exhibit 7.1 as we go along). The company

---

* The year-end amount of total owners' equity is used to calculate ROE. The theoretically more correct amount is the weighted average for the year. As with ROA, the ending balance is a clearer trail to follow and usually is good enough for this type of analysis–unless there was a major infusion of equity capital during the latter part of the year.

had to earn $160,000 operating earnings to cover its cost of debt for the year. To earn $607,200 net income, however, the business had to make the following amount of operating earnings:

$607,200 Net Income ÷ (1 – 34% Income Tax Rate, or .66)
= $920,000 Operating Earnings

Let's see; is this correct? The $160,000 operating earnings for interest plus the $920,000 for net income equals $1,080,000, which is exactly the operating earnings of the business.

Return on Equity

Net income is the "compensation" for the use of owners' equity capital during the period. The company's shareholders put $750,000 in the business over the years for which they received shares of capital stock, called *paid-in capital*. Keep in mind that the stockholders could have invested this money elsewhere.

Also, the company has reinvested a good amount of its annual profits back into the business. In addition to $750,000 paid in for capital stock, the company's balance sheet (Exhibit 4.1) reports that its accumulated retained earnings has grown to $1,431,249 at most recent year-end. Thus, total owners' equity capital is $2,181,249, which is the capital investment amount used in the ROE computation shown earlier and in Exhibit 7.1.

Stockholders' equity capital is at risk; the business may or may not be able to earn enough net income on their capital.

For that matter the company could go belly up and go into bankruptcy. In bankruptcy proceedings, stockholders are paid last, after all debts and liabilities are settled. There's no promise that cash dividends will be paid to stockholders, even if net income is earned. Net income is $607,200 for its most recent year, but only $76,606 was distributed as cash dividends (see Exhibit 5.1).

In any case, equity capital investment performance is not measured by how much dividends are paid but, rather, by the entire amount of net income earned by the business. The cash dividend yield is an important ratio in investment analysis by individuals and institutions who invest in stock shares. It is the most recent 12 months cash dividends divided by the current market value of the stock and is called the *dividend yield* ratio. ROE, in contrast, is the measure of the full yield or complete return on equity capital.*

ROE is 27.8% for the year, which, as a matter of fact, is pretty good. Although, this comment raises a larger question

---

* If there is more than one class of stock (e.g., both preferred and common stock) net income has to be divided between the classes and the share for the common stock is used in computing its ROE. There may be more than one class of common stock, each having different priorities and claims on net income. So, a separate ROE may have to be computed for each class. Also, we do not consider any change in market value of the stock shares here; net income is treated as the total increase of value to the equity shareholders. If the capital stock shares are traded in a public market, then the change in market value during the year should be included in determining the total return on equity for the period.

regarding which yardstick is most relevant. Theoretically the $2,181,249 owners' equity in the business could be pulled out and invested somewhere else and could earn a ROI on the alternative investment.

Should the company's ROE be compared with the ROI that could be earned on a riskless and highly liquid investment, such as short-term U.S. government securities? Surely not. Most everyone would agree that a company's ROE should be compared with *comparable* investment alternatives that generally have the same risk and liquidity characteristics as stockholders' equity.

The earnings rate (ROI) on the most relevant alternative, or the next best investment alternative, is called the *opportunity cost of capital.* To avoid a prolonged discussion here we'll simply assume the stockholders are satisfied with the company's 27.8% ROE performance, which implies that their opportunity cost of capital is lower. Of course, the company should maintain this ROE and even do better if it can. One reason why its ROE is pretty good is that the company uses financial leverage, which we turn to next.

Financial Leverage

Suppose, if you would, that the example company did not use interest-bearing debt—none at all. This presumes that the stockholders could have and would have supplied $2,000,000 more capital, or that the business could have accumulated this much more retained earnings over the years. In any case, suppose the owners' equity had been $2,000,000 more and debt had been $2,000,000 less. In short, assume all the capital needed for its net operating assets came from owners' equity. What would have been the company's net income and ROE for the year?

In this hypothetical scenario, the company's operating earnings would have been the same—$1,080,000 (see Exhibit 7.1). With no interest to pay, the company's taxable income would equal its operating earnings. Its income tax would have been 34% or $367,200. So, net income would have been $712,800, which is higher than the company's actual $607,200 net income. But, and here's the key point, owners' equity would have been $2,000,000 higher.

ROE would have been considerably worse in this alternative situation:

$$\text{ROE} = \text{Net Income} \div \text{Owners' Equity}$$
$$17.1\% = \$712,800 \div \$4,181,249$$

ROE would have been only 17.1%, which is far less than the 27.8% actual ROE attained by the business. To achieve its higher ROE, the company benefited from *financial leverage*.

Financial leverage refers to borrowing money at an interest rate lower than can be earned on the debt capital. The equity capital base of the business is leveraged by using additional debt capital in place of and on top of equity capital. For this reason financial leverage is also called *trading on the equity*. A favorable spread between the interest rate and the company's ROA produces a financial leverage gain that supplements earnings on equity capital and improves ROE.

EXHIBIT 7.2   FINANCIAL LEVERAGE

$516,592	Earnings on Debt Capital @ 25.8% ROA
(160,000)	Interest Expense on Debt Capital
356,592	Pretax Leverage Gain
563,408	Earnings on Equity Capital @ 25.8% ROA
920,000	Total Equity Earnings (Taxable Income)
(312,800)	Income Tax @ 34%
$607,200	Net Income

In Exhibit 7.1, we see that the company earns 25.8% ROA, but only has to pay 8% interest on its borrowed capital.* It doesn't take a rocket scientist to figure out that this is a good deal. Exhibit 7.2 summarizes the effects of financial leverage for this company example.

The company earned $516,592 operating earnings on its $2,000,000 debt capital at the 25.8% ROA rate. But, it had to pay only $160,000 interest on its debt, so the business realized a $356,592 pretax financial leverage gain for the benefit of its stockholders.† The pretax financial leverage gain adds a sub-stantial amount to the pretax $563,408 ROA earned on owners' equity capital. In other words, pretax net income consists of two parts: (1) the financial leverage gain; plus (2) the pretax operating earnings on equity capital. Because the financial leverage gain is so large in this example, ROE is even more than the company's ROA, because the financial leverage gain benefit to net income is so large.

The lesson here is that managers should keep a close and careful eye on how much the financial leverage factor contributes to net income and ROE. Interest rates can change, although it is unlikely that interest rates would increase all the way to the 25.8% ROA level and wipe out all the favorable spread. ROA could drop substantially, although it is unlikely that ROA would fall down to the 8% interest rate. However, even relatively small changes in ROA and the interest rate can have a substantial impact on net income and ROE. And, the company could also shift its mix of debt and equity. If the company had not used so much debt in this example, then the financial leverage gain would have been smaller.

Financial leverage looks good of course, but it has its limits and disadvantages. Lenders will loan only so much money to a business; once a business hits its borrowing capacity, new debt is either not available or lending terms become prohibitive. Any slippage in the spread between ROA and the interest rate has a magnifying effect on ROE. A lower ROA would not only reduce the earnings on equity capital, but it also would take away some of the leverage gain; there would be a twofold negative impact on ROE.

---

* A business usually has two or more loans or debt issues and usually different interest rates are paid on different loans. For this analysis, all interest-bearing liabilities are telescoped into one composite average interest rate. As you can see in Exhibit 7.1, the company's average annual interest rate on all its debt is 8%.

† Alternatively, we could calculate pretax financial leverage gain as follows: 17.8% favorable spread between the 25.8% ROA less the 8% interest rate times $2,000,000 debt equals $356,592, the same as shown in Exhibit 7.2.

Revisiting Income Tax and ROI

Income Tax: Not So Simple

The example company uses the 34% income tax rate. Under current income tax law, corporate taxable incomes starting at $335,000 up to $10,000,000 are taxed at the 34% rate. Annual taxable incomes below $335,000 are taxed at lower rates, and above $10,000,000 at a slightly higher rate. In this example, the company's taxable income is $920,000 ($1,080,000 operating earnings – $160,000 interest expense). So it owes 34% or $312,800 to Uncle Sam. The assumption is that the company is a corporation and is taxed as a domestic C or regular corporation.

A corporation with 35* or fewer stockholders may elect to be treated as an S (for small) corporation. An S corporation pays no income tax itself; its annual taxable income is passed through to its individual stockholders in proportion to their share ownership. Business sole proprietorships (self-employed persons) and partnerships are also tax conduits; they are not subject to income tax as a separate entity but pass their taxable income through to their owner or owners who have to include their shares of the entity's taxable income in their personal income tax returns. As you probably know, personal income tax rates and situations vary widely.

---

* At the time this book went to press Congress was considering legislation that would increase the 35 stockholder limit to 50.

Corporations may have net loss carryforwards that reduce or eliminate taxable income in one year. There is also the alternative minimum tax (AMT) to consider, to say nothing of a myriad of other provisions and options (loopholes) in the tax law. It's very difficult to generalize. The main point is that in a given year in a given situation the taxable income of a business may not result in the normal income tax.

Book Values Versus Current Values

Evaluating the capital investment performance for a business requires dollar values for its debt and equity capital. The amounts generally used are the *book values* for debt and equity as reported in the company's most recent balance sheet. Book values are the values used in the calculations in this chapter.

Book values of most debt instruments are equal to their maturity values—the amounts due at maturity. Book values of debt are generally correct for capital investment analysis, and interest rates based on these maturity values are generally correct.*

---

* There is one major exception. Debt may be issued by a business with very heavy original issue discount, which means the amount received by the business at the time of borrowing is substantially less than the maturity value of the debt. The discount represents additional interest that will be paid eventually; the *effective* interest rate is therefore higher than the rate based on maturity value, which is called the *coupon rate*. Indeed, the business could issue zero-coupon bonds that pay no interest until maturity. The effective interest rate should be used when debt is issued with heavy original issue discount from maturity value.

The book (maturity) value of debt may not be appropriate if the business is in financial distress, has defaulted on its debt payments, or is in bankruptcy proceedings. The capital investment performance of the business would not be the main concern in such a situation. The very survival of the company would be the main concern.

Book value of equity is used for calculating ROE, as explained in this chapter. Keep in mind that book value is *historical recorded* value. The book value of equity is the cumulative sum of paid-in capital amounts for capital stock (which may go back many years) plus the annual additions to retained earnings equal to net income less dividends paid each year (which also may go back many years).

Private corporations have no ready market value information for their capital stock shares. These entities could estimate the market value of their owners' equity or have a formal appraisal done, but they seldom do. Thus, ROE is based on the book value of their owners' equity. Keep in mind, however, that this tends to inflate ROE because the historical book value of owners' equity may be low compared with any reasonable estimate of current value.

In their annual external financial reports, publicly owned corporations report ROE based on the book value of their equity capital, although this disclosure is not required. Stockholders in public corporations have market value information at their fingertips by looking in the *Wall Street Journal*, the *New York Times*, *Barrons*, *Investor's Daily*, and many other sources of financial market information.

Stockholders of publicly owned companies are very interested in two key ratios: the *earnings per share* (EPS) and the *price/earnings ratio* (P/E). EPS is net income divided by the number of common stock shares outstanding. The trend of EPS clearly has more impact on the market value of stock shares than ROE based on book value equity balances.

Stock investors closely watch the stock's P/E ratio, which is the stock's current market price divided by its EPS. In fact, P/E ratios are reported in the *Wall Street Journal*, whereas ROE ratios are not. There's no question that ROE (based on book value) takes a back seat to EPS and P/E ratios for investors in publicly owned corporations.

Summary

This chapter examines a business as an investment enterprise and user of capital. The basic capital investment analysis tools are return on investment (ROI) ratios. Stockholders, being the suppliers of the equity capital to business, are primarily interested in Return on Equity (ROE), which is the ratio of net income divided by stockholders' equity. To earn a satisfactory ROE, a business must first earn a satisfactory Return On Assets (ROA).

ROA is measured by dividing operating earnings before interest and income tax expenses by total net operating assets. The spread between the ROA rate and the interest rate on debt times the amount of debt capital determines the amount of financial leverage gain (or loss!). A large part of bottom-line net income may be due to financial leverage; you don't know until you analyze it. Operating earnings may remain the same, but changes in the ROA rate, the interest rate, or the mix of debt to equity can have a material impact on net income and ROE. Managers should keep a close watch on changes in these factors.

The main premise of this chapter is that every business must meet its cost of capital demands and objectives—interest on debt and net income for equity capital. The cost of capital changes over time. Interest rates fluctuate, income tax laws change, debt to equity ratios shift, and ROE goals change. So, cost of capital is a "moveable feast." The basic concept and theory of cost of capital is constant; but year-to-year calculations change. In developing the financial plans for one year ahead, cost of capital determinants can be predicted fairly accurately. But a five- or ten-year financial plan is much more subject to forecast errors and revisions.

8

BUDGETING FOR PROFIT, CAPITAL NEEDS, AND SOLVENCY

Planning for Growth

This chapter demonstrates budgeting for growth. In our example company, the managers have decided on higher sales revenue and profit objectives for next year. They believe that these targets are realistic. Without some growth the long-run survival of the entity may be threatened. The company's basic strategy is to grow the business on a steady year-to-year trend line.

A higher level of total net operating assets is needed to support the higher level of sales revenue and expenses. It would be very unusual to grow without increasing operating assets and operating liabilities. So, more capital is needed; and, to maintain return on assets (ROA) and return on equity (ROE) performance, the company has to increase its operating profit and net income consistent with the increase in capital. One primary reason for budgeting is to test whether return on investment (ROI) can be maintained, or perhaps, even improved.

In short, managers should keep an eye on both profit and the incremental capital needed for the profit growth. From the capital investment point of view, a business should not seek growth at the expense of its ROE performance, in theory, at least. In practice, ROE performance may be sacrificed to keep the business alive over the short run, in order to reach a better long-run competitive and strategic position.

The Basic Step: Profit Budgeting

Budgeting for next year, which, in this example, means budgeting for moderate growth, can be done on two levels or in two steps. The minimal budgeting approach involves preparing a budgeted income statement. Sales revenue and each of the major expenses are analyzed and forecast for next year. The business then puts together its profit plan in the form of a reasonably detailed budgeted income statement for next year.

Using the minimal approach, the business would make only rough estimates of how much capital is needed to support budgeted sales revenue and expenses. These ballpark estimates of net operating assets and capital sources are used to predict how ROA and ROE should turn out next year. No attempt is made to assemble a budgeted balance sheet or a budgeted cash flow statement.

Exhibit 8.1 illustrates the minimal budgeting approach. Please refer to this exhibit as we go along. The year just ended, labeled Last Year in the exhibit, is the point of departure for preparing next year's budget. Budgeting starts with the year just completed and predicts what changes will or should happen over the coming year. The premise is that to get *there* you have to start from *here*.

Looking down the percent changes and dollar changes columns in the budgeted income statement for next year we see that many changes are predicted next year. Establishing targets and making estimates, forecasts, and predictions are the essence of budgeting. It starts with sales revenue. The company is budgeting sales revenue to increase $1,340,000 next year, a 13.4% increase. This budget goal is based on sales price increases and sales volume increases. Increasing both prices and volume may be a tall order.

The budgeting of expenses pivots off budgeted sales volume. Of course, cost of goods sold and sales volume-driven operat-

EXHIBIT 8.1   BUDGETING PROFIT AND CAPITAL GROWTH

Income Statement

	Actual Last Year	Budgeted % Changes	Plan Next Year	Budgeted $ Changes
Sales Revenue	$10,000,000	13.4%	$11,340,000	$1,340,000
Revenue-Driven Expenses	(850,000)	21.9%	(1,036,193)	(186,193)
Cost of Goods Sold	(6,000,000)	10.7%	(6,642,000)	(642,000)
Volume-Driven Expenses	(500,000)	15.0%	(575,100)	(75,100)
Contribution Profit Margin	$ 2,650,000	16.5%	$ 3,086,708	$ 436,708
Fixed Operating Expenses	(1,570,000)	12.5%	(1,766,250)	(196,250)
Operating Earnings	$ 1,080,000	22.3%	$ 1,320,458	$ 240,458
Interest Expense	(160,000)	0.0%	(160,000)	0
Income Tax	(312,800)	26.1%	(394,556)	(81,756)
Net Income	$ 607,200	26.1%	$ 765,902	$ 158,702

The simplifying assumption is that net operating assets increase the same percent as sales revenue.

Capital increase needed to support profit increase

Net Operating Assets and Capital Sources

	Actual Last Year	Budgeted % Changes	Plan Next Year	
Total Net Operating Assets	$4,181,249	13.4%	$4,741,536	$560,287
ROA (Return on Assets)*	25.8%	2.0%	27.8%	
Total Debt Capital	$2,000,000	no change	$2,000,000	no change
Total Equity Capital	$2,181,249	25.7%	$2,741,536	$560,287
ROE (Return on Equity)*	27.8%	0.1%	27.9%	

*Budgeted change equals the difference between the two and not the percent of change from last year.

Management Planning Questions

Debt policy and availability?

Will new capital stock shares have to be issued?

Can any cash dividends be paid out of net income for year?

ing expenses depend on the quantities sold. Also, fixed costs (in this example) are expanded to support the higher sales volume. The business also forecasts whether the unit costs of its several different expenses will increase (or possibly decrease). For now we step around these details, which are discussed later in this chapter.

At this point we drop down to the bottom line; net income is budgeted to increase $158,702, or 26.1%. We certainly should examine why net income increases 26.1% with only a 13.4% sales revenue increase. Managers definitely should understand how this works. But for now our focus shifts down to the amount of net operating assets needed to support the sales revenue and expenses budgeted for next year.

The income statement in Exhibit 8.1 is based on thorough planning of sales revenue and expenses for next year. But the estimate of net operating assets is based on a shortcut procedure. It is simply assumed that total net operating assets would increase the same percent as sales revenue. (See the balloon on the left side of the exhibit.) Although simplistic, this shortcut is better than altogether ignoring net operating assets.

Additional capital is needed to finance the net operating assets increase. Managers have to give some thought to where the additional capital will come from. And, managers should look at what happens to ROA and ROE. The bottom part of Exhibit 8.1 presents the capital plan for the coming year, including budgeted ROA and ROE, of course.

As you see in Exhibit 8.1, the budgeted profit growth requires $560,287 additional net operating assets. Where does this additional capital come from? Its total debt is already fairly heavy, so the business budgets no increase in borrowings next year. This plan may be changed based on the impact on ROE, however. Despite net income increasing 26.1%, the company's ROE remains virtually the same. Why? The company is using less financial leverage according to its profit plan. To put it another way, owners' equity is supplying a larger portion of the total capital used by the business.

The managers may reconsider and decide to increase total debt by $100,000 or $200,000. Can the company borrow this money? Will the lenders be willing? Steps should be taken now to line up additional borrowing. Bankers don't like to be surprised or rushed into such things. Indeed, a budget report, such as Exhibit 8.1, is a good "talking" document to convince lenders that a profit and capital plan has been developed and how additional debt fits into the capitalization structure of the business.

The budgeting approach shown in Exhibit 8.1 is the essential first step. It's not a bad starting point—indeed a very necessary first step, but, there are several critical loose ends in this profit and capital budget. Many other balance sheet and cash flow questions should be addressed. For instance, how will the company's cash balance be affected by the sales and profit growth? A more comprehensive budget includes the balance sheet (all assets and liabilities) and cash flows.

Developing the Master Budget

The second level of budgeting goes a step further, in fact, a pretty big step up. The assets, liabilities, and owners' equity as well as cash flows for the coming year are budgeted. In short, a complete set of budgeted financial statements are prepared.

As already mentioned, a budget is based on targets, forecasts, estimates, and predictions. It goes without saying that the future numbers in a budget can turn out to be wrong—almost assuredly so! This is the very nature of budgeting. If you want precision, you'll have to do it with hindsight, not foresight. In short, budgets are based on the most reasonable and realistic future numbers you can come up with, knowing in the back of your mind that the actual numbers will turn out different.

Exhibit 8.2 presents the complete set of budgeted financial statements for the business. We have already seen its profit plan, or budgeted income statement, in Exhibit 8.1. What's different now is that we also see the budgeted balance sheet and budgeted cash flow statement. The budgeted income statement is presented again, but with a slight format change. Many businesses use this format, which includes the gross profit line, equal to sales revenue, less only the cost of goods sold expense. Otherwise the format of the income statement is the same as before.

As previously mentioned, many forecasts, estimates, and predictions are built into these three budgeted financial statements. Rather than going through each one in detail I direct your attention to the balloons in the statements, which identify the key forecasts and targets behind the numbers in the financial statements. As you probably know, in actual practice these forecasts are not easy to make. For instance, how did the company arrive at the 8% sales volume increase forecast? Is it realistic, especially given the 5% sales price increase planned for next year?

Every one of the forecasts, estimates, and predictions can be challenged. To move ahead, however, the budgeting process has to make the best guesses about the future that can be made and then put together budgeted financial statements in order to examine consequences and outcomes. We will not spend time considering every forecast, estimate, and prediction, but I encourage you to take the time to read each of the balloons in the budgeted financial statements. It goes without saying that every business is in a different situation, and that every year is a different situation for a business.

How Does the Budget Look?

How does the budget look? What does it tell us? Many things, of course. Most of the news is good. Net income increases, cash dividends increase, and the ending cash balance is up. Free cash flow (cash flow from operating activities) is more than enough to cover the planned capital expenditures. One piece of bad news is that ROE slips a little, although it is still a very respectable 26.9% (see Exhibit 8.2a). Things don't always look so good.

We might compare Exhibit 8.2 (the complete master budget) with Exhibit 8.1 (the abbreviated profit plan). Net operating assets are a little higher than the rough estimate made in the first step of the budgeting process, although not by all that much. In other words, total net operating assets increase slightly more than the 13.4% sales revenue increase.

The approach in Exhibit 8.1 assumes net operating assets would be $4,741,536, whereas the master budget (Exhibit 8.2) shows that the amount is $4,847,151. The two amounts are very close however. In fact, if cash dividends had been budgeted at $205,615 instead of $100,000, then net operating assets and stockholders' equity would have been exactly the same as in Exhibit 8.1.

EXHIBIT 8.2A   MASTER BUDGET FOR NEXT YEAR: INCOME STATEMENTS

INCOME STATEMENTS	Actual Last Year	Budgeted Next Year	Budgeted % Changes
Sales Revenue	$10,000,000	$11,340,000	13.4%
Cost of Goods Sold Expense	(6,000,000)	(6,642,000)	10.7%
Gross Margin	$ 4,000,000	$ 4,698,000	17.5%
Variable Operating Expenses			
Sales Volume-Driven	(500,000)	(575,100)	15.0%
Sales Revenue-Driven	(850,000)	(1,036,193)	21.9%
Contribution Profit Margin	$ 2,650,000	$ 3,086,708	16.5%
Fixed Operating Expenses	(1,570,000)	(1,766,250)	12.5%
Operating Earnings	$ 1,080,000	$ 1,320,458	22.3%
Interest Expense	(160,000)	(160,000)	0.0%
Earnings Before Income Tax	$ 920,000	$ 1,160,458	26.1%
Income Tax Expense @ 34%	(312,800)	(394,556)	26.1%
Net Income	$ 607,200	$ 765,902	26.1%
Year-end Stockholders' Equity	$ 2,181,249	$ 2,847,151	30.5%
ROE (based on year-end balances)*	27.8%	26.9%	-0.9%

*Budgeted change equals the difference between the two, and not the percent of change from last year.

Budgeting Forecasts and Assumptions

Sales prices increase 5% and sales volumes increase 8% on all products across the board.

Sales volume increases 8% and product costs increase 2.5% on all products.

This format is a slight modification from previous management income statement format, to show the gross profit line.

8% sales volume increase and 6.5% cost inflation increases on the components in this expense category.

Increases in the various components of this cost.

Almost all of the components in this expense category increase over last year at higher rates than other expenses.

Remains the same because total debt and interest rates remain the same. See the budgeted balance sheet.

Higher taxable income causes income tax to increase accordingly.

Increases more than sales revenue increase, a key point analyzed later in the book.

See budgeted balance sheets for stockholders' equity amounts.

Slightly less than previous year, which, of course, is not a good trend to start.

EXHIBIT 8.2B   MASTER BUDGET FOR NEXT YEAR: YEAR-END BALANCE SHEETS

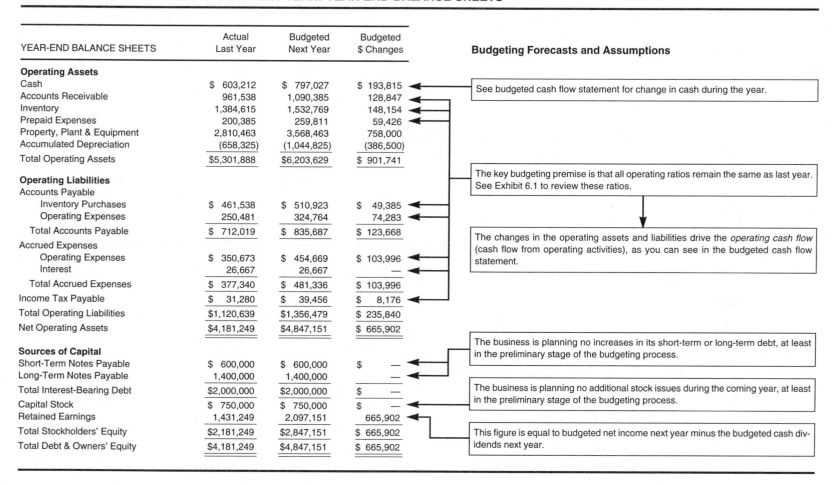

YEAR-END BALANCE SHEETS	Actual Last Year	Budgeted Next Year	Budgeted $ Changes	Budgeting Forecasts and Assumptions
Operating Assets				
Cash	$ 603,212	$ 797,027	$ 193,815	See budgeted cash flow statement for change in cash during the year.
Accounts Receivable	961,538	1,090,385	128,847	
Inventory	1,384,615	1,532,769	148,154	
Prepaid Expenses	200,385	259,811	59,426	
Property, Plant & Equipment	2,810,463	3,568,463	758,000	
Accumulated Depreciation	(658,325)	(1,044,825)	(386,500)	
Total Operating Assets	$5,301,888	$6,203,629	$ 901,741	
				The key budgeting premise is that all operating ratios remain the same as last year. See Exhibit 6.1 to review these ratios.
Operating Liabilities				
Accounts Payable				
Inventory Purchases	$ 461,538	$ 510,923	$ 49,385	
Operating Expenses	250,481	324,764	74,283	
Total Accounts Payable	$ 712,019	$ 835,687	$ 123,668	
Accrued Expenses				The changes in the operating assets and liabilities drive the *operating cash flow* (cash flow from operating activities), as you can see in the budgeted cash flow statement.
Operating Expenses	$ 350,673	$ 454,669	$ 103,996	
Interest	26,667	26,667	—	
Total Accrued Expenses	$ 377,340	$ 481,336	$ 103,996	
Income Tax Payable	$ 31,280	$ 39,456	$ 8,176	
Total Operating Liabilities	$1,120,639	$1,356,479	$ 235,840	
Net Operating Assets	$4,181,249	$4,847,151	$ 665,902	
				The business is planning no increases in its short-term or long-term debt, at least in the preliminary stage of the budgeting process.
Sources of Capital				
Short-Term Notes Payable	$ 600,000	$ 600,000	$ —	
Long-Term Notes Payable	1,400,000	1,400,000	—	
Total Interest-Bearing Debt	$2,000,000	$2,000,000	$ —	
Capital Stock	$ 750,000	$ 750,000	$ —	The business is planning no additional stock issues during the coming year, at least in the preliminary stage of the budgeting process.
Retained Earnings	1,431,249	2,097,151	665,902	
Total Stockholders' Equity	$2,181,249	$2,847,151	$ 665,902	
Total Debt & Owners' Equity	$4,181,249	$4,847,151	$ 665,902	This figure is equal to budgeted net income next year minus the budgeted cash dividends next year.

EXHIBIT 8.2C   MASTER BUDGET FOR NEXT YEAR: CASH FLOW STATEMENTS

CASH FLOW STATEMENTS	Actual Last Year	Budgeted Next Year	Budgeting Forecasts and Assumptions
Cash Flows from Operating Activities			
Net Income	$607,200	$ 765,902 ◄──	See budgeted income statement.
Changes in Operating Cycle			
Assets and Liabilities:			
Accounts Receivable	(135,193)	(128,847) ◄	See the budgeted changes in these operating assets and liabilities from the balance sheet above.
Inventory	(196,970)	(148,154) ◄	
Prepaid Expenses	(31,430)	(59,426) ◄	
Accounts Payable	56,999	123,668 ◄	
Accrued Expenses	(45,665)	103,996 ◄	Because of replacement and expansion of fixed assets (see capital expenditures below), the annual depreciation expense increases.
Income Tax Payable	4,840	8,176 ◄	
Operating Cash Flow			
Before Depreciation	$259,781	$ 665,315	
Depreciation Expense	315,000	386,500 ◄	Certain long-term, fixed assets reached the end of their useful lives and are replaced; also, the company's fixed assets are expanded to support the additional sales volume. So, total capital expenditures are more than last year, which also reflects inflation in the costs of the fixed assets acquired or constructed. Notice that operating cash flow is more than capital expenditures, so the free cash flow more than covers this need and the company does not have to raise additional debt or equity capital.
Cash Flow from Profit			
Making Operations	$574,781	$1,051,815	
Cash Flows from Investing Activities			
Purchases of Property, Plant & Equipment	(491,688)	(758,000) ◄	
Cash Flows from Financing Activities			
Net Increase in Short-Term Debt	100,000	0 ◄	The business is planning no increase in its short-term or long-term debt, at least in the preliminary stage of the budgeting process.
Long-Term Borrowings	100,000	0 ◄	
Capital Stock Issue	50,000	0 ◄	
Cash Dividends to Stockholders	(76,606)	(100,000) ◄	
Increase (Decrease) in Cash	$256,487	$ 193,815 ◄	

The business is planning no additional stock issues during the coming year, at least in the preliminary stage of the budgeting process.

The business is planning to increase total cash dividends to $100,000, subject to approval by the board of directors during the coming year.

What About Solvency?

The other main "lesson" of the master budget concerns the solvency of the business. The standard definition of solvency refers to the ability of a business to pay its liabilities on time. If not paid on time, creditors could threaten or actually take legal action to enforce collection, and that could bring a business to its knees. Without a doubt, to continue as a going concern, a business must remain solvent and avoid the wrath of its creditors.

Two ratios are widely used to gauge the short-term solvency of business: (1) the *current* ratio and (2) the *quick* ratio (also called the *acid test* ratio). Current assets are those converted into cash in one year or less; current liabilities are those due in one year or less. The current ratio is calculated by dividing total current assets by the total current liabilities. Using next year's ending balances (from Exhibit 8.2b), the current ratio is determined as follows:

Current Ratio

Cash	$ 797,027
Accounts Receivable	1,090,385
Inventory	1,532,769
Prepaid Expenses	259,811
Total Current Assets	$3,679,991
Accounts Payable	$ 835,687
Accrued Expenses	481,336
Income Tax Payable	39,456
Short-Term Notes Payable	600,000
Total Current Liabilities	$1,956,479
Current Assets/Current Liabilities	= 1.88

Short-term notes payable are included in total current liabilities in calculating the current ratio, because these liabilities have to be paid within one year or less. This ratio says that the business has $1.88 assets that will be converted into cash within one year or less for every $1.00 of liabilities that come due in one year or less.

The quick, or acid test, ratio limits assets to cash, cash equivalents (highly marketable investments), and accounts receivable. These assets are more readily available for paying current liabilities than inventory and prepaid expenses. Using next year's ending balances (from Exhibit 8.2b), the quick ratio is calculated as follows:

Quick (Acid Test) Ratio

Cash	$ 797,027
Short-Term Marketable Investments	none
Accounts Receivable	1,090,385
Total Quick Assets	$1,887,411
Accounts Payable	$ 835,687
Accrued Expenses	481,336
Income Tax Payable	39,456
Short-Term Notes Payable	600,000
Total Current Liabilities	$1,956,479
Quick Assets/Current Liabilities	= 0.96

The business has $.96 of quick assets for every $1.00 of liabilities falling due during the following year.

Both ratios suggest the business should be able to pay its short-term liabilities. To be frank however, the ratios have limited meaning. The current and quick ratios have their roots in *external* financial reporting. The ratios use information disclosed in external financial statements. The ratios were developed by and for creditors and investors who do not have access to inside information and who want a fast test of solvency. Managers, on the other hand, have access to more information, and they must keep the business solvent day to day and week to week.

One technique for controlling solvency is to prepare weekly, monthly, or quarterly cash flow budgets that plot when cash will be received and when liabilities fall due. More broadly, operating cash flow period by period can be budgeted and compared to all investing and financing demands on the cash flow. This comparison in turn leads to decisions regarding when and where to raise additional debt and equity capital that may be needed, cash dividends levels, and so on.

It is very important to keep in mind that short-term operating liabilities and short-term debt are not really paid off and retired by most businesses. Rather, short-term liabilities are *rolled over*; new liabilities replace the old liabilities. The current and acid test ratios are *payment* tests, not rollover tests. Liability rollover is the name of the game for the great majority of businesses. From the viewpoint of the capitalization of a business, its operating liabilities and short-term interest-bearing debt are, for all practical purposes, part of its "permanent" capital base.

The question is not really whether the business can actually pay off and retire its liabilities, but whether it can convince its creditors to continue to extend credit. The key test of solvency is whether the business can keep recycling its liabilities. Creditors often insist on payment of the old liability before renewing the credit. Banks, for example, may require that a line of credit be "rested" for at least part of the year. Or, a vendor may insist on payment of the old debt before selling on credit again to the business. For this and other operating reasons, a business must keep an adequate working cash balance.

Interestingly, there is no standard ratio or rule of thumb for how much a company's working cash balance should be relative to its short-term liabilities—and I can't give you one either. The budgeted cash balance at next year-end is almost $800,000. Is this adequate? It seems to provide an adequate buffer against unexpected delays in collecting accounts receivable, or selling inventory, or unusual expense outlays.

If all its current liabilities had to be paid within one or two months, the business might have a problem. It's helpful to prepare a schedule, or timeline of liability due dates, so that managers can plan cash needs. This doesn't mean that the liabilities are actually paid off and retired, as we have already discussed. But it gives the managers a look ahead of when the liabilities come due and their schedule for rolling over liabilities. The smaller the working cash balance of the business, the greater the need for such a schedule.

Summary

The central strategy of many businesses is growth. Growth requires careful planning. Budgeting is the best tool to identify and focus on the specific factors and developments that managers must deal with to translate the plan into actualization. A growth plan without a budget is more a wish list than a road map for achieving goals and objectives.

This chapter presents two levels of budgeting, similar to a budgeting appetizer and main course. The minimal budgeting approach (the appetizer) is to prepare an income statement in sufficient detail for sales revenue and major expenses. Also, rough estimates of the increase in net operating assets and the corresponding increase from capital sources should be made. This profit and capital budget is a very useful guideline for reaching the goals and objectives of the coming period.

The more comprehensive budgeting approach (the main course) is to plan and forecast changes in all assets, all liabilities, all debt and equity capital sources, and all cash flows. A budgeted balance sheet and cash flow statement are prepared, in addition to a budgeted income statement. The complete set of budgeted financial statements covers all the bases, providing benchmarks for achieving both profit and financial condition goals and objectives. The master budget also provides critical information for planning and controlling the solvency of the business, which is critical to say the least.

9

MANAGEMENT CONTROL

Management Control: The Essential Steps after Making Decisions

Decision making lays down a plan of action for accomplishing objectives. Actually achieving the objectives requires *management control*. In its broadest sense, management control refers to everything managers do in moving the business toward its objectives. Decisions start things in motion; then control brings things to a successful conclusion. Good decisions made with poor control can turn out just as badly as making poor decisions in the first place.

Management control is both preventive and positive in nature. Managers have to prevent, or at least minimize, wrong things from occurring. Murphy's law is true; if something can go wrong it will. Managers must make sure right things are happening, and happening on time. Managers must do more than be reactive to problems; they must also be proactive and push things along in the right direction. Management control is not just the absence of problems but the presence of actions to achieve the goals and objectives of the business.

One of the best definitions of management control I've heard was told to me by a former student. I asked the class for a good but concise definition of management control. He defined it in two words: "watching everything." This pithy comment captures the essence of management control. All management theorists include control in their conceptual scheme, but there's little consensus on exact definitions of control.

Most definitions of management control emphasize the need for feedback information. Actual performance is compared against goals, objectives, targets, budgets, and plans to detect deviations and variances. Managers then take corrective action to bring performance back on course. Management control is an information dependent process, that's for sure.

Managers need actual performance information reported on a timely basis. Feedback information on actual performance is the main tool of management control. Managers need this information quickly, and in this regard, time itself is a tool of control. Information received too late can result in costly delays before problems are corrected.

Management Control Information

Management control information consists of three basic types: (1) periodic comprehensive financial statements (including supporting schedules) designed for control purposes; (2) periodic limited-scope control reports that focus on critical factors and key variables, such as employee absenteeism; and (3) ad hoc control reports triggered by specific problems that have arisen, which are needed in addition to the regular control reports included in (1) and (2).

Management control information can be divided into either good news or bad news. Good news is when actual performance is going according to plan. Management's job is to keep things moving in this direction. Management control information usually reveals bad news as problems that have come up and unsatisfactory performance areas that need attention. Not all problems come to attention through the accounting system.

Managers draw on a very broad range of information sources for control purposes. Managers monitor customer satisfaction, employee morale, production schedules, and quality control inspection results. Managers listen to customers' complaints, shop the competition, and may even decide that some industrial intelligence and espionage is necessary to get information about the competition. Nevertheless, the accounting system is one of the most important sources for control information.

Managers are primarily concerned with problems that directly affect the financial performance of the business, such as sales quotas not being met, sales prices being discounted lower than predicted, product costs higher than expected, expenses running over budget, cash flow running slower than planned, and so on. Even when things are moving along very close to as planned, managers need control reports to inform them of this satisfactory progress.

Control reports should be designed to fit the specific areas of authority and responsibility of individual managers. For example, the purchasing (procurement) manager gets control reports on inventory and suppliers; the credit manager gets control reports on accounts receivable and customers; the sales manager gets control reports on sales and salespersons; and so on. These periodic control reports are "detail rich." For example, the monthly sales report for a territory may include breakdowns on hundreds or perhaps more than a thousand different products and customers.

Moving up the organization chart, to a product line manager or a division manager for example, the span of management authority and responsibility becomes broader and broader. At the top level of management (president and chief executive officer), the span of authority and responsibility encompasses the whole business.

Financial statements for management control are supplemented with much more detailed schedules, compared with the financial statements illustrated earlier in this book. For example, management control financial statements include detailed schedules of receivables that are past due, inventory that has been in stock too long, products that have unusually high rates of return, which specific expenses are most over budget, and so on.

In addition to regular periodic financial statements, managers usually select specific factors or key items for special attention. An example of this approach is the following:

> During a recent cost-cutting drive, James Orr, chairman and chief executive of Anima Corp., an insurer in Portland, Maine, asked for a daily count on the number of company employees. He was told he couldn't get it. Some data were kept by divisions, and so were hard to gather together in one place. Some were in a payroll database accessible only to programmers.
>
> Mr. Orr persisted, however, and now the answer is at his fingertips whenever he wants it: A specially designed executive information system links personnel data to a personal computer in Mr. Orr's office. "Management knows I'm watching the count very closely," he says. "Believe me, they don't add staff carelessly."*

Managers should identify the relatively few most critical success factors and keep a close and constant watch on them.

---

* William M. Bulkeley, "Special Systems Make Computing Less Traumatic for Top Executives," *Wall Street Journal*, 20 June 1988, p. 17.

Knowing what these factors are is one secret of good management. Product quality is almost always one such key success factor.

By their very nature management control reports are confidential and are not discussed outside the company, because they disclose "mistakes" of decision and how decisions went wrong. Some degree of inherent uncertainty surrounds all business decisions. Unexpected and unpredictable developments may upset the applecart of good decisions. Nevertheless, management control reports have a strong element of "passing judgment" on the manager's ability to make good decisions and forecasts.

Internal Accounting Controls and Audits

The reliability of the accounting system that supplies essential information for management control rests in large measure on the *internal accounting controls* built into the system and how well these controls are working. Specific forms and procedures are instituted to eliminate, or at least minimize, errors in capturing, processing, storing, and retrieving the enormous amount of detailed data and information needed to operate the business. Without well-designed forms and procedures, an organization couldn't function. One danger is that filling out the forms becomes perfunctory and that established procedures are short-circuited.

Internal accounting controls also serve a second critical function—to protect against theft and fraud by employees, suppliers, customers, and managers themselves. Unfortunately my father-in-law was right. He told me many years ago that "there's a little bit of larceny in everyone's heart." He could have added that there's a lot of larceny in the hearts of a few.

It's an unpleasant fact of business life that some customers shoplift, some vendors overcharge or short-count on deliveries, some employees embezzle or steal assets, and some managers commit fraud against the business or take personal advantage of their position of authority and trust in the business organization. Instances of fraud and corruption are reported with alarming frequency in the financial press.

The ideal internal accounting control is one that ensures the integrity of the information being recorded and processed, that deters or at least quickly detects any fraud and dishonesty, and is cost effective. Some controls are simply too offensive to justify, such as a body search of every employee on exit from work, although diamond and gold mines take these precautions, I understand. And a recent article in the *New York Times* on General Electric indicated some of its employees must go through a search on exit from work.*

The national organization of CPAs, the American Institute of Certified Public Accountants (AICPA), has published a very useful guide dealing with internal accounting controls.† It's an excellent summary and reflects the long experience of CPAs in

---

*D. Frantz, "How G. E. Plays for Keeps in Diamonds," *New York Times*, 18 September 1994, Sect. 3, p.1.

† *Statement on Auditing Standards No. 55*, "Consideration of the Internal Control Structure in a Financial Statement Audit," April 1988, issued by the Auditing Standards Board, American Institute of Certified Public Accountants, Inc. (New York, 1988).

auditing a wide range of businesses. The AICPA's guidelines are an excellent checklist for the types of internal accounting controls that a business should establish and enforce with due diligence.

Speaking of CPAs, audits by these independent accountants is one type of control. Based on their audit, the CPA firm expresses an opinion on the external financial statements of the business. Business managers should understand the limits of audits by CPAs regarding discovering errors and fraud. Auditors are responsible for discovering material errors and fraud (called "irregularities" in the official pronouncement). However, it is not cost effective to have the outside auditors do an exhaustive examination that would catch all errors and irregularities. It would take too long and cost too much. The first line of defense is internal accounting controls.

Most larger businesses establish an *internal auditing* department in the organization. Although the internal auditors are employees of the organization, they are given autonomy to act independently. Internal auditors report to the highest levels of management, often directly to the board of directors of the corporation.

Internal auditors constantly monitor the organization's internal accounting controls, regularly reevaluate the cost and benefits of existing internal controls, and carry out special investigations either on their own or at the direction of top management. Different areas of operations are audited either on a surprise basis or on a regular rotation basis.

Recent articles in the financial press have reported gigantic losses from employees or managers trading in financial derivatives. In virtually all of these cases there was a breakdown in important internal controls. Many of these cases show managers violating one of the most important of all internal controls—requiring two or more persons to authorize significant expenditures or taking on major risk exposures. Many of these cases also revealed that another key internal control, called the *separation of duties*, was violated. The authority for making a decision and carrying it out should always be separated from the accounting and record keeping for the decision and its outcome. One person should never do both.

Controlling Fraud

Business fraud is like adultery. It shouldn't happen, but after having done it, every attempt is made to hide it, although it often comes out in the end. The same holds true for business fraud. Businesses handle a lot of money, have a lot of valuable assets, and give managers and other employees a lot of authority. So, it's not surprising that business is so vulnerable to fraud and other dishonest schemes.

Many books have been written on business fraud. Many seminars and training programs are offered dealing with fraud in the business world. Indeed, developments are underway to make the control and detection of business fraud a professional specialty, if you can believe it.

Audits and internal accounting controls are not foolproof. A disturbing amount of fraud still slips through these preventive measures. High-level management fraud is particularly difficult to prevent and detect. By their very nature, high-level managers have a lot of authority and discretion. Their positions of trust and power give high-level managers an unparalleled opportunity to commit fraud and the means to conceal it.

It is argued that business should aggressively prosecute offenders. The record shows, however, that most businesses are reluctant to do this, fearing the adverse publicity surrounding legal proceedings. Many businesses adopt the policy that fraud is just one of the many "costs" of doing business. They don't encourage it of course, and they do everything practical to prevent it. But, in the final analysis, the majority of businesses appear to tolerate some amount of "normal" fraud.

Management Control Reporting Guidelines

How to design management control reports? That's the question addressed in this section, which presents guidelines and suggestions for management control reporting. Unfortunately there is no one best format and system for control reporting. There is no "one size fits all" approach for communicating the vital control information needed by managers, no more than there are simple answers in most areas of business decision making. One job of managers is to know what they need to know, and this includes control reporting.

The Starting Point: Well-Designed Management Financial Statements

Management control reporting begins with the format, layout, and content of each of the primary internal financial statements for managers. These key reports are presented in Chapters 3, 4, and 5. In particular, the internal profit report (management income statement) should not be a look-alike, or simply a more detailed version of the external income statement. Perhaps you should review the internal profit report presented at the start of Chapter 3. Let me remind you that much additional management information is included in the internal profit report as compared with the external income statement.

In the following discussion I assume that the management financial statements have been carefully designed for management use. (If the business formulates its plans in formal budgets these financial statements are the framework for the budget, which Chapter 8 explains.) In short, management control starts with knowing what's going on. Managers depend on the internal accounting reports for this information. We now turn to more specific aspects and features of internal management financial reporting from the control point of view.

Comparative Reports: Goals for This Period or Last Period's Performance?

As previously stated, management control is directed toward achieving profit goals and meeting the other financial objectives of the business. Ideally, the business should adopt goals and objectives for this period in the form of clear-cut benchmarks and standards against which actual performance is compared. Budgeting is one way of doing this, as discussed in Chapter 8.

Instead of setting goals and objectives, many businesses simply compare actual performance this period against last period.

This comparison focuses attention on trends, especially if several past periods, not just the most recent period, are used. But this approach avoids one of management's main responsibilities, which is to forecast changes and plan accordingly. Managers should get in the forward planning mode, which is one main reason for budgeting. Using last period for comparison leads to the "rearview mirror" style of management.

Management by Exception

One key concept of management control reporting is called *management by exception*. Managers have limited time to spend on control reports and therefore should focus mainly on deviations and variances from the plan or budget. Departures and detours from the plan are called *exceptions*. The premise is that most things should be going according to plan but some things will not, and managers need to pay the most attention to the things going wrong or off course.

Frequency of Reports

A tough question to answer is how often to prepare control reports. Managers cannot wait until the end of the year for control reports, although a year-end review is usually a good idea and serves as the platform for developing next year's plan and budget. Daily or weekly control reports are not practical for most businesses, although some companies, such as airlines and banks, monitor sales volume and other vital operating statistics on a day-to-day basis.

Monthly or quarterly management control reports are the most common. Each business develops its own practical solution to the frequency question. The main objective is to strike a balance between preparing control reports too frequently versus too late. With today's computers and other electronic means of communication, it is tempting to bombard managers with too much control information too often. Sorting out the truly relevant information from the less relevant and totally irrelevant information is at the very core of good control reporting.

Highlighting Profit Margins

Profit margins should be the main focus of attention in management profit reports, as demonstrated already in Exhibit 3.1. Profit margins should jump out and catch the eye of managers. Profit margins should be reported for each major product or product line (backed up with detailed schedules on virtually every individual product). This extremely confidential data is not divulged in external income statements, nor for that matter very widely throughout the organization.

Profit control reports should include analyses of *changes in profit margins*. The impact of sales volumes changes should be separated from the impact of sales prices changes. If trade-off decisions were made, for example, cutting sales prices to increase sales volumes, then there should be a follow-up analysis in management control profit reports to track the outcome of the decision. Did sales volume increase as much as expected? Variable operating expenses should be analyzed similarly.

In my opinion, if there is one common fault with internal profit reports for management control purposes, it is the failure of the accounting staff to explain and analyze why different profit lines increased or decreased relative to the last period, or relative to the budget or the established goals for the period. Such profit margin change analysis is extraordinarily useful. But managers generally are left to do this analysis on their own.

Focusing on Profit Robbers

A frustrating fringe of negative pressures constantly threaten profit margins and bloat fixed expenses. Management control profit reports should keep a sharp eye on these negative factors that cut into profit margins, hurt sales volume, and drive up fixed expenses. These are the sinkholes and pitfalls on the road to profit.

The matter of *sales prices* is the logical place to begin. Many businesses advertise or publish list prices, such as sticker prices on new cars, manufacturer's suggested retail prices on consumer products, and standard price sheets for industrial products. List prices often are just the point of departure. Sales price negotiation is the way of life in many industries. The list price simply sets the stage for bargaining. In other cases, the buyer agrees to pay list price, but demands other types of price reductions or other special concessions and accommodations.

Prompt payment discounts usually are offered when making sales on credit to other businesses. A 2% discount off the invoiced sales price may be given for payments received within 10 days after the sales invoice date. (These are also called *sales discounts*.) A business may give *quantity discounts* for large orders or *special customer discounts* for government agencies and educational institutions. *Rebates* and *coupons* that lower the sales price are offered by many consumer product companies.

Sales prices also may be reduced by giving other types of *allowances* or *adjustments* after the point of sale. Some customers may complain about the quality of the product or may discover minor product flaws after taking delivery. Instead of the customer returning the product, the company reduces the original sales price.

Sales *returns* can be a problem, although this varies quite a bit from industry to industry. Many retailers accept sales returns without hesitation as part of their overall marketing strategy. Customers may be refunded their money, or they may exchange one product for a different product. On the other hand, some products, such as new cars, are seldom returned (even when recalled).

For internal management profit reporting, sales revenue should be based on the established list prices; the sales price negatives just discussed are accumulated in separate *sales revenue contra accounts* that are deducted from gross (list price based) sales revenue. If you refer back to Exhibit 3.1 again, sales revenue is reported net of all the sales revenue contra accounts.

For management control, the net sales revenue line should be backed up with a detailed schedule starting with gross sales revenue at list prices minus the several different sales contra accounts—one for each sales price reduction. Managers should monitor each sales revenue reduction account relative to the company's established sales pricing policies, for comparison with previous periods, and with the goals and budgets for the period.

Inventory shrinkage is a serious problem for many businesses, especially most retailers. "Shrinkage" is somewhat of a euphemism for inventory losses caused by shoplifting, employee theft, and short counts from suppliers. The term also includes inventory losses due to product damage and deterioration, as well as inventory write-downs to recognize product obsolescence.

Inventory loss due to theft is a particularly frustrating expense. The business has to buy (or manufacture) these products, then hold them in inventory, which requires carrying costs, only to have them stolen by "customers" or employees. On the other hand, inventory shrinkage due to damage from handling and storing products, and product deterioration over time, as well as product obsolescence is a normal and inescapable cost of doing business.

Internal management profit reports should definitely identify any inventory shrinkage expense and not bury it in cost of goods sold or an operating expense. (Inventory shrinkage is never reported as a separate expense in external financial reports.) Managers need to keep a close watch on inventory shrinkage, and cannot do so if it is buried in the larger expense account. In Exhibit 3.1 no inventory shrinkage expense is reported. But if there had been inventory shrinkage it would have been reported on a separate line above the contribution profit margin line (assuming it were material in amount).

Another reason for separating out inventory shrinkage is that this expense does not behave the same way as cost of goods sold expense. Cost of goods sold expense varies with sales volume.* In contrast, inventory shrinkage may include both a fixed amount that is more or less the same regardless of sales volume, and the remainder may vary with sales volume.

In many business situations there are *hidden costs*; the purchase costs of inventory and other supplies and consumables bought by the business are too high because its purchasing managers are accepting bribes, kickbacks, under-the-table payments, or other favors from vendors. These excessive costs are very difficult to isolate and report in internal profit reports. The reason, of course, is that purchasing managers conceal these costs. Internal audits are one way to detect this. Having lived next door to a purchasing manager for several years, I became aware of how insidious this problem is and how difficult it is to ferret out.

Lost sales due to temporary *stock outs* (zero inventory situations) are important for managers to know about. Such "nonsales" are not recorded in the accounting system. No sales transaction takes place, so there is nothing to record in the sales revenue account. However, missed sale opportunities should be accumulated in the accounting system and reported to managers even though no sales actually took place. Managers need a measure of how much additional profit margin could have been earned on these lost sales.

---

* This general comment is not entirely true unfortunately. The inventory accounting method used by the business may yield a cost of goods sold expense amount that does not vary in strict proportion with changes in sales volume. Both the last-in, first-out (LIFO) method and the first-in, first-out (FIFO) method can cause this problem. Chapter 21 of *How To Read A Financial Report* by John A. Tracy (John Wiley, New York, 4th ed., 1994) discusses this problem.

Many times customers are willing to *back order* the products. Or, if customers do not need their orders immediately, sales are made for future delivery, called *sales backlogs*. Information about back orders and sales backlogs should be reported to managers, but not as sales revenue, of course. If a customer refuses to back order or refuses to wait for future delivery, the sale may be lost. As a practical matter, it is difficult to keep track of lost sales. The manager may have to rely on other sources of information, such as complaints from customers and the company's sales force.

Certain ratios, which have not been mentioned so far, are helpful tools in management profit reports. For example, retailers keep an eye on *sales revenue per employee* and *sales revenue per square foot* of retail space. Most retailers have rough rules of thumb, such as $300/$400 annual sales per square foot of retail space, or $150,000 annual sales per employee. These amounts vary widely from industry to industry.

Trade associations collect such data from their members and publish industry averages. Retailers can compare their performance against local and regional competition, as well as national averages. Hotels and motels carefully watch their *occupancy rates*, which is another example of a useful ratio to measure actual sales against capacity.

Financial Condition and Cash Flow Reports

Managers should keep close tabs on changes in every asset and liability reported in the balance sheet and cash flow statements. In particular, the manager should keep a close watch on changes in each operating asset and each operating liability to spot any change in the operating ratios of the business. These changes have immediate impact on the cash flow of the business as explained in Chapter 5. Such changes need quick management response.

Sales revenue and expenses drive the operating assets and liabilities of the business. Changes in each operating asset and liability need to be compared with changes in the sales revenue or expense that determines the asset or liability. Suppose sales revenue increased by 10%: Did accounts receivable go up 10%? Significant deviations must be investigated. Controlling cash flow from profit means controlling changes in the company's operating assets and liabilities.

Investment Performance

Management financial statements should include business capital investment performance measures, which are explained in Chapter 7. Return on assets (ROA) and return on equity (ROE) are the two key business capital investment performance measures. If the business falls below its ROE goal, there should be a very clear explanation that pinpoints which factors are to blame.

Financial leverage is also explained in Chapter 7. Shifts in the ratio of debt to equity, interest rates changes, and ROA changes can have significant impact on the amount of financial leverage gain, and therefore on bottom-line net income. Financial leverage analysis should be presented in a comparative period-versus-period format in the internal management financial reports. Managers should not have to take the time to do these calculations on their own; the analysis should be ready-made for their attention.

Summary

In short, management control means getting the job done—achieving the goals and objectives of the business for the period. Successful managers know they have to establish and implement definite control procedures; control doesn't just happen. The key ingredient of management control is feedback information that reports actual performance, so that managers can identify where things are going according to plan and where they are not.

In designing internal reports, managers should be protected from information overload. Although extremely important, control is only one of the essential functions of business managers—they can allocate only so much time out of each busy day and week to the control function. Management control reports, therefore, should concentrate on the most important problems and issues, rather than providing reams of data.

I hope this chapter offered guidelines to maximize the usefulness and efficiency of management financial reports for control purposes. Managers should watch everything because anything can go wrong and get out of control. On the other hand, one principle of management control reporting is not to waste a manager's time on all that's going right (according to plan), but to emphasize what's going wrong.

I might draw a comparison with grading student exams. The "red marks" are errors or places where the student made mistakes; the rest of the exam is what the student has done right. Likewise, management control reports should highlight red marks for managers, without overlooking the majority of things that are going according to plan and that are under control.

10

MAKING PROFIT: BREAKEVEN AND BEYOND

How Did Our Company Make a Profit?

As we have previously seen, our example company has made a profit for the year that just ended. Exhibit 3.1 presents the management income statement for the company. The business earned $607,200 net income on $10,000,000 sales revenue. How did it do this? The answer is not as simple as it might appear.

Chapter 7 explains that net income is derived from two basic sources: (1) operating profit earned on the equity capital invested in the business, and (2) financial leverage.* Like most businesses, the business in this example uses borrowed money. Thus, it has either financial leverage gain or loss depending on whether its return on assets (ROA) is higher or lower than the interest rate on its debt (borrowed capital).

To review briefly: The company earned $1,080,000 operating profit, which is earnings before interest and income tax expenses (see Exhibit 3.1). Its debtholders supply about one-half of its total capital, but they do not get one-half of the operating profit, which would be over $500,000. The business pays only $160,000 interest on its debt, so its stockholders realize a sizable pretax financial leverage gain. Exhibit 7.2 shows the exact computations of the financial leverage gain.

This chapter mainly explains the analysis of how a business makes an operating profit and operating profit behavior. We

---

* Net income may also be affected by unusual, nonrecurring, extraordinary gains and losses recorded in the year. Our example company does not include any of these. Reasons for these one-time charges include abandoning major assets, discontinuing business segments, settling law suits, major catastrophes, corporate restructuring, etc.

should not lose sight of the fact that operating profit and ROA determine financial leverage gain (or loss), which can have a big impact on net income. However, in this chapter, operating profit is the focus.

How do successful companies make a satisfactory operating profit year in and year out? To begin with, the business must make sales. No sales, no business; it's as fundamental as that. But, sales is not the whole story of making profit.

Managers must set sales prices and control product costs and variable expenses; these key factors determine unit profit margins. Sales without adequate profit margins will not generate enough total contribution profit margin to cover the fixed operating expenses of the business. This problem is the key concern of this chapter.

Our example company sells many different products, which is typical of most businesses. But, to explain the analysis of operating profit behavior we need an easy-to-follow example. It is much clearer to deal with a one-product company. So, in this chapter we shall imagine that our example company sells just one product.

This sole product becomes the proxy, or average stand-in, for all the company's products. This one product serves as the common denominator for all products. As a matter of fact, many industries measure overall sales activity with a common denominator. Examples are barrels for breweries, tons for steel mills, passenger miles for airlines, number of copies for book stores, and vehicles for car and truck manufacturers.

The management income statement presented in Chapter 3, Exhibit 3.1, is for a multiproduct business. This means that sales revenue for all products is aggregated into the total

$10,000,000 sales revenue reported in the profit report. The cost of all products sold is aggregated into the total $6,000,000 cost of goods sold expense. And the two variable operating expenses are totals across all products sold.

In place of the management income statement format shown earlier, Exhibit 10.1 now presents a different profit report format for our one-product company. What's new? The totals are the same, but now we see the sales price and the per unit costs and the contribution profit margin per unit.

Sales volume is listed at the top of the profit report because everything keys off this critical measure of operating activity. Sales price is $100.00 per unit. Unit product cost is $60.00. Sales volume-driven operating costs are $5.00 per unit. Sales revenue-driven operating costs are 8.5% of sales price and sales revenue. Notice that only the total amount of fixed operating expenses are given in the new exhibit, without the functional breakdown presented earlier.* As a matter of fact we need to take a closer look at these fixed costs before proceeding.

---

* In Exhibit 3.1, the company's fixed expenses are broken down by broad basic functions—occupancy costs; management, general, and administration costs; marketing and advertising costs; and the cost of employee benefits. Instead, fixed costs can be classified by object of expenditure, such as salaries, property taxes, depreciation, office supplies, insurance, and so on. For management analysis, it is more important to see fixed costs classified by basic purpose (function) than by what the money is spent on. (Keep in mind that depreciation expense is not a cash outlay during the period and that depreciation is included in the functions.)

EXHIBIT 10.1   PROFIT REPORT FOR ONE-PRODUCT EXAMPLE COMPANY

Sales Volume	100,000 Units	
Sales Revenue	$100.00	$10,000,000
Revenue-Driven Operating Expenses	8.5%	(850,000)
Cost of Goods Sold Expense	$ 60.00	(6,000,000)
Volume-Driven Operating Expenses	$5.00	(500,000)
Contribution Profit Margin	$ 26.50	$ 2,650,000
Total Fixed Operating Expenses		(1,570,000)
Operating Profit		$ 1,080,000
Interest Expense		(160,000)
Earnings before Income Tax		$ 920,000
Income Tax Expense @ 34%		(312,800)
Net Income		$ 607,200

Fixed Operating Expenses

In contrast to product cost (cost of goods sold) and the variable operating expenses of making sales, the other expenses of the business are fixed for the year. These costs do not vary with sales activity; they are relatively insensitive to changes in sales volume. Fixed expenses often are called *overhead*, or the *nut* of the business. Some fixed expenses are not flexible at all, such as rent, insurance premiums, and annual property taxes.

Some fixed expenses are flexible on the edge, such as total salary expense for the year. The business could switch to more part-time employees if sales volume were to drop off substantially. Conversely, overtime hours could be worked if sales volume surged unexpectedly. Another example of a fixed expense that is a little soft on the edge is when a business extends the hours that it is open, which would slightly nudge up the company's utility bill.

The key point here is that fixed operating expenses would have been the same even if sales volume had been lower or higher than actual sales volume. Fixed costs stay the same over the short run, regardless of whether sales revenue goes down or up—within limits that is. For instance, if sales revenue were to decrease substantially, management may take action to decrease the company's fixed operating costs. Some employees on fixed salaries may be laid off, employees may be asked for salary givebacks, or fringe benefits may be reduced. In the following discussion, the fixed costs are just that—*fixed*—and are not changed as we change sales volume.

Owner/Manager Salaries and Other Expenses

Suppose this business were a privately owned and closely held corporation whose top managers are also its major stockholders. Are the salaries of the owner/managers included in fixed operating expenses? Sure, salaries are included in this expense account. Indeed, where else would the salaries be put? I bring this up because salaries of owner/managers are not based on arm's length bargaining like other expenses of the business.

The owner/managers can more or less set their own salaries. Their salaries may be artificially high or low and may not reflect an objective competitive or market-based salary. I don't mean to suggest anything illegal or unethical here. I just mean to make the point that the user of the financial statement has to keep in mind that the fixed operating expenses may be padded a little or perhaps they are too thin.

Also, the reader of the profit report should look for whether personal expenses are being run through the business for income tax purposes. In my experience, owner/managers often charge off to the business some of their own personal expenses, such as vacation trips and auto expenses that are not deductible on their individual income tax returns.

Last, I assume that in this example there is no skimming of sales revenue and no other type of fraud involving the business. Again, I must say that this is not unheard of. Some business owners/managers will use the business as a vehicle for fraud, as you may have read about. Sales revenue skimming (failing to record all of the business sales revenue) is fairly common in some types of businesses unfortunately.

What About Interest Expense?

As shown in Exhibit 10.1, the company's interest expense is $160,000 for the year. Is this a fixed expense? For minor swings in the sales level the answer is yes, it's a fixed expense. If the company had sold, say, 5,000 or even 10,000 units less or more than it did for the year, would its interest expense have been any less or more? Would the company have changed its interest-bearing debt to adjust to the lower or higher sales volume?

Probably not. Most businesses take on a certain level of debt and tend to stay with it, unless there are major upturns or downturns in their level of sales. But we should keep in mind that a business can adjust its short-term debt without too much trouble. Indeed this is precisely one of the advantages of short-term debt.

As previous chapters explain, a business needs operating assets in carrying on its profit-making activity. A business generates certain spontaneous liabilities in carrying on its profit-making operations, which are called *operating liabilities*. Deducting operating liabilities from the total operating assets needed for its profit-making activities gives the all-important figure of net operating assets. This is the amount of capital the business must raise from debt and equity sources. As you know, most businesses use debt for part of their total capital.

Total net operating assets fluctuate with the total sales revenue and expenses of a business, which means that the total capital investment also fluctuates as sales revenue and expenses go up or go down. Thus, the debt component of the total capital base of the business will probably change, unless, as just discussed, we are talking about relatively minor changes in sales levels. If debt changes, then the interest expense will change.

The following discussion looks at changes in sales volume. So, it is important to keep in mind the point about the total capital being used by the company and the debt component of the total capital. It is not accurate to keep interest as an unchanging fixed expense amount if we make sizable changes in sales vol-ume. In this respect, interest expense is quite different from the fixed operating expenses of the business because it is driven by the total capital needed by the entity and how much of this total capital is debt.

Computing Operating Profit

We now calculate the company's operating profit (earnings before interest and income tax) even though the operating profit amount is already presented in the company's income statement in Exhibit 10.1. This straightforward calculation lays the groundwork for the analysis that follows. The first way to compute operating profit is probably the most intuitive (see Exhibit 10.1 for data):

$ 26.50	Unit Contribution Profit Margin
× 100,000	Units Sales Volume
$2,650,000	Total Contribution Profit Margin
− 1,570,000	Total Fixed Operating Expenses
$1,080,000	Operating Profit

The linchpin in this calculation is the multiplication of unit contribution profit margin times sales volume to get total contribution profit margin. Sales volume needs a good profit margin per unit to start with. Maybe you've heard the old joke: "A business loses a little on each sale but makes it up on volume."

The Break-Even Hurdle

Business managers worry a lot about fixed expenses: There's no operating profit until fixed expenses are overcome. The *break-even point* is that specific sales volume, when multiplied by unit contribution profit margin, gives total contribution margin equal to total fixed expenses. In other words, breakeven is that sales volume necessary just to cover fixed expenses for the period.

The following quotes from articles about Chrysler Corporation illustrate the importance of the break-even point. By the way, notice that *vehicles* is the common denominator for its sales volume even though Chrysler makes a wide variety of autos and trucks.

> Chrysler's break-even point now stands at 1.8 million vehicles a year, far above the 1.1 million point that Mr. Iacocca vowed to maintain two years ago. The rise isn't entirely alarming—Chrysler sold about 2.3 million vehicles last year, partly because the acquisitions have added to its sales base—but the break-even point is higher than Chrysler would like it to be as it heads into the trough of the industry's sales cycle (*Wall Street Journal*, 12 January 1988, p. 17).

> Along with diversification came a top-heavy holding company structure that sent Chrysler's costs soaring. The company must now sell 1.9 million cars and trucks a year just to break even. That's far above the break-even point of 1.1 million vehicles in 1985 and a much bigger increase than can be justified by Chrysler's 1987 purchase of American Motors Corp. (*Wall Street Journal*, 17 September 1990, p. 1A).

Although showing their age a little, both of these articles are useful because they offer a break-even estimate for a major well-known business.

The operating profit break-even point for the example company, which is that sales volume level at which the company's earnings before interest and income tax would be zero, is calculated as follows:

**Computation of Operating Profit
Break-Even Sales Volume**

Fixed Operating Expenses ÷ Unit Contribution Margin
$1,570,000 ÷ $26.50
= 59,245 Units Break-Even Sales Volume*

In other words, suppose the company had sold only 59,245 units during the year. It would have earned an operating profit of zero but would still have interest expense to worry about. Case A in Exhibit 10.2 illustrates this hypothetical operating profit break-even sales volume scenario.

Assume that interest expense does not decrease at the lower sales level. As already mentioned, this assumption is not entirely realistic and accurate. In any case, the company would

---

* Here and in subsequent computations in this chapter, the actual number in the discussion and Exhibit 10.2 is rounded to the nearest whole number. For example, the actual break-even volume is 59,245.28 units.

have to sell more units to cover its interest expense, which is determined as follows based on its interest expense for the year:

Computation of Additional Units over the Operating Profit Break-Even Sales Volume to Cover Interest Expense

Interest Expense ÷ Unit Contribution Margin
$160,000 ÷ $26.50
= 6,038 Additional Units

So, including interest as a fixed expense the company's break-even sales volume level is 65,283 units [59,245 + 6,038]. See Case B in Exhibit 10.2.

Both break-even sales volumes are considerably less than the 100,000 units sales level of the business. At the lower sales level the business would not use nearly as much net operating assets. Thus, less capital would be needed, which means the business might very well decrease its debt, which in turn would lower its interest expense.

In short, how to handle the interest expense in break-even analysis is fairly arbitrary and is based on what assumption you make about the decrease in the capital needed by the business at the lower break-even sales level. In any case, the break-even sales volume level is mainly a point of reference, more than a mathematical curiosity but not worth an extended discussion about the "best" way to deal with interest expense.

EXHIBIT 10.2   HYPOTHETICAL BREAK-EVEN VOLUMES FOR ONE-PRODUCT EXAMPLE COMPANY

Case A   Operating Profit (Earnings before Interest and Income Tax Expenses) Break-Even Point

Sales Volume		59,245 Units
Sales Revenue	$100.00	$5,924,528
Revenue-Driven Operating Expenses	8.5%	(503,585)
Cost of Goods Sold Expense	$ 60.00	(3,554,717)
Volume-Driven Operating Expenses	$ 5.00	(296,226)
Contribution Profit Margin	$ 26.50	$1,570,000
Total Fixed Operating Expenses		(1,570,000)
Operating Profit		$ 0

Case B   Net Income Break-Even Point (Interest Expense Assumed to Be a Fixed Cost)

Sales Volume		65,283 Units
Sales Revenue	$100.00	$6,528,302
Revenue-Driven Operating Expenses	8.5%	(554,906)
Cost of Goods Sold Expense	$ 60.00	(3,916,981)
Volume-Driven Operating Expenses	$ 5.00	(326,415)
Contribution Profit Margin	$ 26.50	$1,730,000
Total Fixed Operating Expenses		(1,570,000)
Operating Profit		$ 160,000
Interest Expense		(160,000)
Earnings before Income Tax		$ 0
Income Tax Expense @ 34%		(0)
Net Income		$ 0

Using Break-Even Sales Volume to Compute Operating Profit

A second way to compute operating profit (earnings before interest expense and income tax) starts with break-even volume. Actual sales volume is compared with break-even volume and profit is computed as follows:

Excess Over Break-Even Method to Compute Operating Profit

Annual Sales Volume	100,000 Units
Less Break-Even Sales Volume	−59,245
Excess over Break-Even Volume	40,755 Units
× Unit Contribution Profit Margin	× $26.50
= Operating Profit	$1,080,000

The first 59,245 units sold during the year are assigned to covering fixed expenses; the total contribution margin from the first 59,245 units is treated as consumed by fixed expenses. The 40,755 units in excess of break-even volume are viewed as the source of operating profit. In other words, sales volume is divided into two groups: (1) the break-even group and,(2) the profit group.

Operating profit is the same both ways of course, although the method of getting there is different. The difference is a little deeper than meets the eye. It's more than an exercise with numbers; it concerns how managers think about making profit in the first place.

The first method of computing operating profit stresses the multiplication of unit contribution profit margin times sales volume to get total contribution profit margin for the period. Fixed expenses are not ignored, but are deducted from total contribution margin to get down to operating profit. In contrast, the excess over break-even method puts fixed expenses first and profit second. The business first has to get over its fixed expenses hump before it gets into the black.

One key point not to overlook is this: Fixed operating expenses provide *capacity*. Why would any rational manager commit to overhead expenses? These costs make available the capacity to carry on the sales activity of the business. Fixed expenses provide the space, the equipment, and the personnel to sell products. By committing to these costs the business buys *capacity*.

The manager should estimate sales capacity, for example, the maximum sales volume possible from the fixed operating expenses of the business, and compare this capacity against actual sales volume. The business may have unused sales capacity. Sales could grow by 10%, 20%, or even 30% before more space would have to be rented, more persons hired, or more equipment installed.

Estimating sales capacity may not be all that precise. Yet a reasonable ballpark estimate can be made. You can start by asking whether a 10% sales volume increase would require any increase in total fixed operating expenses. Perhaps it would not. This answer is especially important for planning ahead and analyzing the profit impact of changes.

A Third Way to Compute Operating Profit

The excess over break-even profit calculation method divides sales volume into two groups: (1) the break-even quantity necessary to cover total fixed operating expenses and (2) the surplus over break-even volume, which provides profit. A third basic method of computing profit divides every unit sold into two parts: (1) the fixed expenses part and (2) the profit part.

The basic idea of the third method is that profit derives from spreading fixed operating expenses over a large enough sales volume so that the average fixed expenses per unit is less than the contribution profit margin per unit. The fundamental thinking is that every unit sold has to do two things: (1) contribute its share to cover fixed expenses and (2) provide a profit residual. The computation steps follow:

Unit Average Method for Computing Operating Profit

First Step: Compute the average fixed operating expenses per unit sold.

Average Fixed Expenses per Unit

$1,570,000 ÷ 100,000 units = $15.70

Second Step: Compute the difference between the average fixed operating expenses per unit and the unit contribution profit margin to determine the average operating profit per unit.

Average Operating Profit per Unit

Contribution Profit Margin per Unit	$26.50
Less Average Fixed Expenses per Unit	15.70
Average Operating Profit per Unit	$10.80

Third Step: Multiply the average operating profit per unit times sales volume to get total operating profit for the year.

$10.80	×	100,000	=	$1,080,000
Average Operating Profit per Unit		Sales Volume		Operating Profit Before Interest and Income Tax

This method spreads fixed expenses for the year over all units sold, which gives $15.70 per unit. Profit is viewed as the *spread* between this average cost and the $26.50 unit contribution profit margin. So, the business makes $10.80 profit per unit. Each unit sold is viewed on equal terms—sort of the "one unit, one vote" idea. Of course operating profit for the year is the same as the other two computation methods.

Suppose the business had sold only 59,245 units (which we already know is its operating profit break-even sales volume). The average fixed expenses per unit sold would have been much higher. In fact, it would have been $26.50 per unit: $1,570,000 total fixed expenses ÷ 59,245 units = $26.50. This is exactly equal to the unit contribution profit margin. So, the business would have made precisely zero operating profit per unit; and, total operating profit would be zero.

Margin of Safety

One purpose of break-even analysis is to figure the company's *margin of safety*. This term refers to how far sales volume would have to drop before the business slips out of the black into the red—from profit to loss. The company in this example has a fairly good margin of safety—its operating profit break-even sales volume is 40,755 units lower than its actual sales volume for the year. Sales volume would have to drop off by more than 40% for the company to slip into the red.

Of course this big margin of safety does not necessarily guarantee a profit next year. Sales could drop dramatically or expenses could get out of control. The following chapters explore what would happen based on changes in the factors that determine operating profit.

Summary

Because of fixed expenses, the business manager has to worry about its break-even point, which is determined by dividing its total fixed expenses by its contribution profit margin per unit.

Breakeven is the sales volume at which the business would have exactly zero profit. Of course a company does not deliberately try to earn a zero profit.

The chapter closely examines the nature of fixed expenses and why fixed expenses are not really 100% fixed and unchangeable. However, over the short run they are treated as if they were in break-even analysis.

The value of the break-even analysis tool is not to focus on the zero profit volume, but to use break-even volume as a useful reference point for understanding how profit is made and to analyze how profit changes with changes in sales volume, which is a major topic discussed in later chapters.

Three different ways are explained for computing operating profit, each of which has its unique insights into how to make profit. In any given situation, a manager may find one more advantageous or beneficial than the others to explain the profit strategy of the business.

11

SALES VOLUME, PROFIT, AND CASH FLOW

The Business Environment: Constant Change

Business managers face constant change. All profit factors are subject to change because of external changes beyond the control of the business and changes initiated by the managers themselves. Many management decisions are triggered by change. Indeed, managers are characterized as change agents.

There are many examples of changes: Suppliers may increase the purchase costs of the products sold by the business; the company may raise wages for some or all of its employees, or wage rates might be actually reduced by employee givebacks or downsizing; the landlord may raise the rent; competitors may drop their sales prices and the business may follow them down; or managers may decide that they have to raise sales prices.

One basic function of managers is to keep a close watch on all relevant changes and to know how to deal with them when they occur. Changes set in motion a new round of profit-making decisions. In this chapter we concentrate mainly on the profit and operating cash flow impacts of sales *volume* changes. Sales volume, of course, is one of the most important determinants of operating profit and operating cash flow.

Chapter 10 explains break-even analysis, often called cost-volume-profit analysis to indicate that we are not just interested in the break-even point, but rather the bigger picture of how profit behaves relative to changes in volume. In this chapter we analyze how sales volume changes have an impact both on profit performance and on cash flow from profit, which, by

the way, is typically overlooked in books and other writings on profit behavior. In my opinion, a most serious oversight.

Sales Volume Increases

Business managers, quite naturally, are sales oriented. No sales, no business. As they say in marketing: "Nothing happens until you sell it." Many businesses do not make it through their start-up phase because it's very difficult to build up and establish a sales base. Customers have to be won over. Once established, sales volume can never be taken for granted. Sales are vulnerable to competition, shifts in consumer preferences and spending decisions, and domestic and global general economic conditions.

Thinking more positively, sales volume growth is the most realistic way to increase profit. Sales price increases are met with some degree of customer resistance in most cases as well as competitive response. Indeed, demand may be extremely sensitive to sales prices. Cost containment and expense control are important to be sure but are more of a defensive tactic, and, as such, don't constitute a profit growth strategy.

Suppose in our business example that the company's annual sales volume had been 10% higher at the same sales price than in the original example in Exhibit 10.1. In other words, suppose the business had sold 10,000 more units than in our baseline example. Sales volume would have been 110,000 units instead of the 100,000 units sales level in Exhibit 10.1.

An experienced manager would ask: How could the business increase its sales volume? Would customers buy 10%

more without any increase in advertising, without any sales price incentives, without some product improvements or other inducements? It's not too likely. Increasing sales volume usually requires some stimulant, such as more advertising.

Another question an experienced manager might ask is whether the business has enough capacity to handle a 10% increase in sales volume. It's always a good idea to run a capacity check whenever looking at sales volume increases. Fixed operating expenses may have to be increased to support the additional sales volume. However, we'll assume that the company has enough untapped capacity to take on an additional 10% in sales volume, without having to increase any of its fixed operating expenses.

The example company makes $26.50 contribution profit margin per unit (see Exhibit 10.1). Selling 10,000 additional units would increase total contribution profit margin by $265,000, computed as follows:

$26.50	×	10,000	=	$265,000
Contribution Profit Margin per Unit		Additional Units		Contribution Profit Margin Increase

Exhibit 11.1 shows the profit impacts for the 10% higher sales volume scenario. Notice the changes caused by the higher sales volume. All unit values remain the same, as do fixed operating expenses and interest expense. Total sales revenue, total product cost (cost of goods sold), and the two variable operating expenses all increase by 10%. Thus, contribution profit margin (profit before fixed operating expenses, interest, and income taxes) would be 10% higher, as you see in Exhibit 11.1.

Fixed operating expenses do not increase at the higher sales volume level. Keeping fixed expenses constant at a moderately higher sales volume level is generally reasonable. As mentioned previously, we assume that the company has enough slack or idle sales capacity to take on an additional 10% volume increase without any increase in these expenses.

I should stress that these assumptions should be made very carefully! One or more of the company's fixed operating expenses might have to be increased to support a higher sales volume. For instance, the company might have to rent more retail floor space, or hire additional salaried employees, or purchase new equipment on which depreciation has to be recorded.

At the higher level of sales, the company's investment in its net operating assets would be higher, which means more capital from debt and equity sources would be needed. As a result, interest-bearing debt may have to be secured, which in turn would increase the interest expense. For now, however, interest expense is held constant at the higher sales level, for purposes of analyzing the profit increase. Implicitly, this assumes that the amount of incremental capital that would be needed at the higher sales volume level would be provided entirely by equity and not by debt sources.

Chapter 8 presents the comprehensive budgeting approach that analyzes changes in operating assets and liabilities when sales revenue changes. On the other hand, the purpose of this chapter, and the several chapters that follow it, is to isolate the changes in profit and cash flow from operating activities when certain key profit factors are changed.

Our first concern is what happens to profit as a result of the 10% sales volume increase. As you can see from Exhibit 11.1,

EXHIBIT 11.1   PROFIT IMPACTS OF 10% SALES VOLUME INCREASE

	Actual Income Statement (see Exhibit 10.1)			Pro Forma Changes Caused by 10% Higher Sales Volume		
Sales Volume		100,000 Units		10,000 Units		
	Per Unit	**Totals**		**Per Unit**	**Totals**	
Sales Revenue	$100.00	$10,000,000			$1,000,000	
Revenue-Driven Operating Expenses	8.5%	850,000			85,000	
Cost of Goods Sold Expense	60.00	6,000,000			600,000	
Volume-Driven Operating Expenses	5.00	500,000			50,000	
Contribution Profit Margin	$ 26.50	$ 2,650,000			$ 265,000	10%
Total Fixed Operating Expenses		1,570,000				
Operating Profit		$ 1,080,000				
Interest Expense		160,000				
Earnings Before Income Tax		$ 920,000			$ 265,000	
Income Tax Expense @ 34%		312,800			90,100	
Net Income		$ 607,200			$ 174,900	28.8%

Note: Expenses are shown without parentheses, which is different than in earlier income statements. Of course, expenses are deducted from sales revenue and profit subtotals. Expenses are shown both ways in financial reports. However, it is clearer to show expenses without parentheses in this and future exhibits.

Notice the *Operating Leverage* effect: total contribution profit margin increases by 10%, the same percentage as the increase in sales volume. But bottom-line profit increases 28.8% because, in this example, fixed costs and interest expense do not increase.

net income would be $174,900 higher, a 28.8% profit increase. Just a minute here. How can only a 10% sales volume increase generate a 28.8% profit increase?

Operating Leverage

The net income percent increase is 2.88 times the sales volume percent increase. This "multiplier" effect is called *operating leverage*. In this example, a 10% sales volume increase causes nearly a three times percent increase in net income. To understand this leverage effect please recall the second way to compute profit explained in Chapter 10—the excess over the break-even method.

This method divides annual sales into two groups: (1) the number of units needed to reach the break-even point and (2) the excess of sales volume over this number. The company sold 34,717 units over and above its break-even volume. (See Chapter 10, page 100; interest is included as a fixed expense, so the company's total break-even volume is 65,283 units.)

Each unit sold in excess of the break-even volume earns $26.50 contribution profit margin, which can be thought of as "pure profit" because fixed expenses have already been covered by the break-even sales volume. Now please notice the following:

10,000	÷	34,717	=	28.8%
Additional Units Sold		Units in Excess of Breakeven		

The 10% additional units sold add 28.8% more units to the "profit pile" of units. This is the nub of operating leverage. You have to be above your break-even point. But if you are, then the profit swing is more than the sales volume swing.

Operating leverage means that profit percent changes are usually a multiple of sales volume percent changes. There's hardly ever a one percent for one percent relationship. This rule is based on fixed operating and interest expenses remaining constant at the higher sales level. If fixed expenses increased by 10% right along with the sales volume increase—that is, if fixed operating expenses and interest all went up by 10% as well—then net income would have gone up by only 10%.

Operating leverage reflects the notion that a business has not been fully using its sales capacity. When capacity is reached, and sooner or later it will be with continued sales volume growth, fixed expenses will have to be increased to provide more capacity. If the company had already been selling at its maximum capacity, then its fixed expenses would have to be increased. This points out the importance of knowing where you are presently relative to the company's capacity.

What About Cash Flow?

Managers cannot overlook the impact of higher sales volume on operating cash flow. Of course, the 28.8% net income increase is good. But what would be the cash flow effects of this change?

Chapter 8 discusses budgeting for growth and the capital needs of growth. Budgeted financial statements were prepared based on several critical assumptions about financing the capital needs of growth, such as whether cash dividends would be paid, new debt would be borrowed, new capital stock shares would be issued, and so on. Such a full-blown set of budgeted financial statements are too much to repeat here.

However, we can and should at least look at the impact of sales volume growth on operating cash flow—that is, cash flow from the profit-making operating activities of the business. For this purpose we keep the company's operating ratios the same as first presented in Exhibit 6.1. Exhibit 11.2 shows the differences that would be caused by the sales volume increase. This cash flow analysis extends down to operating cash flow from profit before depreciation expense. Recall that depreciation by its very nature is a fixed expense, and we are assuming that fixed expenses remain the same.

In this 10% sales volume increase scenario we see in Exhibit 11.2 that cash flow from profit would be only $16,218 more than in the original example, even though net income would be $174,900 higher. You can see why in the exhibit. The changes in the company's operating assets and operating liabilities would cause a negative drag of $158,682 against the increase in net income, causing only a $16,218 operating cash flow increase.

The $1,000,000 sales revenue increase causes ending Accounts Receivable to increase by $96,154: $1,000,000 x 5/52 = $96,154 Accounts Receivable increase. Recall that the company's accounts receivable/sales revenue operating ratio equals 5/52 of annual sales revenue. An increase in accounts receivable decreases cash flow from profit, as explained in Chapter 5.

From Exhibit 11.2, we see that the cost of goods sold expense increases $600,000. This increase causes ending inventory to increase by $138,462, which is equal to 12/52 times the cost of goods sold expense increase. (Recall that the company's average inventory holding period is 12 weeks.) This inventory increase is based on the company's operating ratio, which we assume remains the same. However, there may be a danger of an even larger increase in inventory.

In the heat and pressure of a marketing campaign to increase sales volume, unbridled enthusiasm and overly optimistic sales quotas can lead to a buildup of inventory to levels not justified by the actual sales growth. However, the sales staff doesn't want to be caught short of inventory that would delay delivery of products and cause lost sales. So, ending inventory may be considerably above what would be needed for the actual sales volume increase. Or, very liberal credit terms may be offered to customers, and the accounts receivable collection period may stretch out.

I won't explain in detail the changes in the other operating assets and liabilities shown in Exhibit 11.2. Like the changes in accounts receivable and inventory, the other changes are based on the operating ratios of the company (from Exhibit 6.1). You can check the other changes by applying the appropriate operating ratio to each of the changes in expenses.

To sum up, cash flow from profit would not nearly keep pace with the net income increase in the sales volume increase scenario. The additional profit from the sales volume increase would not immediately add a significant amount to the company's cash balance. In fact, given the higher level of sales and expenses the business might have to increase its capital sources by taking on more debt, or by issuing more capital stock, or by cutting its cash dividend.

EXHIBIT 11.2   CASH FLOW IMPACTS OF 10% SALES VOLUME INCREASE

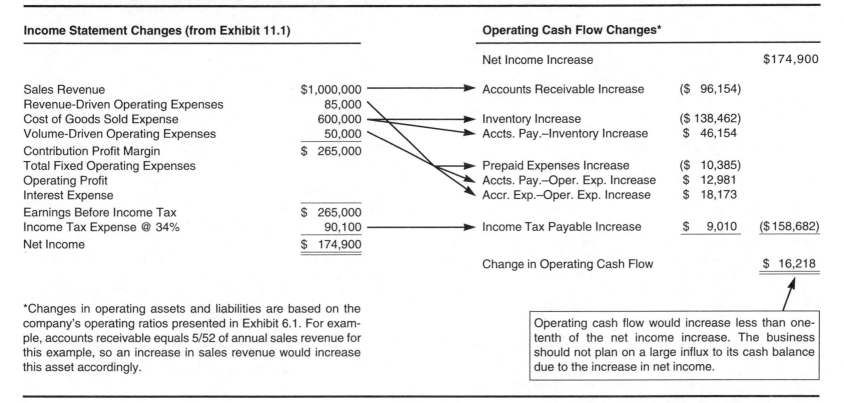

Income Statement Changes (from Exhibit 11.1)

Sales Revenue	$1,000,000
Revenue-Driven Operating Expenses	85,000
Cost of Goods Sold Expense	600,000
Volume-Driven Operating Expenses	50,000
Contribution Profit Margin	$ 265,000
Total Fixed Operating Expenses	
Operating Profit	
Interest Expense	
Earnings Before Income Tax	$ 265,000
Income Tax Expense @ 34%	90,100
Net Income	$ 174,900

Operating Cash Flow Changes*

Net Income Increase		$174,900
Accounts Receivable Increase	($ 96,154)	
Inventory Increase	($ 138,462)	
Accts. Pay.–Inventory Increase	$ 46,154	
Prepaid Expenses Increase	($ 10,385)	
Accts. Pay.–Oper. Exp. Increase	$ 12,981	
Accr. Exp.–Oper. Exp. Increase	$ 18,173	
Income Tax Payable Increase	$ 9,010	($ 158,682)
Change in Operating Cash Flow		$ 16,218

*Changes in operating assets and liabilities are based on the company's operating ratios presented in Exhibit 6.1. For example, accounts receivable equals 5/52 of annual sales revenue for this example, so an increase in sales revenue would increase this asset accordingly.

Operating cash flow would increase less than one-tenth of the net income increase. The business should not plan on a large influx to its cash balance due to the increase in net income.

Cash flow analysis of sales volume changes draws management's attention to these important points. And, it reminds managers that a profit increase does not necessarily lead to an immediate cash flow increase of equal amount (and, in some cases, could even decrease cash flow in the short run). Profit analysis without cash flow analysis is like putting on only one shoe. You have to wear both shoes to get where you're going.

Sales Volume Decreases

Suppose the business had sold 10% less sales volume than it actually did. Its managers should be very concerned and probe into the reasons for the decrease. Did it result from more competition? Are people switching to substitute products? Are hard times forcing customers to spend less? Is the location deteriorating? Has service to customers slipped? Are total quality management (TQM) techniques needed to correct the loss of sales?

Sales volume declines are one of the most serious problems confronting any business. Unless quickly reversed, the business has to make extremely wrenching decisions regarding how to downsize that would require laying off employees, selling off fixed assets, shutting down plants, and so on. The late economist Kenneth Boulding has called downsizing *the management of decline*, which I think really hits the nail on the head. It's a very unpleasant task, to say the very least.

The immediate (short-run) operating profit impact of a 10% sales volume decrease would depend heavily on whether the company could reduce its fixed expenses at the lower sales level. Assume, however, that most companies could not. Generally, fixed operating expenses would remain the same, as would the interest expense since total debt could not be decreased at the lower sales level, at least not in the short run.

Exhibit 11.3 shows the impact on profit performance at the 10% lower sales volume level. Bottom-line profit would decrease $174,900. This is what you would expect because fixed expenses do not change. Notice that operating leverage compounds the felony. Net income decreases by 28.8% in this scenario, caused by only a 10% drop in sales volume.

What about cash flow in this case? In the previous 10% growth case, cash flow from profit increases by $16,218. In the 10% lower sales volume case, operating cash flow decreases by $16,218, which is presented in Exhibit 11.4. Net income takes a big dive, by $174,900. But accounts receivable and inventory are reduced (because we hold the company's operating ratios the same). Notice in Exhibit 11.4 that the net effect of the changes in the operating assets and liabilities is to offset all but $16,218 of the drop in profit.

The lower sales revenue and lower cost of goods sold expense would lead to decreases in accounts receivable and inventory, assuming of course, that the company's two operating ratios remain the same. Basically the cash flow impacts would be just the opposite between the two sales volume change cases, as you can see in comparing Exhibits 11.2 and 11.4.

A Final Word

All profit factors are subject to change. Management neglect or ineptitude can lead to profit deterioration, and sometimes very

EXHIBIT 11.3 PROFIT IMPACTS OF 10% SALES VOLUME DECREASE

	Actual Income Statement (see Exhibit 10.1)			Pro Forma Changes Caused by 10% Lower Sales Volume		
Sales Volume		100,000 Units		-10,000 Units		
	Per Unit	**Totals**		**Per Unit**	**Totals**	
Sales Revenue	$100.00	$10,000,000			($1,000,000)	
Revenue-Driven Operating Expenses	8.5%	850,000			(85,000)	
Cost of Goods Sold Expense	60.00	6,000,000			(600,000)	
Volume-Driven Operating Expenses	5.00	500,000			(50,000)	
Contribution Profit Margin	$ 26.50	$ 2,650,000			($ 265,000)	-10%
Total Fixed Operating Expenses		1,570,000				
Operating Profit		$ 1,080,000				
Interest Expense		160,000				
Earnings Before Income Tax		$ 920,000			($ 265,000)	
Income Tax Expense @ 34%		312,800			(90,100)	
Net Income		$ 607,200			($ 174,900)	-28.8%

Note: You might recall that expenses are shown without parentheses. Of course, they are still deducted from sales revenue and profit subtotals.

Notice the *operating leverage* effect: Total contribution profit margin decreases by 10%, the same as the sales volume decrease. But bottom-line profit decreases by 28.8% because fixed costs and interest expense do not decrease in this example.

EXHIBIT 11.4   CASH FLOW IMPACTS OF 10% SALES VOLUME DECREASE

Income Statement Changes (from Exhibit 11.3)

Sales Revenue	($1,000,000)
Revenue-Driven Operating Expenses	(85,000)
Cost of Goods Sold Expense	(600,000)
Volume-Driven Operating Expenses	(50,000)
Contribution Profit Margin	($ 265,000)
Total Fixed Operating Expenses	
Operating Profit	
Interest Expense	
Earnings Before Income Tax	($ 265,000)
Income Tax Expense @ 34%	(90,100)
Net Income	($ 174,900)

Operating Cash Flow Changes*

Net Income Decrease		($ 174,900)
Accounts Receivable Decrease	$ 96,154	
Inventory Decrease	$138,462	
Accts. Pay.–Inventory Decrease	($ 46,154)	
Prepaid Expenses Decrease	$ 10,385	
Accts. Pay.–Oper. Exp. Decrease	($ 12,981)	
Accr. Exp.–Oper. Exp. Decrease	($ 18,173)	
Income Tax Payable Decrease	($ 9,010)	$158,682
Change in Operating Cash Flow		($ 16,218)

*Changes in operating assets and liabilities are based on the company's operating ratios that are presented in Exhibit 6.1. For example, accounts receivable equals 5/52 of annual sales revenue for this example, so a decrease in sales revenue would decrease this asset accordingly.

> Operating cash flow would decrease only about one-tenth of the net income decrease. The business would not immediately suffer a large decrease to its cash balance due to the decrease in net income.

quickly. Increases in product cost, as well as increases in variable and fixed expenses can do serious damage to profit performance. But, managers may not be able to improve certain factors much.

Fixed expenses may already be cut to the bone. Product costs may be controlled by one vendor or alternative vendors may offer virtually the same prices. Competition may put a fairly tight straitjacket on sales prices. Customers are sensitive to sales price increases.

Sales volume is the key success factor for most businesses, which explains why managers are so concerned about market share. Market share is often mentioned in later chapters because of its central importance to a company's success.

In any case, this chapter demonstrates the impact on profit and operating cash flow from 10% sales volume changes. If fixed operating expenses and interest expense do not change with the change in sales volume, net income will change by a greater percent than the change in sales volume. This multiplier effect is called *operating leverage*.

Cash flow from profit, also called operating cash flow, is not equal to the change in profit due to a sales volume change—no more than operating cash flow equals net income. A change in sales volume changes sales revenue and cost of goods sold and operating expenses. Thus, the operating assets and liabilities of a business change, and these changes cause pronounced effects on operating cash flow. The examples in the chapter demonstrate that operating cash flow changed only about one-tenth the movement in profit!

12

SALES PRICE, COSTS, PROFIT, AND CASH FLOW

In this chapter we are going to hold sales volume constant and change the per unit profit factors—sales price, product cost, and operating expenses. Before we get going in this chapter, however, let me ask you a basic question. Suppose you could have either 10% sales volume increase or a 10% sales price increase but not both; which option would you prefer? You may be surprised to find that there's a huge difference between the two. In any case, you should be very certain about the differences.

Sales Price Changes

Setting sales prices is one of the most perplexing decisions facing business managers. Competition normally dictates the basic range of sales prices. But, there is usually some room for deviation from your competitors' prices because of product differentiation, brand loyalty, location advantages, and quality of service—to cite only a few of the many reasons that permit higher sales prices than those set by the competition.

Fixed expenses are generally insensitive to sales price increases. In contrast, sales volume increases very well could require increases in fixed operating expenses, especially when sales volume is already pushing on the limit of the company's capacity. Very few fixed expenses are directly affected by raising sales prices, even if the company were operating near full capacity. Advertising (a fixed cost once spent) might be stepped up to persuade customers that the hike in sales prices is necessary or beneficial. Other than this, it's hard to find many fixed operating expenses that are tied directly to sales price increases.

With this point in mind, let's consider the hypothetical case in which our example company could have sold the same volume but at 10% higher sales prices. Exhibit 12.1 presents this scenario for our example company. Profit almost doubles; it increases by 99.5%, as shown in the exhibit. Would this be realistic? Well, only to the extent that a 10% sales price increase would be realistic. In this situation only one variable operating expense increases—the one driven by sales revenue.

Notice that cost of goods sold does not increase because the volume sold remains the same. In the sales volume increase situation (Chapter 11) the sales revenue increase is offset substantially by the increase in cost of goods sold expense. In contrast, 91.5% of the $1,000,000 incremental sales revenue flows through to operating profit (earnings before interest and income tax) in the sales price increase case.

Chapter 3 explains the internal income statement for managers. One key point in the design of this management accounting report is that expenses should be classified according to their behavior, or what drives them.* Certain operating expenses depend directly on the *dollar amounts* of sales and not the quantity of products sold. As total sales revenue (dollars) increases, these expenses increase directly in proportion.

Most retailers accept national credit cards, such as VISA, MasterCard, Discover, American Express, Diners Club, and so

---

* *Cost driver* is a popular term these days, which means that managers should identify which factors determine, or push, or drive a particular cost. Identifying cost drivers is the key step in the method of cost analysis and allocation called *activity-based costing*, or *ABC*. More on this in Chapter 14.

EXHIBIT 12.1 PROFIT IMPACTS OF 10% SALES PRICE INCREASE

	Actual Income Statement (see Exhibit 10.1)		**Pro Forma Changes Caused by 10% Higher Sales Price**	
Sales Volume		100,000 Units	*No Change in Sales Volume*	

	Per Unit	Totals	Per Unit	Totals	
Sales Revenue	$100.00	$10,000,000	$ 10.00	$1,000,000	
Revenue-Driven Operating Expenses	8.5%	850,000	0.85	85,000	
Cost of Goods Sold Expense	60.00	6,000,000			
Volume-Driven Operating Expenses	5.00	500,000			
Contribution Profit Margin	$ 26.50	$ 2,650,000	$ 9.15	$ 915,000	34.5%
Total Fixed Operating Expenses		1,570,000			
Operating Profit		$ 1,080,000			
Interest Expense		160,000			
Earnings Before Income Tax		$ 920,000		$ 915,000	
Income Tax Expense @ 34%		312,800		311,100	
Net Income		$ 607,200		$ 603,900	99.5%

One final reminder: Expenses are shown without parentheses. It is clearer to show increases and decreases in expenses without parentheses.

Notice the *sales price leverage* effect: Total contribution profit margin increases 34.5% due to the sales price increase. Bottom-line profit increases by 99.5%, or almost doubles because fixed costs and interest expense do not increase in this example.

on. The credit card charge slips are deposited daily with a local participating bank. The bank then discounts the total amount and credits the net balance in the business's checking account. Discount rates vary between 2% and 4% (sometimes lower or higher).

In short, the business nets only 98¢ to 96¢ on each dollar of its credit card sales. The credit card discount expense comes right off the top of the sales dollar and the business avoids the expenses of extending and administering credit directly to its customers. Therefore, the discount may be a bargain. Clearly the credit card discount expense is a sales revenue-driven expense.

Sales commissions are another common example of sales revenue-dependent expenses. As you probably know, many retailers and other businesses pay their sales representatives on a commission basis, which usually is a certain percent of the total sales amount, such as 5% or 10%. The salespersons may receive a base salary, which would be the fixed floor of the expense; only the commission over and above the fixed base would be variable. (This situation requires the separation of the fixed part from the variable part in the management income statement.)

In selling to other businesses, a company usually extends short-term credit, called *trade credit*. No matter how carefully customers are screened before extending credit, a few never pay their accounts owed to the business. Eventually, after making repeated collection efforts, the business ends up having to write off all or part of these receivables' balances as uncollectible. These losses are called *bad debts* and are a normal expense of doing business on credit. This expense depends on the sales amount, not sales volume (number of units sold).

Another example of an expense that varies with sales revenue is one you might not think of—*rent*. Companies often sign lease agreements that call for rental amounts based on gross sales. There may be a base amount or fixed minimum monthly rent. In addition there may be a variable amount equal to a percent of total sales revenue. This situation is common for retailers renting space in shopping centers. There are several other examples of expenses that vary with total sales revenue, such as franchise fees based on gross sales.

To sum up, sales revenue would increase by 10% but this increase would be offset by a 10% increase in the sales revenue-driven expenses, yielding a net $915,000 increase in contribution profit margin as shown in Exhibit 12.1. We assume that the company's fixed operating expenses and interest expense do not change at the higher sales price level. Thus, taxable income increases by the same amount. Uncle Sam takes a 34% cut of the action, leaving a $603,900 increase in the bottom-line net income.

The 10% sales price increase produces a rather hefty 99.5% gain in net income. In other words, net income just about doubles, which could also be viewed as a type of leverage—sales price leverage.* The reason for such a large percent increase in

---

* Usually the operating leverage concept refers only to sales *volume* changes, so the multiplier effect on profit caused by a sales price increase is not called operating leverage.

net income is the huge jump in the contribution profit margin per unit, which increases $9.15; an increase of 34.5%. This change is key.

The company bumps its sales price by $10.00, and its revenue-driven operating expenses are 8.5% percent of sales revenue. So, $.85 comes off the top leaving a $9.15 net sales price gain per unit. The 100,000 units sold times the $9.15 gain in unit contribution profit margin equals $915,000, the increase in total profit contribution margin and taxable income.

Quite frankly, a 10% increase in sales price without increase in the product cost or in other company expenses is not too likely. However, such a scenario is presented here to illustrate the powerful impact of a sales price increase and to contrast it with a 10% increase in sales volume. If you recall, a 10% sales volume increase results in a net income increase of only $174,900, or 28.8%. As we have just seen, a 10% sales price increase would bump up net income $603,900, or almost double the bottom line.

The reason for the difference is brought out in the following side-by-side computations of the changes in net income:

Contribution Profit Per Unit		Sales Volume Units		Total Contribution Profit Margin
$26.50	×	10,000	=	$265,000
+ $9.15	×	100,000	=	$915,000

Selling 10,000 additional units at $26.50 profit per unit is not nearly as good as selling 100,000 units at $9.15 more profit per unit. To put it another way, in the sales volume case you increase contribution margin 10% by selling 10% more units. In the 10% sales price case you sell the same number of units but increase your contribution margin per unit by 34.5%.

Also we need to consider the cash flow impacts of a 10% sales price increase, which also differs like day from night compared with the sales volume increase case.

Cash Flow at Higher Sales Price

Exhibit 12.2 presents the operating cash flow effects of increasing the sales price by 10%. Cash flow increases $551,933—a huge increase. Accounts receivable increases because of the sales revenue, which is a drag against cash flow. Variable operating expenses and income tax expense increase their respective operating assets and liabilities. Overall the operating cash flow increase is nearly as much as the profit increase.

Indeed, the increase in cash flow from profit would almost double the cash balance of the company, which in the baseline example is $603,212 (from Exhibit 4.1). This big increase in the cash balance would raise questions about what to do with the excess cash. Should you increase cash dividends? Reduce debt? Retire some capital stock? The double-barreled analysis of both profit and operating cash flow effects of sales price increases calls such questions to the attention of managers who have to make intelligent decisions about what to do with this information.

EXHIBIT 12.2 CASH FLOW IMPACTS OF 10% SALES PRICE INCREASE

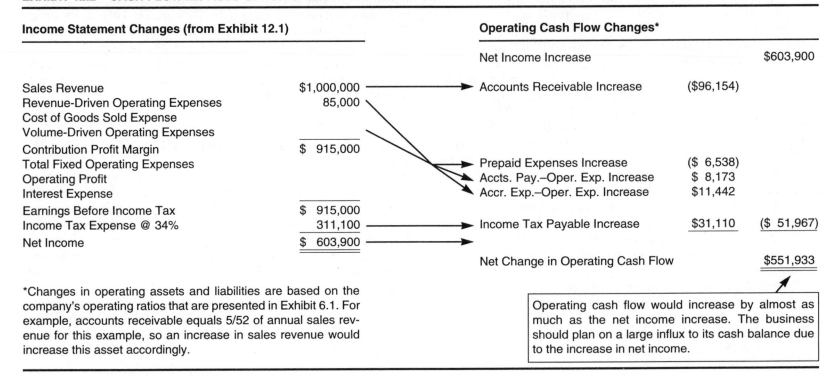

Income Statement Changes (from Exhibit 12.1)

Sales Revenue	$1,000,000
Revenue-Driven Operating Expenses	85,000
Cost of Goods Sold Expense	
Volume-Driven Operating Expenses	
Contribution Profit Margin	$ 915,000
Total Fixed Operating Expenses	
Operating Profit	
Interest Expense	
Earnings Before Income Tax	$ 915,000
Income Tax Expense @ 34%	311,100
Net Income	$ 603,900

Operating Cash Flow Changes*

Net Income Increase		$603,900
Accounts Receivable Increase	($96,154)	
Prepaid Expenses Increase	($ 6,538)	
Accts. Pay.–Oper. Exp. Increase	$ 8,173	
Accr. Exp.–Oper. Exp. Increase	$11,442	
Income Tax Payable Increase	$31,110	($ 51,967)
Net Change in Operating Cash Flow		$551,933

*Changes in operating assets and liabilities are based on the company's operating ratios that are presented in Exhibit 6.1. For example, accounts receivable equals 5/52 of annual sales revenue for this example, so an increase in sales revenue would increase this asset accordingly.

Operating cash flow would increase by almost as much as the net income increase. The business should plan on a large influx to its cash balance due to the increase in net income.

Sales Price Decreases

What goes up can go down. We now consider the sales price decrease scenario. Managers hardly need to be reminded of the bad effects of decreasing sales prices, but they may not realize how damaging decreasing sales price can be on the bottom line. It takes a very large sales volume increase to offset sales price decreases, which we examine in Chapter 13. At this point, I'll simply mention that an equal percent of sales volume increase does not even come close to offsetting a sales price decrease.

Here, we analyze the damage done by a sales price decrease, assuming sales volume remains the same. Instead of showing a 10% sales price decrease, which would be the reverse mirror image of the 10% sales price increase scenario analyzed earlier, we examine just how devastating even a minor sales price decrease can be. Suppose that the company had come under competitive pressure to lower its sales price by, say, 4%, which doesn't seem that bad on the surface.

Exhibit 12.3 shows that a 4% sales price cut would have been a minor disaster. The company would give up $400,000 off the top (from sales revenue), and only one operating expense would decrease. Thus, contribution profit margin would decrease $366,000, which would reduce taxable income the same amount. Net income would fall $241,560, or 39.8%!

Furthermore, operating cash flow would decrease by approximately the same amount as the net income decrease (see Exhibit 12.4). Its cash balance would have been $220,773 less (from the $603,212 year-end balance in the baseline example). Thus, the company may have to cut its cash dividend, or borrow additional money, or convince its stockholders to put more money into the business to finance the sales price cut—not an easy task to say the least.

Changes in Product Cost and Operating Expenses

Changes in sales volume and sales prices usually have the biggest impact on operating profit. For most businesses (except for service businesses that do not sell products; see Chapter 16), product cost would rank the next most critical factor. A retailer needs smart, tough-nosed, sharp-pencil, aggressive purchasing tactics to control its product costs. On the other hand, this philosophy can be carried to an extreme.

When I lived in California some years ago, my neighbor George was a purchasing agent who was a real tiger. For instance, he would even return new calendars sent by vendors at the end of the year with a note saying "Don't send me this calendar; give me a lower price." This may be overkill, although George eventually became general manager of the business.

Even with close monitoring and relentless control, the variable and fixed operating expenses of a business may increase. Salaries, rent, insurance, utility bills, audit and legal fees—virtually every operating expense is subject to inflation. To illustrate this situation, let's consider the case in which sales prices and sales volume remain the same, but the company's product cost (cost of goods sold) and its variable and fixed operating expenses increase by, say, 5%, which is a

EXHIBIT 12.3   PROFIT IMPACTS OF 4% SALES PRICE DECREASE

Actual Income Statement (see Exhibit 10.1)			**Pro Forma Changes Caused by 4% Lower Sales Price**		
Sales Volume		100,000 Units	*No Change in Sales Volume*		
	Per Unit	**Totals**	**Per Unit**	**Totals**	
Sales Revenue	$100.00	$10,000,000	($4.00)	($400,000)	
Revenue-Driven Operating Expenses	8.5%	850,000	(0.34)	(34,000)	
Cost of Goods Sold Expense	60.00	6,000,000			
Volume-Driven Operating Expenses	5.00	500,000			
Contribution Profit Margin	$ 26.50	$ 2,650,000	($3.66)	($366,000)	-13.8%
Total Fixed Operating Expenses		1,570,000			
Operating Profit		$ 1,080,000			
Interest Expense		160,000			
Earnings Before Income Tax		$ 920,000	($366,000)		
Income Tax Expense @ 34%		312,800	(124,440)		
Net Income		$ 607,200	($241,560)	-39.8%	

Notice the *sales price leverage* effect: Total contribution profit margin decreases by 13.8% due to the sales price decrease. Bottom-line profit decreases by 39.8%, or almost three times as much because fixed costs and interest expense do not decrease in this example.

EXHIBIT 12.4 CASH FLOW IMPACTS OF 4% SALES PRICE DECREASE

Income Statement Changes (from Exhibit 12.3)

Operating Cash Flow Changes*

Net Income Decrease	($241,560)

Sales Revenue	($400,000)	Accounts Receivable Decrease	$38,462
Revenue-Driven Operating Expenses	(34,000)		
Cost of Goods Sold Expense			
Volume-Driven Operating Expenses			
Contribution Profit Margin	($366,000)		
Total Fixed Operating Expenses		Prepaid Expenses Decrease	$ 2,615
Operating Profit		Accts. Pay.–Oper. Exp. Decrease	($ 3,269)
Interest Expense		Accr. Exp.–Oper. Exp. Decrease	($ 4,577)
Earnings Before Income Tax	($366,000)		
Income Tax Expense @ 34%	(124,440)	Income Tax Payable Decrease	($12,444) $ 20,787
Net Income	($241,560)		
		Change in Operating Cash Flow	($220,773)

*Changes in operating assets and liabilities are based on the company's operating ratios that are presented in Exhibit 6.1. For example, accounts receivable equals 5/52 of annual sales revenue for this example, so a decrease in sales revenue would decrease this asset accordingly.

Operating cash flow would decrease just about as much as the net income decrease. The business would suffer a substantial decrease in its cash balance due to the decrease in net income.

EXHIBIT 12.5   PROFIT IMPACTS OF 5% COST INFLATION

Actual Income Statement (see Exhibit 10.1)			Pro Forma Changes Caused by 5% Higher Costs		
Sales Volume		100,000 Units	No Change in Sales Volume		
	Per Unit	**Totals**	**Per Unit**	**Totals**	
Sales Revenue	$100.00	$10,000,000			
Revenue-Driven Operating Expenses	8.5%	850,000	$ 0.425	$ 42,500	
Cost of Goods Sold Expense	60.00	6,000,000	3.000	300,000	
Volume-Driven Operating Expenses	5.00	500,000	0.250	25,000	
Contribution Profit Margin	$ 26.50	$ 2,650,000	$(3.675)	($367,500)	-13.9%
Total Fixed Operating Expenses		1,570,000		78,500	
Operating Profit		$ 1,080,000		($446,000)	
Interest Expense		160,000			
Earnings Before Income Tax		$ 920,000		($446,000)	
Income Tax Expense @ 34%		312,800		(151,640)	
Net Income		$ 607,200		($294,360)	-48.5%

Total contribution profit margin decreases by 13.9% due to the cost factors' increases. But bottom-line profit decreases by 48.5%.

modest rate of cost inflation. For convenience we hold interest expense constant.

Exhibit 12.5 presents the impact on profit performance for the 5% cost inflation scenario. As you can see, the 5% increases in product cost and operating expenses would cause net income to drop $294,360, or 48.5%. The company could ill afford to let its product cost and operating expenses get out of control by 5%. The business has to take action either to prevent this cost inflation or will have to raise sales price enough to offset the cost inflation impact.

Operating cash flow would suffer even more than the net income decrease. Instead of a complete cash flow exhibit as shown earlier, only the changes in operating assets and liabilities are summarized here:

Operating Cash Flow Impacts of Changes in Operating Assets and Liabilities Caused by 5% Cost Inflation

Net Income Decrease		($294,360)
Inventory Increase	($69,231)	
Accts. Pay–Inventory Increase	$23,077	
Prepaid Expenses Increase	($11,231)	
Accts. Pay.–Oper. Exp. Increase	$14,038	
Accr. Exp.–Oper. Exp. Increase	$19,654	
Income Tax Payable Decrease	($15,164)	($ 38,856)
Operating Cash Flow		($333,216)

The $333,216 decrease in operating cash flow is more than the net income decrease. This would cause the company's cash balance to drop to a very dangerous level.

Summary

If you had your choice as to whether you should increase sales volume or sales price, the best change, as you have seen, is a sales price increase—assuming all other profit factors remain the same (which is hardly ever true). A sales price increase yields the largest profit increase and the best cash flow result, much better than a sales volume increase of equal magnitude. A sales volume increase is a distant second.

Competition may put a fairly tight straitjacket on sales prices. Customers are sensitive to sales price increases. Sales volume is the key success factor for most businesses, which explains why managers are rightly concerned about protecting and building market share.

Sales volume and sales price are the "big two" factors. However, no profit factor should be overlooked. Increases in product cost, as well as increases in variable and fixed operating expenses can do serious damage to profit performance.

13

SALES PRICE AND VOLUME TRADE-OFFS

The World of Trade-Offs

Customers are sensitive to sales prices. So, when a business raises sales prices, its sales volume may drop. If the company decreases sales prices, its sales volume may increase, unless competitors also lower their prices. Higher sales prices may be driven by higher product costs and higher operating costs. By deliberately spending more on its fixed operating expenses, such as bigger advertising budgets, higher rent for larger stores, or more expensive furnishings, the business may pull in more customer traffic and increase its sales volume.

None of this is news to experienced business managers. They know the business world is one of *trade-offs* among profit factors. A change in one profit factor causes, or is in response to, a change in another factor. Business managers make many trade-off decisions.

Chapters 11 and 12 analyze changes in profit factors one at a time; the other profit factors are held the same in order to isolate the effects of the change in that one particular profit factor. However, you can seldom change just one thing at a time. In this chapter, we look at trade-off decisions involving two or more profit factors, and analyze the effects on profit and cash flow. We begin with a basic decision facing business managers, that being whether to cut sales prices in an effort to increase sales volume.

Business managers face this decision day in and day out. Some customers are very price aggressive and suggest that they would buy larger quantities at lower prices.

Cutting Price for More Volume

The Basic Strategy

Suppose you're the sales manager for our example company. You're considering decreasing sales price by 5%, which you predict would increase sales by 10%. I select this example because a two for one trade-off appears to be a good move. Giving up just 5% of your sales price for 10% more in sales volume appears to be a good trade-off—or does it?

Your competition may follow you down in price, so the sales volume may not increase. But, you don't think so. Your product is differentiated from the competition. (Two types of differentiation, for example, are established brand names and differences in product specifications.) There always has been some sales price spread between your product and the competition. In your opinion, a 5% price cut should not trigger price reductions by competitors.

One reason for reducing sales price is that the business is not selling up to its capacity. This is not unusual; many companies have some slack, or untapped sales capacity provided by their fixed operating expenses. In this example, assume the company's total fixed operating expenses provide enough space and personnel to handle a 20% to 25% larger sales volume. Total fixed operating expenses would not increase, unless sales volume increases more than this percentage.

Demand by customers may not respond to the sales price reduction as much as you predict. Or, sales volume may increase by more than 10%. You plan to closely monitor the reaction of customers. There is a serious risk here. If sales volume doesn't increase, you may not be able to reverse directions. You may not be able to roll back the sales price decrease without losing those customers who forget about the sales price decrease and see only the reversal.

What About Interest and Capital?

A higher sales volume level would increase total net operating assets. Thus, more capital from debt and equity sources would be needed, which means more interest-bearing debt may be borrowed, which would increase interest expense. Interest expense is held fixed at the higher sales level in analyzing this trade-off decision. However, let's keep this in the back of our minds.

Chapter 8 presents a comprehensive budgeting example that captures the changes in all operating assets and liabilities caused by sales revenue and operating expense increases next year. On the other hand, the purpose of this chapter and Chapter 14 is to focus on changes in profit and operating cash flow for certain basic trade-off decisions.

Analysis of Profit Effects

We will shortly look at the income statement that would result from the trade-off decision to cut sales price 5% in an effort to achieve a 10% sales volume increase. First we'll do a very condensed analysis that excludes fixed operating expenses, interest expense, and income tax.

A quick analysis of the trade-off decision is as follows:

Cut Sales Prices 5%; Sales Volume Increases 10%

Profit Factors	Before	After	Change
SP	$ 100.00	$ 95.000	-5.0%
SRDOE	8.50	8.075	-5.0%
COGS	60.00	60.000	
SVDOE	5.00	5.000	
CPM/U	$ 26.50	$ 21.925	-17.3%
Volume	100,000	110,000	+10.0%
Total CPM	$2,650,000	$2,411,750	-9.0%

SP = sales price; SRDOE = sales revenue-driven operating expenses; COGS = cost of goods sold; SVDOE = sales volume-driven operating expenses; CPM/U = contribution profit margin per unit.

Total CPM would drop by 9.0% as you can see. A 5% sales price reduction causes CPM/U to drop by more than 17%! *This is the key to the analysis.* A 10% sales volume increase cannot recoup, or make up for a 17% give-up in the profit margin. At the lower $21.925 CPM/U, the business would have to sell more than 120,000 units just to keep total CPM the same, which is not too likely. And, if volume goes up more than 20%, the company's fixed costs would increase.

The Income Statement

Exhibit 13.1 presents the income statement for your sales price reduction plan. Your bottom line would drop one-fourth! This trade-off decision would reduce total contribution profit margin by $238,250, or 9.0%. The contribution profit

EXHIBIT 13.1   TRADE-OFF ANALYSIS CUT PRICE 5%; VOLUME INCREASES 10%

Income Statement	Before*	After	Changes	
Sales Volume	100,000 Units	110,000 Units	10,000 Units	+ 10.0%
Sales Revenue	$10,000,000	$10,450,000	$450,000	+4.5%
Revenue-Driven Operating Expenses	850,000	888,250	38,250	+4.5%
Cost of Goods Sold Expense	6,000,000	6,600,000	600,000	+10.0%
Volume-Driven Operating Expenses	500,000	550,000	50,000	+10.0%
Contribution Profit Margin	$ 2,650,000	$ 2,411,750	($238,250)	-9.0%
Fixed Operating Expenses	1,570,000	1,570,000	0	
Operating Profit	$ 1,080,000	$ 841,750	($238,250)	-22.1%
Interest Expense	160,000	160,000	0	
Earnings Before Income Tax	$ 920,000	$ 681,750	($238,250)	-25.9%
Income Tax Expense @ 34%	312,800	231,795	(81,005)	-25.9%
Net Income	$ 607,200	$ 449,955	($157,245)	-25.9%

* See Exhibit 10.1.

Sales volume increases by 10.0%, but contribution profit margin actually *decreases* by 9.0%. Since fixed expenses do not decrease (and might even increase at the higher sales volume level) net income falls by 25.9%! In short, this would be a lousy trade-off decision on bottom-line profit. However, this move might increase the company's *market share*, and thus, position the company for better long-run profit performance.

margin reduction would decrease taxable income the same amount. Therefore, the after-tax impact on net income is $157,245, which would be a 25.9% decrease in net income.

On the surface, it might seem that a 10% sales volume gain is more than enough for only a 5% sales price reduction. However, sales price is the wrong place to look. As mentioned above, the key factor to keep your eye on is not sales price but the contribution profit margin per unit. The CPM/U drops 17.3%—this is the "killer" in the trade-off strategy. Sales volume does not increase enough.

The 5% sales price reduction needs a fairly large sales volume increase and thus is not a good decision. Yet, we frequently see sales price reductions of 10% or more. What's going on? First of all, many sales price reductions are from *list* prices, which no one takes seriously as the final price—such as the sticker price on new cars. List prices are only the point of departure for getting to the real price. Everyone wants a discount. I'm sure you've heard the line "I can get it for you wholesale."

Our example company uses the *real* price, the sales revenue per unit actually received by the business. Can a business cut its (real) sales price 5% and increase profit? Unless a company's CPM/U were extraordinarily high, its sales volume would have to increase much more than 10%, as we have just seen. So we have settled this question—haven't we? Well, there is one situation that brings up a critical point.

"Sunk" and Irrelevant Costs

Notice that the $60.00 unit product cost (cost of goods sold per unit) remains the same at the higher sales volume. Total cost of goods sold increases by 10% with the 10% sales volume increase. This seems pretty obvious doesn't it? Well, the business would sell more volume and thus would have to buy or manufacture more units, so there is the possibility that its unit product cost might increase, which would further squeeze its profit margin.

One basic premise of decision making analysis is that the products sold are replaced. Thus the cost of replacement, which is the purchase or manufacturing cost to the business, is a key factor in the analysis. Now, what if the units to be sold will not be replaced because these units are at the end of the product's life cycle? For instance, the product may be in the process of being replaced with a newer model or demand for the product has simply dried up. These orphan-type products generally face sales price pressure.

The historical accounting cost of a product that will not be replaced is called a *sunk* cost. The historical cost is like water over the dam. A business should write down the original cost of these products according to the lower of cost or market (LCM) accounting rule. The rule is somewhat complicated, but the basic idea is to record the loss of value as soon as it becomes apparent that the products cannot be sold for as much as their costs.

The recorded cost value of products that will not be replaced should be disregarded in making decisions. There will be no future outlay to replace the units. In other words, the relevant cost of these products for decision making is zero. The business should seek out the highest sales price that would move all the units out of inventory.

Sunk costs are one example of *irrelevant* costs in decision making. Any cost that would be the same and would not change in the future as a result of the decision is not relevant and should not influence the decision. We have already seen this exclusion of irrelevant costs. Recall that the company's fixed costs do not change at the higher sales volume, and therefore are not included in the analysis for deciding yes or no in the trade-off decision.

Short-Term Sales Promotions

The foregoing analysis applies the sales price reduction to all sales over the entire year. Many sales price reductions are limited to a relatively few items and are short-lived, perhaps for just a day or weekend. Furthermore, the sale may bring in customers who may buy other items that are not on sale. Profit margin is sacrificed on selected items to make additional sales of other products at normal profit margins.

Indeed, many retailers seem to always have some products on sale virtually every day of the year. In this case, the normal profit margin is hard to pin down, since almost every product takes its turn at being on sale. In short, every product may have two profit margins—one when not on sale and one when on sale. The *average* profit margin for the year depends on how often the item goes on sale weighted by the relative sales volumes at each price.

In any case, the same basic method of analysis just explained applies to short-term, limited sales price reductions. A manager should calculate, or at least estimate, how much additional sales volume would be needed on the sale items just to remain even with the profit that would have been earned at normal sales prices. What complicates the picture is keeping track of the sales of other products (not on sale), which would not have

been made without the increase in customer traffic resulting from the sale items. Clearly the additional sales made at their normal profit margins is an important factor to consider, although it may be very hard to estimate with any precision.

Operating Cash Flow

What would happen to operating cash flow (cash flow from operating activities) for this lower price/higher volume trade-off scenario? It would be a minor disaster, as we see in Exhibit 13.2. Cash flow from profit (before depreciation) would be $287,346 lower. This decrease in operating cash flow is almost half the company's $603,212 cash balance (see Exhibit 4.1). The company likely would have to go to external capital sources to provide enough working cash balance and eliminate its cash dividends.

The net income decrease is the largest reason for the negative impact on cash flow. But notice in Exhibit 13.2 that accounts receivable and inventory would have sizable increases that hurt cash flow. In short, operating cash flow would be much worse if sales price were reduced 5% in exchange for a 10% higher sales volume. The operating cash flow decrease would be almost double the decrease in net income. Talk about double jeopardy!

Giving Up Volume for Higher Price

Assume, the company's president is thinking of a 5% sales price increase knowing that sales volume would decrease. The pres-

Income Statement Changes (from Exhibit 13.1)

Sales Revenue	$450,000
Revenue-Driven Operating Expenses	38,250
Cost of Goods Sold Expense	600,000
Volume-Driven Operating Expenses	50,000
Contribution Profit Margin	($238,250)
Fixed Operating Expenses	0
Operating Profit	($238,250)
Interest Expense	0
Earnings Before Income Tax	($238,250)
Income Tax Expense @ 34%	(81,005)
Net Income	($157,245)

Operating Cash Flow Changes*

Net Income Decrease		($157,245)
Accounts Receivable Increase	($ 43,269)	
Inventory Increase	($138,462)	
Accts. Pay.–Inventory Increase	$ 46,154	
Prepaid Expenses Increase	($ 6,788)	
Accts. Pay.–Oper. Exp. Increase	$ 8,486	
Accr. Exp.–Oper. Exp. Increase	$ 11,880	
Income Tax Payable Decrease	($ 8,101)	($130,101)
Change in Operating Cash Flow		($287,346)

* Changes in operating assets and liabilities are determined by the company's operating ratios presented in Exhibit 6.1. For example, inventory equals 12/52 of annual cost of goods sold. So, an increase in cost of goods sold increases this asset accordingly.

> Operating cash flow decreases much more than the drop in net income. The business has higher sales revenue and expenses, which increase the net amount of operating assets less operating liabilities.

ident predicts volume will drop about 10%. The sales manager doesn't think along these lines. Sales managers generally are opposed to giving up sales volume, especially any loss of market share that is hard to recapture later. Any decision that deliberately decreases sales volume should be considered very carefully. For the moment we put aside these warnings.

The analysis of this trade-off decision is as follows:

Raise Sales Price 5%; Sales Volume Decreases 10%

Profit Factors	Before	After	Change
SP	$ 100.00	$ 105.00	+5.0%
SRDOE	8.50	8.925	+5.0%
COGS	60.00	60.000	
SVDOE	5.00	5.000	
CPM/U	$ 26.50	$ 31.075	+17.3%
Volume	100,000	90,000	-10.0%
Total CPM	$2,650,000	$2,796,750	+5.5%

SP = sales price; SRDOE = sales revenue-driven operating expenses; COGS = cost of goods sold; SVDOE = sales volume-driven operating expenses; CPM/U = contribution profit margin per unit.

The president is right: total contribution profit margin would increase 5.5%. The CPM/U would increase 17.3%, which is more than enough to offset the 10% drop in sales volume.

The income statement for the higher sales price/lower sales volume trade-off is shown in Exhibit 13.3. You see that sales revenue decreases. But cost of goods sold expense and both variable operating expenses decrease, and the total of these expense decreases is more than the sales revenue decrease.

In short, the company would give up $550,000 sales revenue and would avoid $696,750 expenses, for a net gain of $146,750 in total contribution margin. After income tax, the bottom-line net income would increase by 16%. And, at the lower sales volume level, the company may be able to lower its fixed operating expenses and interest expense.

But, and this is a big BUT, any loss of market share should be taken very seriously. By and large, successful companies have built their success on getting and keeping a loyal and satisfied customer base who make repeat purchases from the business. With its significant market share, the business is a major player and perhaps a dominant force in the marketplace, which provides very important competitive advantages.

The profit increase is based on the prediction that sales volume would drop only 10%. However, volume might fall by 15%, or 20%, or 25%. Net income can be calculated for any particular sales volume decrease. Generally speaking, it is difficult to predict how sales volume would respond to a 5% sales price increase. Sales may not decrease at all. The higher price might enhance the "prestige" or "premium" image of the product and attract more of an upscale clientele who are quite willing to pay the higher price. At the other extreme, sales may drop more than 25% because customers search for better prices elsewhere.

What sales volume would keep total contribution margin the same? This keep-even sales volume is computed as follows:

$2,650,000 Total CPM ÷ $ 31.075 CPM/U
= 85,278 units

EXHIBIT 13.3   TRADE-OFF ANALYSIS RAISE PRICE 5%; VOLUME DECREASES 10%

Income Statement	Before*	After	Changes	
Sales Volume	100,000 Units	90,000 Units	(10,000) Units	-10.0%
Sales Revenue	$10,000,000	$9,450,000	($550,000)	-5.5%
Revenue-Driven Operating Expenses	850,000	803,250	(46,750)	-5.5%
Cost of Goods Sold Expense	6,000,000	5,400,000	(600,000)	-10.0%
Volume-Driven Operating Expenses	500,000	450,000	(50,000)	-10.0%
Contribution Profit Margin	$ 2,650,000	$2,796,750	$146,750	+5.5%
Fixed Operating Expenses	1,570,000	1,570,000	0	
Operating Profit	$ 1,080,000	$1,226,750	$146,750	+13.6%
Interest Expense	160,000	160,000	0	
Earnings Before Income Tax	$ 920,000	$1,066,750	$146,750	+16.0%
Income Tax Expense @ 34%	312,800	362,695	49,895	+16.0%
Net Income	$ 607,200	$ 704,055	$ 96,855	+16.0%

*See Exhibit 10.1

Sales price increases by 5% but sales revenue is lower because sales volume decreases by 10%. Cost of goods sold and operating expenses also drop by 10%, which is more than the sales revenue decrease. Thus, contribution profit margin actually increases by 5.5%. Fixed expenses do not decrease (although they might at the lower sales volume level), so net income rises by 16%. However, the company may be giving up some market share, which is a decision that might hurt its long-term profit performance.

Income Statement Changes (from Exhibit 13.3)

Operating Cash Flow Changes*

Net Income Increase		$ 96,855

Income Statement		Operating Cash Flow	
Sales Revenue	($550,000)	Accounts Receivable Decrease	$ 52,885
Revenue-Driven Operating Expenses	(46,750)		
Cost of Goods Sold Expense	(600,000)	Inventory Decrease	$138,462
Volume-Driven Operating Expenses	(50,000)	Accts. Pay.–Inventory Decrease	($ 46,154)
Contribution Profit Margin	$146,750		
Fixed Operating Expenses	0	Prepaid Expenses Decrease	$ 7,442
Operating Profit	$146,750	Accts. Pay.–Oper. Exp. Decrease	($ 9,303)
Interest Expense	0	Accr. Exp.–Oper. Exp. Decrease	($ 13,024)
Earnings Before Income Tax	$146,750		
Income Tax Expense @ 34%	49,895	Income Tax Payable Increase	$ 4,990	$135,297
Net Income	$ 96,855		
		Net Change in Operating Cash Flow	$232,152

* Changes in operating assets and liabilities are determined by the company's operating ratios presented in Exhibit 6.1. For example, inventory equals 12/52 of annual cost of goods sold. So, a decrease in cost of goods sold decreases this asset accordingly.

Operating cash flow increases much more than the rise in net income. The business has lower sales revenue and expenses, which decrease the net amount of operating assets less operating liabilities.

Sales may not drop off this much, at least in the short run, and, fixed operating expenses could probably be reduced at the lower sales level.

Given their choice, the large majority of business managers probably would rather keep their market share and not give up any sales volume, even though profit could be maximized in the short run with the higher sales price/lower sales volume trade-off. Protecting sales volume and market share is deeply ingrained in the thinking of most business managers. True, some companies don't have a very large market share. They carve out a relatively small niche and build their business on low sales volume at premium prices. The foregoing analysis demonstrates the profit potential of this niche strategy, which is built on higher unit contribution profit margins that make up for smaller sales volume.

Operating Cash Flow Again

Cash flow from profit would be an even better story than the profit increase for the higher price/lower volume trade-off—as we see in Exhibit 13.4. The cost of goods sold expense would decrease, leading to a decrease of inventory. The higher profit would be made on a smaller inventory. Also, accounts receivable would decrease because of the sales revenue decrease. The large increase in operating cash flow would raise questions about what to do with the additional cash—a pleasant task for management to deal with.

Summary

Seldom does one profit factor change without changing or being changed by one or more of the other profit factors. The joint interaction effects of the changes should be carefully analyzed before making final decisions and locking onto a course of action that may be hard to reverse.

Managers should keep their attention riveted on contribution profit margin per unit. A seemingly small percent decrease in sales price causes a much larger percent decrease in the contribution profit margin per unit. The consequence is that a corresponding large percent increase in sales volume is needed just to maintain profit and an even larger percent volume increase to improve profit.

Sales prices are the most external, or visible, part of the business—the factor most exposed to customer reaction. In contrast, product cost and variable expenses are more internal and less visible. Customers may not be aware of these expense decreases, unless such cost savings show through in lower product quality or worse service, which Chapter 14 examines.

The importance of protecting sales volume and market share is mentioned several times in this chapter. Marketing managers know what they're talking about on this point. Recapturing lost market share is not easy. Once gone, customers may never return.

14

INFLATION VERSUS QUALITY COST CHANGES

Two Types of Cost Increases

This chapter examines two types of cost changes that are quite different but tend to get confused with each other:

- First we look at one of the most common cost changes in the economy—*inflation*. The defining characteristic of inflation is that the real quality and quantity (or size) of an economic factor or good doesn't change but its price increases.
- Second we look at those cost changes that are the result of deliberate changes in products sold by a business and deliberate increases (or decreases) in its operating expenses—changes not the result of inflation but, rather, changes made to protect or improve sales volume, or to improve profit margins.

Inflation means that a particular product remains the same, but now costs more per unit. On the other hand, product cost increases occur where the product itself is changed as a result of quality or size improvements that tend to justify a higher price.

Inflation is external to the business—the cost increases are driven by outside forces over which the business has little or no control. However, other product cost increases are just the opposite; they are the result of deliberate decisions made by the business to change its products (or to change its operating expenses), knowing that there will be an impact on sales price or sales volume, and possibly both.

Inflation Pass-Through Pricing

One basic function of business managers, which is not often stressed, is to raise sales prices in an effort to pass along to customers increases in product costs and operating expenses caused by inflation. Managers must get customers to pay higher prices to cover the higher costs of the business, which is not a simple task to say the least. The purpose is not to improve profit margins, but rather simply to increase sales prices to pay for cost increases.

As you know, the costs of the large majority of products (with some notable exceptions) tend to rise over time. Customers generally accept higher sales prices if they perceive that the company is operating in an inflationary environment. In their minds everything is going up. A particular product does not cost more relative to price increases of other products they purchase.

Sales volume may not be adversely affected by higher sales prices in an "inflation mentality" market. Assuming its competitors also face general product cost inflation, a company's sales volume may not suffer from passing along product cost increases in higher sales prices—the competition would be doing the same thing. On the other hand, if customers' incomes are not rising in proportion with sales price increases, demand would likely fall off at higher sales prices.

Because of inflation, suppose that our example company's cost of goods sold increases by $3.66 from $60.00 to $63.66 per unit, an increase of 6.1%. An overall inflation rate of 6.1% would certainly worry the Federal Reserve. However, we do not consider what action the Fed might take; we are interested in what action the business should take.

The business cannot simply raise its sales price by $3.66. In our example, the company's sales revenue-driven operating expenses are 8.5% of sales revenue. The required sales price increase is determined as follows:

$3.66 Product Cost Increase ÷ (1 - .085)
= $4.00 Sales Price Increase

Dividing by (1 − .085), or .915, recognizes that only 91.5¢ from each sales revenue dollar is available to provide for the increase in the unit product cost. If the company were to raise its sales price exactly $4.00, its contribution profit margin per unit would remain exactly the same, shown as follows:

**Sales Price Increase Needed to Pass Through
Inflation-Driven Product Cost Increase**

Notice that sales price has to increase by $4.00 to cover the $3.66 product cost increase.

Profit Factors	Before	After	Change
SP	$100.00	$104.00	+4.0%
SRDOE	8.50	8.84	+4.0%
COGS	60.00	63.66	+6.1%
SVDOE	5.00	5.00	
CPM/U	$ 26.50	$ 26.50	no change

SP = sales price; SRDOE = sales revenue-driven operating expenses; COGS = cost of goods sold; SVDOE = sales volume-driven operating expenses; CPM/U = contribution profit margin per unit.

As you see, the company's contribution profit margin per unit remains the same. Assuming sales volume remains the same, total contribution profit margin would hold steady. Total fixed operating expenses should be the same. But would interest expense remain the same at the higher sales price, product cost, and revenue driven operating expenses per unit?

At the higher sales price, total sales revenue would be higher so accounts receivable would be higher; and, at the higher product cost, total cost of goods sold would be higher so inventory would be higher. Also, the higher level of operating expenses would cause prepaid expenses and operating liabilities to increase. In short, total net operating assets would be higher.

In light of the previous discussion, the company probably would need more capital, some of which might very well come from increasing its debt. To cover the higher interest expense, and to provide additional net income to maintain its return on equity (ROE) on a higher owners' equity capital base, the business probably would have to raise its sales price by more than $4.00. Determining the exact sales price increase needed to compensate for the increase in interest expense and to provide additional net income to maintain ROE requires the more comprehensive (main course) budgeting approach, which was explained in Chapter 8.

Inflation-driven cost changes are only one type of the many changes in the business environment that managers have to deal with. In many situations, the manager must deal with two or more fundamental changes at the same time. So, a shift in the sales price may be the composite reaction to several basic underlying changes.

Making Cost Increases to Improve Sales Volume

It's one thing when the cost of a product increases as a result of inflation (and the product remains unchanged). But, it's quite another thing when a product's cost increases because a business makes a conscious decision to improve the product's quality or size, in order to make it more attractive to customers.

Customers may be willing to pay more for the improved product. The sales price is increased enough to offset the cost increase, and sales volume remains more or less the same. This case is analogous to the inflation-driven, pass-through pricing situation just discussed. Alternatively, product improvements may be part of a marketing strategy to give customers a better product while keeping the sales price the same, in an effort to stimulate demand. At the same sales price, customers may buy more—perhaps a lot more.

Also, certain variable operating expenses may be deliberately increased to improve the quality of the service to customers. For example, faster delivery methods, such as overnight Federal Express, could be used, even though this service would cost more than the traditional delivery methods and would increase the sales volume-driven operating expenses. Or, the company could increase sales commissions to improve the personal time and effort the sales staff spends with each customer, which would increase the sales revenue-driven operating expense.

Such a "quality upgrade" scenario may be customer driven. In fact, if a company failed to improve its product and/or service, then it might lose sales because customers want the improvements and are willing to pay for them. This state of affairs may seem strange, but you see examples everyday where the customer wants a better product and/or service and is willing to pay more for the improvements.

Suppose in our business example that the company has developed a quality improvement plan. After careful and detailed analysis of all the changes, the business has budgeted the following cost changes:

- Product cost would increase by 7.5% from $60.00 to $64.50 per unit
- Revenue dependent operating expenses would be pushed up from 8.5% to 10% of sales revenue (higher sales commissions for better service to customers)
- Volume driven operating expenses would increase by 6%, from $5.00 to $5.30 per unit.

Tentatively, and I should say very tentatively, management has decided *not* to increase the sales price; they predict demand should increase by 15% or even 20% for the improved product and service. (It goes without saying that demand would increase only if customers are made aware of and become convinced of the product and service improvements.) Is this a good trade-off decision? Would profit increase as the result of this higher cost/higher sales volume decision?

For a first cut at the analysis we shall hold fixed operating expenses and interest expense the same and also assume that sales volume increases by 20%. Using the same analysis tool we have applied before, this decision would produce the following results:

**Costs Are Increased; Don't Change Sales Price;
Sales Volume Increases 20%**

Profit Factors	Before	After	Change
SP	$ 100.00	$ 100.00	no change
SRDOE	8.50	10.00	+17.6%
COGS	60.00	64.50	+7.5%
SVDOE	5.00	5.30	+6.0%
CPM/U	$ 26.50	$ 20.20	-23.8%
Volume	100,000	120,000	+20.0%
Total CPM	$2,650,000	$2,424,000	-8.5%

> Even with a 20% increase in sales volume, total contribution profit margin would decrease because of the steep fall-off in the contribution profit margin per unit; sales volume does not increase enough to make up for 23.8% decrease in CPM/U.

SP = sales price; SRDOE = sales revenue-driven operating expenses; COGS = cost of goods sold; SVDOE = sales volume-driven operating expenses; CPM/U = contribution profit margin per unit.

**Sales Volume Needed at Higher Costs to
Keep Total Contribution Profit Margin the Same**

Profit Factors	Before	After	Change
SP	$ 100.00	$ 100.00	no change
SRDOE	8.50	10.00	+17.6%
COGS	60.00	64.50	+7.5%
SVDOE	5.00	5.30	+6.0%
CPM/U	$ 26.50	$ 20.20	-23.8%
Volume	100,000	131,188	+31.2%
Total CPM	$2,650,000	$2,650,000	no change

> Because of the steep fall-off in the contribution profit margin per unit, sales volume would have to increase to 131,188 units to keep the total contribution profit margin the same.

SP = sales price; SRDOE = sales revenue-driven operating expenses; COGS = cost of goods sold; SVDOE = sales volume-driven operating expenses; CPM/U = contribution profit margin per unit.

The three cost increases add up to $6.30 per unit, which drives down the contribution profit margin per unit to $20.20—a 23.8% drop. The 20% sales volume increase is not enough to overcome the large drop in the CPM/U.

At the lower $20.20 CPM/U, the business would have to sell 131,188 units just to earn the same total contribution profit margin as before:

Would demand for the improved product increase more than 30%? Even if the answer to this question is yes, and sales volume did indeed increase this much, the business may have to expand its capacity and increase its fixed operating expenses. This question leads to one conclusion: the business should plan on a sales price increase.

Suppose that the company decides to load all of the cost increases into the sales price with no increase at all in sales volume. The sales price increase that would then be needed is as follows:

$$\$6.30 \text{ Total Cost Increases per Unit}$$
$$\div \ (1 - 10\% \text{ Revenue-Driven Expenses per Unit})$$
$$= \$6.30 \div .9 \ = \ \$7.00 \text{ Sales Price Increase}$$

So the sales price would have to be raised to $107.00. In the following analysis, we see that this sales price increase is indeed correct.

Setting the Sales Price to Recover All the Cost Increases; Volume Remains the Same

Profit Factors	Before	After	Change
SP	$ 100.00	$ 107.00	+7.0%
SRDOE	8.50	10.70	+25.9%
COGS	60.00	64.50	+7.5%
SVDOE	5.00	5.30	+6.0%
CPM/U	$ 26.50	$ 26.50	no change
Volume	100,000	100,000	no change
Total CPM	$2,650,000	$2,650,000	no change

The 7% sales price increase covers all the cost increases so that the contribution margin per unit remains the same. On the same sales volume, total contribution margin would also be the same.

SP = sales price; SRDOE = sales revenue-driven operating expenses; COGS = cost of goods sold; SVDOE = sales volume-driven operating expenses; CPM/U = contribution profit margin per unit.

A warning might be repeated here: Any sales price increase has to be considered very carefully! Customer reaction is never easy to predict.

A more optimistic scenario would be that sales price could be raised more than $7.00 and sales volume would nevertheless increase because of the improvements in product quality and service. This case is examined in the next section.

Making Cost Increases to Improve Profit Margin

We continue with the company's quality improvement plan introduced earlier and its attendant cost increases. Now, however, assume that the company takes the quality upgrade program as an opportunity to improve both its profit margin and sales volume. This might work, especially if the perception by customers is that substantial improvements have been made by the company that convinces old customers to pay more and attracts new customers.

To raise sale prices for quality improvements, a business usually needs a carefully orchestrated advertising and marketing promotion program—one that makes customers aware of the changes and that convinces them that they are getting more value added at the higher prices.

To illustrate this scenario, assume the company were to raise its sales price $8.50 and would sell 5% additional sales volume. We have already seen that $7.00 is needed to cover the cost increases, so the additional $1.50 sales price increase would improve the company's contribution profit margin per unit (CPM/U). The analysis of the outcome is as follows:

Improving Both Profit Margin and Sales Volume Based on Quality Improvement Plan

Profit Factors	Before	After	Change
SP	$ 100.00	$ 108.50	+8.5%
SRDOE	8.50	10.85	+27.6%
COGS	60.00	64.50	+7.5%
SVDOE	5.00	5.30	+6.0%
CPM/U	$ 26.50	$ 27.85	+5.1%
Volume	100,000	105,000	+5.0%
Total CPM	$2,650,000	$2,924,250	+10.3%

> The "extra" $1.50 sales price increase over and above the $7.00 needed to cover the cost increases would improve the contribution profit margin per unit, which combined with the modest 5% volume increase would increase total contribution profit margin by over 10%.

SP = sales price; SRDOE = sales revenue-driven operating expenses; COGS = cost of goods sold; SVDOE = sales volume-driven operating expenses; CPM/U = contribution profit margin per unit.

To see the full impacts of this strategy, refer to Exhibit 14.1, which presents the income statement for this combination (improving both profit margin and sales volume). Net income would increase by almost 30%! Of course, whether the company could pull this off is the question. If it could, then net income would show a very substantial increase.

What about the issue of cash flow? As mentioned many times before, managers should always look at the operating cash flow consequences of a decision before moving ahead. Exhibit 14.2 lays out the cash flow effects of this plan. This news is bad, but not too bad. Operating cash flow would decrease about $10,000 from this decision even though net income would increase over $180,000. It's doubtful that a $10,000 decrease in its cash balance would dissuade the business from moving ahead with this decision.

Cost Decreases Causing Volume Decrease but Yielding Profit Increase

Suppose a business were able to lower its unit product costs and certain of its variable operating expenses per unit. Such savings may be a true efficiency or productivity gain. Purchase costs may be reduced by sharper bargaining. (If the business is a manufacturer, labor productivity gains reduce unit product costs.) Or, wasteful expenses could be eliminated. This situation, the reverse of inflation, is called *deflation*; the product remains the same, but it now costs less. The business can also have cost deflation in some of its operating expenses.

Some key questions are whether the product itself remains the same, whether the product's real and perceived quality remains unchanged, in the eye of the customer, and whether the quality of service to customers remains the same. Maybe so, maybe not. Product cost decreases may represent quality

Income Statement	Before*	After	Changes	
Sales Volume	100,000 Units	105,000 Units	5,000 Units	
Sales Revenue	$10,000,000	$11,392,500	$1,392,500	+13.9%
Revenue-Driven Operating Expenses	850,000	1,139,250	289,250	+34.0%
Cost of Goods Sold Expense	6,000,000	6,772,500	772,500	+12.9%
Volume-Driven Operating Expenses	500,000	556,500	56,500	+11.3%
Contribution Profit Margin	$ 2,650,000	$ 2,924,250	$ 274,250	+10.3%
Fixed Operating Expenses	1,570,000	1,570,000		
Operating Profit	$ 1,080,000	$ 1,354,250	$ 274,250	+25.4%
Interest Expense	160,000	160,000		
Earnings Before Income Tax	$ 920,000	$ 1,194,250	$ 274,250	+29.8%
Income Tax Expense @ 34%	312,800	406,045	93,245	+29.8%
Net Income	$ 607,200	$ 788,205	$ 181,005	+29.8%

* See Exhibit 10.1.

Sales price would have to increase to $107.00 just to cover the cost increases, as this chapter explains. In this example, the company increases its sales price to $108.50, which improves its contribution profit margin per unit. Also, sales volume increases by 5%. The overall result of these two seemingly modest increases is a sizable 29.8% increase in net income.

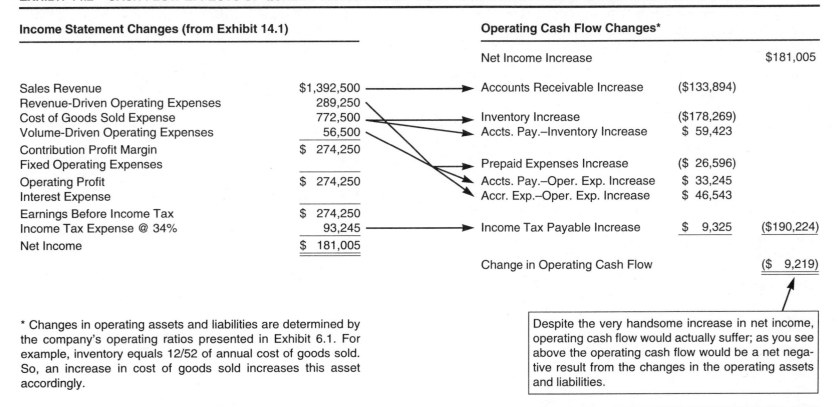

Income Statement Changes (from Exhibit 14.1)

Sales Revenue	$1,392,500
Revenue-Driven Operating Expenses	289,250
Cost of Goods Sold Expense	772,500
Volume-Driven Operating Expenses	56,500
Contribution Profit Margin	$ 274,250
Fixed Operating Expenses	
Operating Profit	$ 274,250
Interest Expense	
Earnings Before Income Tax	$ 274,250
Income Tax Expense @ 34%	93,245
Net Income	$ 181,005

Operating Cash Flow Changes*

Net Income Increase		$181,005
Accounts Receivable Increase	($133,894)	
Inventory Increase	($178,269)	
Accts. Pay.–Inventory Increase	$ 59,423	
Prepaid Expenses Increase	($ 26,596)	
Accts. Pay.–Oper. Exp. Increase	$ 33,245	
Accr. Exp.–Oper. Exp. Increase	$ 46,543	
Income Tax Payable Increase	$ 9,325	($190,224)
Change in Operating Cash Flow		($ 9,219)

* Changes in operating assets and liabilities are determined by the company's operating ratios presented in Exhibit 6.1. For example, inventory equals 12/52 of annual cost of goods sold. So, an increase in cost of goods sold increases this asset accordingly.

Despite the very handsome increase in net income, operating cash flow would actually suffer; as you see above the operating cash flow would be a net negative result from the changes in the operating assets and liabilities.

decreases or degradations, or may result from reducing sizes (such as smaller candy bars or fewer ounces in breakfast cereal boxes). Reducing variable operating expenses may adversely affect the quality of service to customers, for instance, spreading fewer sales personnel over the same number of customers.

If the company can lower its costs and still deliver the same product and the identical quality of service, then sales volume should not be affected. Customers should see no differences in the products or service. The cost savings would improve the unit contribution margin and profit would increase accordingly. Improvements in the unit contribution profit margin are very powerful and have a *multiplier effect* similar to that which occurs as a result of operating leverage.

Total quality management (TQM) is getting a lot of press today, indicated by the fact that it has been reduced to an acronym. Managers have always known that product quality and quality of service to customers are absolutely critical for maintaining a successful business. However, in the past (the 1980s) some managers may have lost sight of this point in pursuit of short-term profits. Today, however, managers have been made acutely aware of how quality conscious customers really are.

Cost savings may cause degradation in the quality of the product or service to customers. Thus, it would be no surprise to find that sales volume decreased as a result of a cost reduction technique. The unit contribution margin would improve, but the drop in sales volume could offset the gain in the profit margin. Therefore the sales price may have to be dropped to protect sales volume.

To demonstrate a cost savings example, suppose the business could lower its unit product cost by 4%, or $2.40 per unit,

because of true efficiency and productivity gains that do not cause any degradation in the product or customer service. Assuming all other product factors remain the same, the quick analysis of this deflation impact is as follows:

Product Cost Decreases; No Other Changes

Profit Factors	Before	After	Change
SP	$ 100.00	$ 100.00	no change
SRDOE	8.50	8.50	no change
COGS	60.00	57.60	-4.0%
SVDOE	5.00	5.00	no change
CPM/U	$ 26.50	$ 28.90	+9.1%
Volume	100,000	100,000	no change
Total CPM	$2,650,000	$2,890,000	+9.1%

The 4% reduction in product cost per unit improves the contribution margin per unit by 9.1%. At the same sales volume, total contribution profit margin also increases by 9.1%.

SP = sales price; SRDOE = sales revenue-driven operating expenses; COGS = cost of goods sold; SVDOE = sales volume-driven operating expenses; CPM/U = contribution profit margin per unit.

The $2.40 per unit product cost reduction yields a 9.1% increase on the $26.50 original contribution profit margin per unit, which has more than twice as much impact as the percent savings in product cost. Since sales volume stays the same, total fixed operating costs should not increase. So, the $240,000 increase in total contribution profit margin would carry down to earnings before tax. After-tax net income would increase by $158,400, assuming a 34% income tax rate.

Fixed Operating Expenses Changes

Why do a company's fixed operating expenses increase? First of all, such increases may be due to general inflationary pressures. For instance, utility bills, real estate taxes, and insurance premiums drift relentlessly upward and they seem hardly ever to go down. You don't find very many fixed expenses that follow a steady downward trend line, do you? There may be a few, but certainly not very many.

On the other hand, fixed operating expenses may be deliberately increased to expand *capacity*. A business may rent a larger space or hire more employees on fixed salaries to provide for a larger sales capacity. A manufacturer may expand its facilities and workforce to provide greater production capacity. Over time, a business has to keep its capacity (and thus its fixed operating costs) in alignment with its sales volume. In any one year, a business may have some idle or unused capacity. But the business has to plan carefully to keep its capacity consistent with sales volume, of course, allowing for some normal standby or safety margin.

There's a third reason for increases in fixed costs: These expenses may be increased by a business to improve demand for its product and to improve the sales value of its present location. The business could invest in better furnishings and equipment. Of course, fixed expenses could decrease for the opposite reasons. But, we'll focus on increases in fixed expenses.

Suppose that in our example company, total fixed operating expenses were to increase due to general inflationary trends. In such a situation, there would be no change in business capacity or in the retail space or its appearance (attractiveness of the space). As far as customers could tell, there would be no changes benefiting them. The company could attempt to increase its sales price—the additional fixed expenses could be spread over its present sales volume.

However, this assumes sales volume would remain the same at the higher sales price, which it might. But sales volume might decrease at the higher sales price, unless customers accept the increase as a general inflationary-driven increase. Sales volume might be sensitive to even small sales price increases. As you know, many customers keep a sharp eye on prices. As a general rule, the business should probably allow for some decrease in sales volume when sales prices are raised. This clearly puts pressure on managers to maintain and, if possible, improve contribution profit margin per unit.

Summary

Both this chapter and the previous one rest on the premise that a change in one profit factor hardly ever occurs without changing or being changed by one or more of the other profit factors. It has been consistently mentioned, but bears repeating here, that managers must keep their attention riveted on *contribution profit margin per unit*. Profit performance is extremely sensitive to changes in this critical operating profit factor. Several different examples demonstrate this point.

Sales prices are the most external part of the business. In contrast, product cost and operating expenses are internal to the business and invisible to customers. Customers may not be aware of such expense decreases, unless they see the results in the form of lower product quality or worse service. Frequently cost "savings" are not true cost savings at all, because they affect demand and cause sales volume to decrease.

One type of cost increase is caused by inflation. Quite another type is caused by product improvements and improvements in the quality of service to customers. Cost increases have to be recovered through higher sales volume or higher sales prices. This chapter examines the critical differences between these two alternatives.

It may not be realistic to depend on increasing sales volume to offset cost increases. Generally speaking, sales volume would have to increase too much to justify a cost increase. Cost increases generally have to be recovered through higher sales prices. The tools of analysis explained in this chapter give managers an invaluable frame of reference for making these critical decisions.

15

SALES MIX AND COST ALLOCATION

Two Peas in a Pod

This chapter explores two issues confronting business managers: (1) *sales mix* and (2) *cost allocation*. It's indeed true that these two subjects are quite different, and may even seem to be unrelated, but, as you will soon see, they are in fact closely connected. Sales mix refers to the relative weights or proportions of the different products making up the sum total of sales revenue. Cost allocation refers to the dividing up or apportioning of a pool of indirect fixed costs over the various products whose sales benefit from and depend on the costs.

As I'm sure you know, many businesses sell a broad range and diversity of products. The different products almost always have different contribution margins per unit. It is extremely important that internal management profit reports highlight profit margin information for decision making and control. The optimal sales mix is the one that maximizes total contribution profit margin. In this way, the business gets the best return from its indirect fixed costs.

If you look at almost any business, you'll find that the different products making up its sales mix share a common base and foothold of indirect fixed operating expenses, also called *overhead* expenses. Indirect means that there is no direct cause and effect relationship between the products and the overhead costs; the costs are far removed from individual products. For example, consider a retail department store operating in one building. Owning and using the building requires many fixed operating costs, such as depreciation, utilities, security guards, property taxes, fire and hazard insurance, and many more such costs. These fixed operating expenses provide *sales capacity—*the space, personnel, and facilities to make sales and to deliver service to customers. Product costs and variable expenses can be directly matched with each product's sales revenue. In contrast, there is no clear-cut basis to couple the building's occupancy costs with each product.

A natural question is whether indirect fixed expenses should be allocated and charged against the contribution profit margins earned from individual products. Allocation may appear to be logical and to make good accounting sense, but does allocation help decision making and control? That's management's key question. First we explore the analysis of sales mix, and then we move on to the allocation question.

Sales Mix Analysis

A Closer Look at Our Example Company

We now return to the example company used throughout previous chapters and take a closer look at how the company is organized. The company has two separate divisions: One division sells consumer products and the other sells industrial products to other businesses. The organization chart, in brief, is as follows:

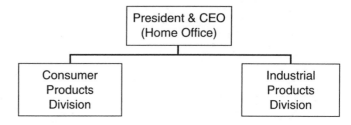

Each of the "boxes" in this organizational structure has fixed costs. If you recall from earlier discussion, total fixed operating expenses of the company as a whole is $1,570,000 for the year just ended. The fixed costs of each organizational unit are as follows:

$ 365,000	Home Office (the corporate headquarters), consisting of the President and CEO and staff
766,000	Consumer Products Division
439,000	Industrial Products Division
$1,570,000	Total Fixed Operating Expenses

The home office fixed costs consist of the president's and other corporate staff salaries and fringe benefits, legal fees of the corporation, the annual audit cost for the company, and so on. The Consumer Products Division's fixed costs consist of the salaries and benefits of the general manager and administrative staff, advertising expenses for the products sold by this division, depreciation of the autos and other fixed assets used in the division, and other administrative and operating costs of the division. The scenario is the same for the Industrial Products Division.

Reporting Sales Mix to Managers

Suppose you're the general manager of the Consumer Products Division. Your division is an autonomous *profit center* in the organization structure. You report to the president but you have broad authority and responsibility for your division.

Your primary job is to meet or exceed the budgeted operating profit objectives for the year. Your annual salary increase and bonus depend on the division's operating profit performance.

The Consumer Products Division sells one product line consisting of four products sold under the company's brand name plus one product sold as a generic (no label) product to a supermarket chain. Exhibit 15.1 presents your division's profit report for the most recent year. Notice in this report that the $766,000 in total fixed operating expenses of your organizational unit is not allocated among the five products.

Your division generates slightly more than half of the $10,000,000 sales revenue of the company and slightly more than half of the company's $2,650,000 total contribution profit margin. All five products earn a contribution margin, although the unit margins vary in dollar amount and by percent of sales price across the five products. The Premier product has the highest percent of profit margin (35%), as well as the highest dollar contribution profit margin per unit ($33.25). Notice that the Generic model has a higher percent of contribution profit margin and generates more total contribution margin than the Economy model.

On the Generic product, production costs are cut to the bone. No advertising or sales promotion of any type is done on the Generic product; the volume-driven expenses are delivery costs. Product cost is highest for the Premier product because the best raw materials are used and additional labor time is required to make its quality the top of the line. The variable sales promotion costs (dealer incentives mainly) are fairly heavy for this product.

The sales revenue, cost of goods (products) sold, and variable expenses should be broken out for each separate product—as

EXHIBIT 15.1   CONSUMER PRODUCTS DIVISION PROFIT REPORT

	Products					Product Line Totals	
	Generic	Economy	Standard	Deluxe	Premier	Units	Dollars
Sales Volume in Units	28,000	18,000	35,000	10,000	9,000	100,000	
% of Total Sales Volume	28%	18%	35%	10%	9%	100%	
Sales Price	$28.25	$42.50	$60.00	$75.00	$95.00		$5,261,000
Revenue-Driven Expenses	none	(0.80)	(2.70)	(6.00)	(9.50)		(254,400)
Product Cost	(20.05)	(26.65)	(32.00)	(36.00)	(40.60)		(2,886,500)
Volume-Driven Expenses	(1.13)	(6.00)	(9.10)	(10.50)	(11.65)		(667,990)
Unit Contribution Profit Margin	$ 7.07	$ 9.05	$16.20	$22.50	$33.25		
% of Sales Price	25%	21%	27%	30%	35%		
Total Contribution Profit Margin	$197,960.00	$162,900.00	$567,000.00	$225,000.00	$299,250.00		$1,452,110
% of Total Contribution Margin	14%	11%	39%	15%	21%		
Fixed Operating Expenses Direct to This Consumer Products Division	?	?	?	?	?		($ 766,000)
Operating Profit*	?	?	?	?	?		$ 686,110

*Operating profit excluding allocation of any home office (general companywide) fixed overhead costs that are indirect to this division.

The question is whether to allocate the total fixed operating expenses among the five products to determine the operating profit attributable to each product.

you see in Exhibit 15.1. For management decision-making analysis this information is absolutely essential. Managers need this data to analyze shifts in sales mix and trade-offs among the products and to reach the optimal sales mix. Managers would be operating in the dark without this information.

One key element in the marketing strategy of many companies is to get their customers to *trade up*, which means to buy higher-priced items in their product lines. Higher priced products generally have higher dollar amount contribution profit margins per unit, which is true in this example. Many new products in the early stages of their life cycles enjoy high profit margins, until competition catches up and forces down sales price and/or sales volume.

Managers should not become complacent about the present sales mix of their products; they should ask whether it is the optimal mix. Would certain trade-offs yield a higher total contribution profit margin?

Trade-Offs within the Product Line

Let's compare two products—the Standard versus the Deluxe. You make a $6.30 higher contribution profit margin per unit on the Deluxe product: $22.50 Deluxe – $16.20 Standard = $6.30. Giving up one Standard unit in trade-off for one Deluxe unit would increase total contribution profit margin. This shift should not affect your total fixed expenses. Of course, there are many possible trade-offs among the five products. The purpose here is to call your attention to how important it is to focus on comparative unit contribution profit margins.

The position of the Economy model is interesting: its unit contribution profit margin is the lowest of the company brand name models, and not that much more than the Generic model. The Economy model may be in the nature of a *loss leader* or, more accurately, a minimum profit leader—a product you don't make much margin on, but a necessary one to fill out the product line and one that serves as a springboard or stepping stone for customers to trade up to higher priced products. However, managers should keep an eye on loss leaders because rather than serve as a springboard for customers to trade up to higher priced products, the opposite may result. In other words, tough times may cause customers to trade down from higher priced models to lower end products. Many customers may trade down to the Standard product, or even down another step to the Economy model. If you see this shift taking place, perhaps you could raise sales prices somewhat on the lower end products because of the increased demand for these products, or, perhaps not.

Should you be selling the Generic product? In other words, should you be allocating 28% of your sales capacity to this product? On the one hand, this product brings in 14% of your total contribution profit margin, even though it uses up 28% of your sales capacity. As a hypothetical exercise, suppose that you could decrease your division's fixed operating expenses by $250,000, which would reduce your sales capacity to 72,000 units. You'd have to sacrifice 28,000 units of sales, which is the sales volume of the Generic model. So, you would have to give up a $197,960 contribution profit margin from the Generic model but at the same time you would save $250,000 in fixed expenses. Strictly speaking, on the basis of the numbers, this would be a good move, as it would increase operating profit by $52,040, but would you be willing to downsize and give up the Generic sales to a competitor?

Suppose, on the other hand, that you could not reduce your fixed operating expenses over the short run. You are "stuck with" 100,000 units of sales capacity over the near term. Selling any of the five products is better than not making a sale—they all earn contribution profit margin. You possibly could introduce a new product, even though it would take sales capacity away from one or more of the five products. Doing so may be beneficial if, as a result, you could increase total contribution profit margin.

The Generic model may be drawing sales away from your four brand-name products—although this is hard to know for sure. If the Generic product were not available in supermarkets, would these customers buy one of your other models? Of course, they might shift to your competitors' products. If all the Generic customers would switch and buy the Economy model you would be better off. You'd be giving up sales on which you make $7.07 unit contribution profit margin for replacement sales on which you earn $9.05, an increase of almost $2.00 per unit.

In making such a decision, many different marketing questions can be and should be raised. Indeed, your job as general manager is precisely this—to identify strategic marketing questions. You have to decide how to position each product; you have to set sales prices; you have to select the most effective media for advertising; and so on. One thing is clear. The information presented in Exhibit 15.1 is essential. Managers can never stray too far away from unit contribution profit margin numbers, as we have seen again and again in previous chapters.

Let's Allocate Fixed Expenses and See What Happens

In our example company, all $766,000 of the Consumer Products Division's fixed operating expenses are *indirect* costs, which means that these costs cannot be matched or coupled with sales of individual products. These fixed costs are necessary to carry on the sales activities of the division. But there are no direct cause and effect connections between any of the fixed costs and the separate products sold by the division.

This is not to ignore the fact that in some situations *direct* fixed costs should be assigned to particular products. Suppose, for example, that you run a one-time insertion in the *Wall Street Journal* for the Premier product. Only the Premier product is targeted in this advertisement. The ad's cost should be deducted against the contribution margin earned from the Premier product. None of this particular advertising expense should be allocated to any other product. Likewise, if a salesperson works exclusively on one product and no others, then his or her salary and benefit costs should be deducted directly against the contribution profit margin of that product. However, generally speaking, most fixed costs are indirect specific products.

In Exhibit 15.1 fixed expenses are not allocated to products, but the question marks raise the possibility. Fixed costs can be allocated on the basis of *sales volume*, which means each unit sold would be assigned an equal amount of the total fixed expense ($766,000 ÷ 100,000 units = $7.66 average per unit). Alternatively, fixed costs can be allocated on the basis of *sales revenue*, which means that each dollar of sales revenue would be assigned an equal amount of total fixed costs ($766,000 ÷ $5,261,000 = 14.56¢ average cost per dollar of sales revenue).

Exhibit 15.2 compares these two methods of allocating indirect fixed expenses. Total operating profit for the division is the same by both methods, but, as you see in the exhibit, the operating profit of each product depends on which allocation basis is used. Both methods for allocating fixed costs are suspect. There may be a justification for using one method over the other method, but, then again, there may not be.

Under the first method, the theory is that each and every unit should be given the same fixed cost because each unit uses one unit of sales capacity. Under the second method the premise is that each and every sales revenue dollar should be given the same fixed-cost burden. Really?

Both sales volume and sales revenue are rather gross and crude methods for allocating fixed costs. Neither method attempts to differentiate between the products relative to whether one product needs more of particular fixed costs than other products. One product may require more legal expense, for instance, because it has more safety problems and may attract more lawsuits from customers.

Activity-Based Costing (ABC)

Instead of allocating the total amount of indirect fixed expenses, one alternative is to divide the total pool of fixed expenses into separate subpools—one for each identifiable, distinct function or support activity. The idea is to lift the veil

covering overhead costs and ask exactly what types of supporting services and value-added functions are provided by the fixed costs. This component-by-component scrutiny of fixed costs should make for better management control of the costs. Indeed, this technique has garnered a lot of attention recently; it is called *activity-based costing* (ABC).

The ABC method subdivides total fixed operating expenses into separate cost pools for each basic activity or support function. Each product is then analyzed to measure the extent to which the product uses or benefits from each activity. If one product uses an activity twice as much as another product, then it is allocated twice as much cost.

In this example all products except the Generic model are advertised. All advertising is done through the advertising department of your division. The advertising department is defined as one fixed cost pool, and its activity, is measured, according to a common denominator of activity such as number of advertising pages in print media (newspapers and magazines). Each product is allocated its share of the advertising department's cost based on how many ad pages were run for the product. The advertising function is called a cost driver. This sales promotion activity drives the amount of the fixed cost subpool, which is allocated among the products.

Different types of advertising (print, electronic media, billboards) could be identified. There would be a separate cost pool within the advertising department for each type of advertising. Each product would be charged with its share of advertising cost based on two or more separate cost drivers—one for the number of print media pages, the second for the number of minutes on television or radio, and so on.

EXHIBIT 15.2 TWO METHODS OF ALLOCATING FIXED EXPENSES
(PRODUCT CONTRIBUTION PROFIT MARGINS ARE FROM EXHIBIT 15.1)

Method A   Fixed Expenses Allocated on Basis of Sales Volume

	Generic	Economy	Standard	Deluxe	Premier	Totals
Sales Volume in Units	28,000	18,000	35,000	10,000	9,000	100,000
Contribution Profit Margin	$197,960	$162,900	$567,000	$225,000	$299,250	$1,452,110
Allocated Fixed Expenses	(214,480)	(137,880)	(268,100)	(76,600)	(68,940)	(766,000)
Operating Profit (Loss)	($ 16,520)	$ 25,020	$298,900	$148,400	$230,310	$ 686,110

Method B   Fixed Expenses Allocated on Basis of Sales Revenue

	Generic	Economy	Standard	Deluxe	Premier	Totals
Sales Revenue	$791,000	$765,000	$2,100,000	$750,000	$855,000	$ 5,261,000
Contribution Profit Margin	$197,960	$162,900	$567,000	$225,000	$299,250	$1,452,110
Allocated Fixed Expenses	(115,169)	(111,384)	(305,759)	(109,200)	(124,488)	(766,000)
Operating Profit (Loss)	$ 82,791	$ 51,516	$261,241	$115,800	$174,762	$ 686,110
Differences: Method B less Method A	+$99,311	+$26,496	($37,659)	($32,600)	($55,548)	$ 0

Additional Operating Profit due to sales revenue basis of allocating fixed expenses.

Operating Profit taken away from the products due to sales revenue method of allocating fixed expenses.

No difference.

The ABC method certainly looks good in theory. However, the actual application of this method presents many practical problems. (Of course, it's not unusual for something that looks good in theory to break down in actual practice.) In particular, certain fixed expenses are very indirect and far removed from particular products, such as fixed costs of the company's accounting department, the annual CPA audit fee, cost of security guards, general liability insurance, and many more.

The cost driver (separate activity or supporting function) concept gets stretched to the limit for certain fixed expenses. Also, the number of separate activities (each with its own expense pool to be allocated based on a cost driver measure) can get out of hand. Three to five, perhaps even seven to ten separate cost drivers for fixed cost allocation may be understandable and feasible, but there is a limit.

Back to Basic Questions

The fundamental management question is whether any allocation scheme is worth the effort. What's the purpose? Does allocation help decision making and control? The basic management purpose should not be to find the "true" operating profit for each product or other sales revenue source. The fundamental question is whether management is making optimal use of the resources and capacity provided by the company's indirect fixed operating expenses.

The bottom line is to find that particular sales mix that maximizes the total contribution profit margin of the entity.

Allocation of indirect fixed expenses in and of itself doesn't help to do this. The advocates of the ABC method would quickly argue here that this technique gives managers better information about how products differ with regard to their "utilization" of and demands on certain indirect fixed costs.

Their basic point is that certain products burn up fixed costs at faster rates than other products, and this should be taken into account in the search for the optimal sales mix. However, as alluded to already, some fixed costs are so indirect to particular products that the ABC method is of little or no help. One example that comes to mind is charitable contributions made in the name of the entire organization.

Indirect fixed expenses may have to be allocated for legal or contract purposes. If so, the method(s) for such allocation should be spelled out in advance, rather than waiting until after the fact to select the allocation rationale.

Sometimes a business may allocate fixed expenses to minimize the apparent operating profit on a product. For example, I was hired to be an expert witness for the plaintiff in a patent infringement lawsuit against a well-known corporation. The defendant had already lost in the first stage; the company had been found guilty of patent infringement. For three years, the defendant business had manufactured and sold a product, the patent of which the plaintiff owned, without compensating the plaintiff. The second stage was to assess the amount of damages to be awarded to the plaintiff. The plaintiff was suing for recovery of the profit made by the defendant corporation on sales of the product. To minimize the profit that was allegedly earned from sales of the product, the defendant allocated every indirect fixed cost it could think of to the product, including part of the CEO's annual salary. The jury threw out this heavy-handed allocation and awarded $16 million to the plaintiff.

In our example company, should any of the $365,000 home office fixed costs be allocated to the two divisions of the company? More generally, should home office or headquarters type of overhead costs that benefit the entire organization be allocated to the profit centers in the organization? It's not unusual for costs "from above" to be allocated across different organizational units. Managers should be aware of the methods, or bases, or formulas that are used to allocate costs. The worst mistake is to assume that there is some natural or objective basis for cost allocation. The great majority of cost allocation schemes are arbitrary, and therefore, subject to manipulation.

Questions about the proper method of allocation should be settled before the start of the year. Raising such questions after the fact—after the profit performance results are reported for the period—is too late. In any case, if you argue for less (a smaller allocation of fixed expenses to your unit), then you are also arguing that other units should get more of the organization's general overhead fixed costs, which will initiate a counterargument from those units. Also, it may appear that you're making excuses rather than fixing the problem.

Finally, it should be mentioned that there is one kind of indirect fixed costs that must be allocated among different products; nonallocation is not an option. Fixed *manufacturing* overhead (indirect production) costs are allocated among the different products manufactured during the period. Manufacturing accounting methods are explained in Chapter 17.

Summary

Sales mix analysis is very important in profit management. Different products have different contribution profit margins. The manager should carefully consider whether the present mix of products being sold can be improved by strategic trade-offs among the products, especially by moving customers from lower margin to higher margin products. Also, the manager should know the profit impact of customers moving down the product line.

Multiple products bring with them an unavoidable side effect—indirect fixed expenses that cannot be directly matched with individual products. These fixed expenses benefit a broad range of products, but the expenses are indirect to any one of the products. The question facing managers is whether to allocate the fixed expenses among the products to determine an operating profit (after fixed expenses) for each product. The premise is that these operating profit numbers would be good guides for making decisions and for assessing the relative profit performance of different products.

However, the allocation of indirect fixed costs does not help and may actually hinder decision making and developing better marketing strategies, particularly if managers don't understand the arbitrary basis on which indirect costs are allocated. The key information managers should focus on in analyzing sales mix and developing new strategies is product contribution profit margins before fixed costs are subtracted.

The new method, called *activity-based costing* (ABC), offers remedies to some of the shortcomings of traditional allocation methods, although the ABC technique is certainly not a cure-all. The value of the ABC technique is that it distinguishes between those fixed costs that have a cost driver relationship with products versus other fixed costs that do not and thus, should not be allocated. The ABC method focuses on the value-added nature of the functions and supporting activities included in fixed costs, and this sharper definition may lead to heightened management attention and better control of these costs.

16

SERVICE BUSINESSES

Different Yet Much the Same

This chapter applies the management analysis and budgeting techniques discussed in previous chapters to *service* businesses. These business entities do not sell a product, or whatever product is sold is quite incidental to the service they provide.

Service businesses range from dry cleaners to film processors, hotels to hospitals, airlines to freight haulers, CPAs to barbers, rental firms to photocopying stores, movie theaters to amusement parks, gambling casinos to professional sports teams, gas and electricity utilities to on-line electronic networks, and so on. The service sector is the largest general category in the economy, and it is also extremely diverse.

To this point we have studied product-oriented businesses—companies that sell products. All businesses sell service with their products. It's hard to think of any business where the quality of service to customers is not important. In fact, the quality of service often is the main competitive advantage of the business. The impact of cutting costs on the quality of customer service has been discussed in previous chapters. I won't preach any further about the importance of service quality. I'm sure you're convinced about this.

Ask managers about their business and one of the first things they will tell you is that their particular business is different from other businesses. Which is true of course; every business is unique. There are some fundamental differences between product and service businesses, but as we look into these differences, we should not lose sight of the fact that most things are the same.

Businesses, like people, draw on a common core of concepts, principles, and techniques. Every individual is different and unique. Yet, basic principles of behavior and motivation apply to all of us, whether we are customers, employees, or suppliers. Take products. Breakfast cereals are different from computers, which are different from autos, and so on. Yet, basic principles of marketing apply to all products. Likewise, the basics of management analysis and budgeting techniques are the same for both service and product businesses.

Applying the basics is the really hard part, which managers are paid to do and do well. A manager must adapt basic concepts and general techniques to specific circumstances of a particular business. Likewise, the examples used in previous chapters have to be adapted and modified to fit the characteristics of your particular business.

Service Business Example

We need an example that serves as a good frame of reference for a large segment of service businesses. By now you should be fairly familiar with the example product company used since Chapter 2. Instead of introducing a completely new example, just convert the example to a service company, Exhibit 16.1, which serves to point out the differences between the two types of business entities.

Exhibit 16.1 presents the three primary financial statements of the product company with certain accounts shaded. These are the accounts not found in the financial statements of a ser-

EXHIBIT 16.1   ACCOUNTS (SHADED) TO OMIT FROM STATEMENTS FOR SERVICE BUSINESS

Income Statement

Sales Revenue	$10,000,000
Revenue-Driven Operating Expenses	(850,000)
Cost of Goods Sold Expense	(6,000,000)
Volume-Driven Operating Expenses	(500,000)
Contribution Profit Margin	$ 2,650,000
Total Fixed Operating Expenses	(1,570,000)
Operating Profit	$ 1,080,000
Interest Expense	(160,000)
Earnings Before Income Tax	$ 920,000
Income Tax Expense @ 34%	(312,800)
Net Income	$ 607,200

> A service business does not sell products, so it has no cost of goods sold expense. Any product type expenses are included in the sales volume-driven expense category.

Balance Sheet

Operating Assets

Cash	$ 603,212
Accounts Receivable	961,538
Inventory	1,384,615
Prepaid Expenses	200,385
Property, Plant & Equipment	2,810,463
Accumulated Depreciation	(658,325)
Total Operating Assets	$5,301,888

Operating Liabilities

Accounts Payable	
Inventory	$ 461,538
Operating Expenses	250,481
Accrued Expenses	
Operating Expenses	350,673
Interest Expense	26,667
Income Tax Payable	31,280
Total Operating Liabilities	$1,120,639
Net Operating Assets	$4,181,249

Sources of Capital

Short-Term Notes Payable	$ 600,000
Long-Term Bonds Payable	1,400,000
Total Debt	$2,000,000
Capital Stock	$ 750,000
Retained Earnings	1,431,249
Total Stockholders' Equity	$2,181,249
Total Debt & Owners' Equity	$4,181,249

Cash Flow Statement

Cash Flows from Operating Activities

Net Income	$607,200
Changes in Short-Term Operating Assets and Liabilities:	
Accounts Receivable	($135,193)
Inventory	(196,970)
Prepaid Expenses	(31,430)
Accts. Payable–Inventory	24,963
Accts. Payable–Operating Expenses	32,036
Accr. Expenses–Operating Expenses	(48,002)
Accr. Expenses–Interest Expense	2,337
Income Tax Payable	4,840
	($347,419)
Operating Cash Flow before Depr.	$259,781
Depreciation Expense	315,000
Operating Cash Flow	$574,781

Cash Flows from Investing Activities

Purchases of Property, Plant & Equip.	($491,688)

Cash Flows from Financing Activities

Net Increase in Short-Term Debt	$100,000
Long-Term Debt Borrowings	100,000
Capital Stock Issue	50,000
Cash Dividends to Stockholders	(76,606)
Increase (decrease) in Cash	$256,487

> A service business does not have inventory or accounts payable from inventory purchases.

vice company. A service company does not sell a product, so the inventory account and the other inventory-related accounts are deleted. In the income statement, the cost of goods sold expense is eliminated. In the balance sheet, inventory and accounts payable for inventory purchases are eliminated. In the cash flow statement, the changes in inventory and accounts payable for inventory purchases are deleted.

Exhibit 16.1 is the stepping stone to Exhibit 16.2, which presents the service business example used later in this chapter. A service company does not have to carry an inventory, so it needs less capital. Accordingly, debt and equity capital sources are decreased in the example service company. The notes in Exhibit 16.2 comment further on the changes from the example product company.

Operating profit before interest and income tax is the same as for the product company, but bottom-line profit (net income) is slightly higher because interest expense is lower due to the smaller amount of debt. The most important change involves the removal of cost of goods sold expense from the income statement. Notice in Exhibit 16.2 that all $6,000,000 of the cost of goods sold expense is transferred to the service company's fixed operating expenses, which is the largest expense category in the service company's income statement.

By definition, a service business sells a service and not a product; even so an incidental product is often sold with the service. For example a copying business sells paper to its customers, but the main item sold is the copying service, not the paper. Likewise, airlines sell transportation service, but they also provide food and beverages in flight. Hotels are not really in the business of selling towels and ballpoint pens, but many guests take these with them when they check out. Many personal and professional service firms, such as architect and CPA firms, sell no product at all. (Well, you could argue that some paper is sold by these professionals.)

The cost of any incidental products sold by a service business is included in the sales *volume*-driven expense category. In detailed management control reports, such product costs should be monitored closely, like all other specific expenses. In the management profit report, it is one of several volume-driven operating expenses. In addition to incidental product costs, service businesses have other expenses that vary with sales volume. For example, the number of passengers flown by an airline or the number of hotel guests directly affect certain variable expenses of these two service businesses.

Like product companies, service businesses have operating expenses that vary with total sales *revenue*. Credit card discounts and sales commissions come to mind. In short, service businesses are much like product businesses regarding sales volume and sales revenue-driven operating expenses. However, when it comes to fixed operating expenses, it's a different story. As you can see in Exhibit 16.2, our example service company includes a much larger amount of fixed operating expenses relative to annual sales revenue.

Most service businesses are saddled with very large fixed expenses. Service takes people, and most service businesses have a large number of employees on fixed salaries. Some service businesses, such as public utilities, movie theaters, and airlines, have to make large capital investments in long-term fixed

Income Statement

Sales Revenue	$10,000,000
Revenue-Driven Operating Expenses	(850,000)
Volume-Driven Operating Expenses	(500,000)
Contribution Profit Margin	$ 8,650,000
Total Fixed Operating Expenses	(7,570,000)
Operating Profit	$ 1,080,000
Interest Expense	(40,000)
Earnings Before Income Tax	$ 1,040,000
Income Tax Expense @ 34%	(353,600)
Net Income	$ 686,400

> Operating profit before interest and income tax is the same as for the product company.

> Interest expense is lower for the service company because its total net operating assets are considerably lower, and the company has less debt.

> All $6,000,000 of the cost of goods sold expense has been moved down to fixed operating expenses in this example. Service companies generally are characterized by relatively large fixed costs (mainly salaries of employees).

Balance Sheet

Operating Assets	
Cash	$ 603,212
Accounts Receivable	961,538
Prepaid Expenses	686,154
Property, Plant & Equipment	2,810,463
Accumulated Depreciation	(658,325)
Total Operating Assets	$4,403,042

Operating Liabilities	
Accounts Payable	$ 857,692
Accrued Expenses	
Operating Expenses	1,200,769
Interest Expense	26,667
Income Tax Payable	31,280
Total Operating Liabilities	$2,116,408
Net Operating Assets	$2,286,634

Sources of Capital	
Short-Term Notes Payable	$ 250,000
Long-Term Bonds Payable	250,000
Total Debt	$ 500,000
Capital Stock	$ 750,000
Retained Earnings	1,036,634
Total Stockholders' Equity	$1,786,634
Total Debt & Owners' Equity	$2,286,634

Note: Inventory is deleted because service companies do not sell a product. Property, Plant & Equipment and its Accumulated Depreciation are kept the same as before, although some service companies do not need large amounts of fixed assets.

Prepaid Expenses, Accounts Payable, and Accrued Expenses for Operating Expenses are higher because the company's fixed operating expenses are higher in the example service company. The operating ratios first presented in Exhibit 6.1 are kept the same in this example.

Net operating assets are smaller than in the example product company, so both debt and equity sources of capital are reduced in this example service business.

operating assets, and they annually record large fixed depreciation expense. (Personal service firms generally do not need large amounts of fixed assets.)

Because service companies do not have a cost of goods sold expense their contribution profit margin is a very large percent of sales revenue. In our example (data from Exhibit 16.2), the company's contribution profit margin is 86.5%, figured as follows:

$8,650,000 Contribution Profit Margin
÷ $10,000,000 Sales Revenue
= 86.5% Contribution Margin

A service company's sales volume is measured in a common denominator of "units" of service. For a law firm it's billable hours; for a movie theater it's number of tickets sold; for an airline it's passenger seat miles; for a hospital it's bed days; for a gambling establishment it's total handle (amount bet); for long-haul trucking companies it's ton miles; and so on.

If we assume 100,000 units of sales activity in this example the service company's sales price is $100.00 and the business earns $86.50 contribution profit margin per unit. For comparison, the product company's unit contribution profit margin is only $26.50. This wide spread in unit contribution profit margins leads to some very interesting differences between service and product businesses.

Ten Percent Changes

We have seen in previous chapters that, for a product company, there is a huge difference on profit performance between a 10% sales *price* increase versus a 10% sales *volume* increase. The sales price increase is much better by a country mile. Is this also true for a service company? No, not at all! Exhibit 16.3 shows that the increase in net income caused by the price change is not that much more than the increase caused by the volume increase for the service company.

Net income increases only $33,000 more from the sales price increase: $603,900 − $570,900 = $33,000. The sales volume-driven expense would not increase in the higher sales price case, which accounts for the difference.

It's very instructive to compare the 10% increases for the service company with its product company "twin." Information for the product company is included in Exhibit 16.3. The 10% sales price increase for the product company yields exactly the same effects—net income increases by $603,900, as it does for the service company. For both companies the contribution profit margin increases by $915,000 which carries down to a $603,900 after-tax net income increase. The two companies are identical regarding the sales price increase.

For contrast, compare the two companies for the sales volume increase scenario. The product company's contribution profit margin increases by only $265,000 compared with the $865,000 increase for the service company. The $600,000 difference is caused by the fact that the product company sells 10% more products, so its cost of goods sold expense increases $600,000. The service company does not sell a product and does not have this cost. In short, it's better not to sell a product when you increase sales volume.

Suppose sales volume were to drop 10%. There's always this downside risk. In our mind's eye we can put negative signs on

EXHIBIT 16.3   PRICE VERSUS VOLUME INCREASE OF 10% FOR SERVICE BUSINESS

	10% Higher Price Case			10% Higher Volume Case		
	Before	Dollar Changes	Percent Changes	Before	Dollar Changes	Percent Changes
Service Company						
Sales Revenue	$10,000,000	$1,000,000	+10.0%	$10,000,000	$1,000,000	+10.0%
Variable Expenses						
Sales Revenue-Driven	850,000	85,000	+10.0%	850,000	85,000	+10.0%
Sales Volume-Driven	500,000			500,000	50,000	+10.0%
Contribution Profit Margin	$ 8,650,000	$ 915,000	+10.6%	$ 8,650,000	$ 865,000	+10.0%
Fixed Operating Expenses	7,570,000			7,570,000		
Operating Profit	$ 1,080,000			$ 1,080,000		
Interest Expense	40,000			40,000		
Earnings Before Income Tax	$ 1,040,000	$ 915,000	+88.0%	$ 1,040,000	$ 865,000	+83.2%
Income Tax @ 34%	353,600	311,100	+88.0%	353,600	294,100	+83.2%
Net Income	$ 686,400	$ 603,900	+88.0%	$ 686,400	$ 570,900	+83.2%

	From Exhibit 12.1			From Exhibit 11.1		
Product Company						
Sales Revenue	$10,000,000	$1,000,000	+10.0%	$10,000,000	$1,000,000	+10.0%
Variable Expenses						
Sales Revenue-Driven	850,000	85,000	+10.0%	850,000	85,000	+10.0%
Cost of Goods Sold	6,000,000			6,000,000	600,000	
Sales Volume-Driven	500,000			500,000	50,000	
Contribution Profit Margin	$ 2,650,000	$ 915,000	+34.5%	$ 2,650,000	$ 265,000	+10.0%
Fixed Operating Expenses	1,570,000			1,570,000		
Operating Profit	$ 1,080,000			$ 1,080,000		
Interest Expense	160,000			160,000		
Earnings Before Income Tax	$ 920,000	$ 915,000	+99.5%	$ 920,000	$ 265,000	+28.8%
Income Tax @ 34%	312,800	311,100	+99.5%	312,800	90,100	+28.8%
Net Income	$ 607,200	$ 603,900	+99.5%	$ 607,200	$ 174,900	+28.8%

the numbers in the changes columns of Exhibit 16.3. The service company would suffer a decrease of $865,000 in its contribution profit margin, but the product company would experience only a $265,000 decrease. The service company would give up the lion's share of its net income, but the product company would not be hurt nearly so badly.

The analysis in Exhibit 16.3 for both the 10% increases makes a critical assumption: that the company's fixed operating expenses remain constant. For the sales price increase situation, this assumption is probably reasonable, although managers should examine carefully for any potential increases in fixed costs that might be triggered by a sales price increase. For example, employees might demand wage increases commensurate with the sales price increase, which would, of course, drive up fixed costs.

A higher sales volume definitely could cause an increase in a service company's fixed costs. As explained before, fixed operating costs provide *capacity*, which refers to the total number of hours its employees can work over the year, or the number of passenger miles an airline can fly, and so on for different types of service businesses. Some slack or unused capacity is normal. A 10% volume increase could be possible without any increase in fixed costs only if the service company is not presently operating near its capacity. This matter is very important, and we will return to it later.

Cash Flow Changes

The cash flow impacts of price and volume increases are much better for a service company. The sales volume increase sce- nario is the more conservative of the two, so we will examine the cash flow consequences for this situation. Based on the operating ratios first presented in Exhibit 6.1, the impact on operating cash flow (cash flow from operating activities) is as follows:

Service Company: Operating Cash Flow Impact from 10% Sales Volume Increase

Net Income Increase (see Exhibit 16.3)		$570,900
Accounts Receivable Increase	($ 96,154)	
Prepaid Expenses Increase	($ 10,385)	
Accts. Pay.–Oper. Exp. Increase	$ 12,981	
Accr. Exp.–Oper. Exp. Increase	$ 18,173	
Income Tax Payable Increase	$ 29,410	($ 45,975)
Operating Cash Flow		$524,925

The $1,000,000 sales revenue increase would increase accounts receivable; also, as you see above, prepaid expenses and the three operating liabilities would increase. Although operating cash flow does not increase quite as much as net income, it's not far behind. The lag in cash flow is not nearly so severe as compared with a product company that has to increase its inventory at the higher sales volume.

Trade-Off Decisions

Suppose the service company is considering reducing its sales price 5%. Management predicts that sales volume would increase by at least 10% or perhaps more. We analyzed this same trade-off scenario for the product business in Chapter 13. The result was a very large decrease in profit. Is this also true for the service business?

Exhibit 16.4 shows the trade-off results for the example service company with comparative information for the example product company. For the service company net income would improve by 34.8%! The main reason for this sizable increase is that the sales volume increase does not increase variable expenses very much relative to its sales revenue increase. The large part of the sales revenue increase flows through to the contribution profit margin, which increases by $361,750 (see Exhibit 16.4). In sharp contrast, notice that the product company's cost of goods sold expense increases by $600,000 at the higher sales volume level and thus, its contribution profit margin decreases.

Another way to explain the difference between the two types of businesses is the following: The service company gives up only $5.00/$86.50, or 5.8% of its contribution margin per unit from the sales price decrease, which is more than made up for by the 10% sales volume increase. But the product company sacrifices $5.00/$26.50, or 18.9% of its contribution margin per unit from the sales price decrease, which is not made up for by only a 10% sales volume increase.

So, the service company looks to have the clear advantage. Well, there may be a fatal flaw in our analysis. Some service companies, particularly those that are labor intensive as opposed to those that are fixed asset intensive, tend to operate close to their practical capacity levels. They adjust their workforce up and down with sales volume and do not have much idle capacity, or employees with time on their hands.

For these service companies a 10% sales volume increase may cause a significant increase in their fixed costs; they would have to hire additional employees to handle the additional sales volume. Please refer to Exhibit 16.4 again—in particular the increase in contribution profit margin caused by the trade-off. If, in our example, fixed operating expenses were to increase by $361,750 (which is only a 4.8% increase), there would be no advantage in making the trade-off.

The higher sales volume may give the company a larger market share, which may have long-term benefits. But there would be no immediate short-run profit benefit. So it bears repeating that whenever sales volume increases, managers should take a hard look at their fixed operating expenses to ascertain whether capacity driven costs would have to be increased to provide additional capacity for the higher sales volume.

What about the opposite trade-off? Suppose sales price were increased by 5%, causing a 10% decrease in sales volume. For product businesses, this trade-off results in a modest profit increase. Is this also true for a service company?

Exhibit 16.5 presents the analysis for this higher price/lower volume trade-off for both the service and product companies. The product company would decrease its cost of goods sold by $600,000 in this situation. The service company has no cost of goods sold expense to decrease. Unless the service company could substantially reduce its fixed operating expenses at the lower sales volume level, this trade-off decision would put a big dent in profit.

Summary

In most respects the financial statements of service businesses are not fundamentally different from those of product companies, although there are some distinctions that managers

EXHIBIT 16.4   SERVICE COMPANY TRADE-OFF ANALYSIS:
REDUCE SALES PRICE 5%; SALES VOLUME INCREASES 10%

	Before	After	Changes	
Sales Volume in Units	100,000	110,000	10,000	+10.0%
Service Company				
Sales Revenue	$10,000,000	$10,450,000	$450,000	+4.5%
Revenue-Driven Operating Expenses	850,000	888,250	38,250	+4.5%
Volume-Driven Operating Expenses	500,000	550,000	50,000	+10.0%
Contribution Profit Margin	$ 8,650,000	$ 9,011,750	$361,750	+4.2%
Fixed Operating Expenses	7,570,000	7,570,000		
Operating Profit	$ 1,080,000	$ 1,441,750	$361,750	+33.5%
Interest Expense	40,000	40,000		
Earnings Before Income Tax	$ 1,040,000	$ 1,401,750	$361,750	+34.8%
Income Tax Expense @ 34%	353,600	476,595	122,995	+34.8%
Net Income	$ 686,400	$ 925,155	$238,755	+34.8%
Product Company (from Exhibit 13.1)				
Sales Revenue	$10,000,000	$10,450,000	$450,000	+4.5%
Revenue-Driven Operating Expenses	850,000	888,250	38,250	+4.5%
Cost of Goods Sold Expense	6,000,000	6,600,000	600,000	+10.0%
Volume-Driven Operating Expenses	500,000	550,000	50,000	+10.0%
Contribution Profit Margin	$ 2,650,000	$ 2,411,750	($238,250)	−9.0%
Fixed Operating Expenses	1,570,000	1,570,000		
Operating Profit	$ 1,080,000	$ 841,750	($238,250)	−22.1%
Interest Expense	160,000	160,000		
Earnings Before Income Tax	$ 920,000	$ 681,750	($238,250)	−25.9%
Income Tax Expense @ 34%	312,800	231,795	(81,005)	−25.9%
Net Income	$ 607,200	$ 449,955	($157,245)	−25.9%

EXHIBIT 16.5   SERVICE COMPANY TRADE-OFF ANALYSIS:
INCREASE SALES PRICE 5%; SALES VOLUME DECREASES 10%

	Before	After	Changes	
Sales Volume in Units	100,000	90,000	(10,000)	−10.0%
Service Company				
Sales Revenue	$10,000,000	$9,450,000	($550,000)	−5.5%
Revenue-Driven Operating Expenses	850,000	803,250	(46,750)	−5.5%
Volume-Driven Operating Expenses	500,000	450,000	(50,000)	−10.0%
Contribution Profit Margin	$ 8,650,000	$8,196,750	($453,250)	−5.2%
Fixed Operating Expenses	7,570,000	7,570,000		
Operating Profit	$ 1,080,000	$ 626,750	($453,250)	−42.0%
Interest Expense	40,000	40,000		
Earnings Before Income Tax	$ 1,040,000	$ 586,750	($453,250)	−43.6%
Income Tax Expense @ 34%	353,600	199,495	(154,105)	−43.6%
Net Income	$ 686,400	$ 387,255	($299,145)	−43.6%
Product Company (from Exhibit 13.3)				
Sales Revenue	$10,000,000	$9,450,000	($550,000)	−5.5%
Revenue-Driven Operating Expenses	850,000	803,250	(46,750)	−5.5%
Cost of Goods Sold Expense	6,000,000	5,400,000	(600,000)	−10.0%
Volume-Driven Operating Expenses	500,000	450,000	(50,000)	−10.0%
Contribution Profit Margin	$ 2,650,000	$2,796,750	$ 146,750	5.5%
Fixed Operating Expenses	1,570,000	1,570,000		
Operating Profit	$ 1,080,000	$1,226,750	$ 146,750	13.6%
Interest Expense	160,000	160,000		
Earnings Before Income Tax	$ 920,000	$1,066,750	$ 146,750	16.0%
Income Tax Expense @ 34%	312,800	362,695	49,895	16.0%
Net Income	$ 607,200	$ 704,055	$ 96,855	16.0%

should understand. From the profit analysis and budgeting point of view, the key difference is that service companies have very large contribution margins as a percent of their sales revenue. However, most service companies also have large fixed operating costs.

Generally speaking, the profit advantage of a sales *price* increase is not significantly different between a service and a product company. However, a service company has the clear advantage on sales *volume* increases because a product company has to increase its cost of goods sold expense with the volume increase, but a service company does not. When it comes to sales volume decreases, the shoe is on the other foot. Product companies experience a large decrease in their cost of goods sold expense but service companies do not.

The profit consequences of trade-offs between sales price and sales volume is different for a service company compared with that of a product company. A service company can cut its sales price and does not need a huge sales volume increase. Its contribution profit margin per unit is relatively large compared with sales price, so the sales price reduction does not take a big chunk out of the contribution margin per unit. A modest sales volume increase can make up for the sales price decrease.

In contrast, a product company needs a large sales volume increase to make up for even a small sales price cut. The sales price reduction takes a big slice out of the contribution margin per unit, which has to be made up with a large volume increase by a product company.

A service company's operating cash flow benefits much more from a sales volume increase, mainly because it does not have to increase inventory at the higher sales level. A product company normally has to increase its inventory level to keep up with the higher sales level, and this hurts its operating cash flow.

17

MANUFACTURING ACCOUNTING AND BUDGETING

Even if You're Not a Manufacturer

This chapter presents a concise explanation of the fundamental accounting methods and problems of manufacturers. Budgeting and standard cost methods used by manufacturers for management planning and control are also briefly explained.

If you're not in the manufacturing business you may have your enthusiasm for this chapter under control. I would point out, however, that all managers use product cost information and all products begin their life by being manufactured. Business managers need to understand how manufacturing costs are assigned to products and how certain accounting problems are dealt with by manufacturers. This background information is very helpful in running any business, and can be particularly useful in bargaining with suppliers who are manufacturers.

Product Makers Versus Resellers

Manufacturers are producers; they make the products they sell. Retailers, wholesalers, and distributors do not make the products they sell; they are channels of distribution. For resellers, product cost is *purchase* cost. Product cost is much different for manufacturers; it's the composite and amalgam of many diverse costs of production.

Unlike resellers, manufacturers must compute product cost. There is no purchase invoice to find product cost; manufacturers have to carefully accumulate costs step by step over the entire production process. Every manufacturer needs to know its product costs to set sales prices, to control costs, to develop strategic plans, to determine inventory cost in the balance sheet and cost of goods sold expense in the income statement, and for other purposes as well.

The manufacturing process may be simple and short or complex and long. It may be either labor intensive or capital (fixed asset) intensive, or both. Products such as breakfast cereal and gasoline may roll nonstop off the end of a continuous process and mass-production assembly line, or, production may be discontinuous and discrete and done on a one-batch-at-a-time basis. Printing and binding 10,000 copies of this book is an example of a job order manufacturing process.

The example company in this chapter is an established manufacturing business that has been operating for many years. The business has assembled and organized machines, equipment, tools, and employees into a smooth running production process that is dependable and efficient, which is a monumental task to say the least. Plant location is critical; so is plant layout, as well as employee training, materials procurement, compliance with an ever-broadening range of governmental regulations, employee safety laws, environmental protection laws, and so on. These points are mentioned in passing and deserve much more discussion if we had the time.

Manufacturing Company Example

Exhibit 17.1 presents a manufacturing company's sales and production budget together with its actual results for the year just ended and includes its management income statement. This example company is new; it is not the same product com-

EXHIBIT 17.1 BUDGETED AND ACTUAL MANUFACTURING ACTIVITIES FOR YEAR, WITH INCOME STATEMENT FOR YEAR

Units

Production and Sales Budget	Budget	Variance	Actual
Production Capacity	120,000	0	120,000
Production Output	110,000	0	110,000
Sales Volume	105,000	(5,000)	100,000
Inventory Change	5,000	5,000	10,000

Totals

Manufacturing Costs	Budget	Variance	Actual
Raw (Direct) Materials	$20,350,000	$1,336,500	$21,686,500
Direct Labor	7,150,000	(550,000)	6,600,000
Indirect Variable Overhead Costs	4,950,000	275,000	5,225,000
Total Variable Manufacturing Costs	$32,450,000	$1,061,500	$33,511,500
Indirect Fixed Overhead Costs	28,980,000	208,500	29,188,500
Total Manufacturing Costs	$61,430,000	$1,270,000	$62,700,000

Notes:
1. Budgeted variable manufacturing costs are based on total actual output.
2. Budgeted fixed overhead costs depend on company's unavoidable commitments for the year, not on actual production output.

Costs per Unit

Manufacturing Costs	Standard	Variance	Actual
Raw (Direct) Materials	$185.00	$12.15	$197.15
Direct Labor	65.00	(5.00)	60.00
Indirect Variable Overhead Costs	45.00	2.50	47.50
Total Variable Manufacturing Costs	$295.00	$ 9.65	$304.65
Indirect Fixed Overhead Burden	241.50	23.85	265.35
Total Manufacturing Costs	$536.50	$33.50	$570.00

Notes:
1. The three budgeted variable costs come from detailed standard cost work-ups for the product: standard quantity is multiplied by standard price for every element making up the total cost per unit.
2. The $241.50 standard fixed overhead burden rate is based on 120,000 units production capacity.

INCOME STATEMENT

Sales Revenue		$85,000,000
Actual Manufacturing Costs	$62,700,000	
Costs Assigned to Inventory Increase	(5,700,000)	
Costs Assigned to Expense		57,000,000
Gross Margin Before Operating Expenses		$28,000,000
Sales Volume Operating Expenses	$ 5,312,500	
Sales Revenue Operating Expenses	4,575,000	9,887,500
Contribution Profit Margin		$18,112,500
Fixed Operating Expenses		8,235,000
Operating Earnings		$ 9,877,500
Interest Expenses		1,850,000
Earnings before Income Tax		$ 8,027,500
Income Tax Expense		2,729,350
Net Income		$ 5,298,150

Notes:
1. Inventory increase: $570.00 actual cost per unit × 10,000 units increase = $5,700,000.
2. The manufacturing cost assigned to cost of goods sold expense equals $570.00 × 100,000 units sold = $57,000,000. However, the manager should not overlook the cost of idle production capacity and excessive production costs (if there are any). The company did not use 10,000 units of its production capacity. And, its total $1,270,000 unfavorable variance over budget may be due to manufacturing inefficiencies.
3. Manufacturing costs are accumulated in a Work-In-Process Inventory asset account during the production process. Costs are transferred to Finished Goods Inventory when the production process is completed. When products are sold, Finished Goods Inventory is relieved of the appropriate amount of cost, and Cost of Goods Sold Expense is recorded. The key decision is whether to record all manufacturing costs into inventory. In certain situations some of the manufacturing cost should not be put into inventory, but instead charged off to expense immediately.

pany that we have used in previous chapters. As you can see, this manufacturer is a fairly large business; its total manufacturing costs for the year were about $63 million. Exhibit 17.1 is referred to frequently in the following discussion. You might take a few minutes to become acquainted with the details, and, to be honest, there are quite a few.

Some manufacturers determine their product costs monthly; others do so quarterly. There is no one standard period. It could be done weekly or even daily, although such short periods are not common. The fiscal year is a natural time period for management planning and financial reporting. In this example, one year serves as the time period.

The company in this example manufactures one product in one production plant. Most manufacturers make a number of different products and may have two or more production plants. However, basic procedures and problems are much easier to illustrate and explain with a one-product manufacturing business example. The additional accounting problems faced by the multiproduct manufacturer are discussed later in this chapter in the section on tracing and allocating manufacturing costs.

This company has established a formal budgeting and standard cost system, which many manufacturers find very useful if not essential. Before the start of the year the company forecasts sales volume and develops its production plan and budget. As you see in Exhibit 17.1, the company budgeted sales at 105,000 units, but fell a little short and sold 100,000 units. The company budgeted production output at 110,000 units. Although actual sales fell short of budget, the company did not scale down its actual production output. So, inventory increased 10,000 units, which is more than the originally budgeted increase of 5,000 units.

The company's budgeted manufacturing costs come from its standard cost system, which is based on the detailed engineering analysis of all steps and requirements of its production process. Most production processes are subject to constant change, and thus standard costs have to be revised frequently. Our concern is not with the technical details nor the specific accounting forms and procedures used by manufacturers. Rather, we focus on what managers should understand about the basic accounting methods to determine product cost and to analyze manufacturing costs for decision making and control.

Manufacturing costs consist of four distinct components: (1) raw materials, (2) direct labor, (3) variable overhead, and (4) fixed overhead (please refer to Exhibit 17.1 again). *Raw materials* are purchased parts and materials that become part of the finished product. *Direct labor* refers to those employees who work on the production line. Direct labor costs should include both base wages and employee benefits. The employer's social security and Medicare tax presently is 7.65% of base wages; unemployment taxes, employee retirement and pension plan contributions, health and medical insurance, worker's compensation insurance, and paid vacations and sick leaves add 15%–20% to base wages, perhaps even more.

All manufacturing operations require *indirect* production costs, also called *overhead* costs. Some of these costs, such as electricity that powers machinery and equipment, vary with total output. Variable overhead costs are separated from fixed overhead costs in Exhibit 17.1. Fixed manufacturing costs are those that do not vary with actual production output; examples are property taxes on the production plant, fire insurance, plant security guards and nurses (on fixed salaries), the salary of the vice president of production, and many, many other costs.

Raw materials added with direct labor is called *prime cost*. Direct labor added with manufacturing overhead costs (fixed and variable) is called *conversion cost*. Conversion cost is the measure of the *value added* by the manufacturing process. Generally speaking, the best opportunity for making profit lies in the value added, or conversion cost, area of manufacturing.

Fixed manufacturing overhead costs provide *production capacity*. In this example, the company's annual production capacity is 120,000 units. Its total annual fixed overhead costs provide the physical facilities and human resources to produce up to a maximum of 120,000 units under normal practical conditions of production operations. This works out to be $241.50 for each unit of capacity based on its *budgeted* fixed manufacturing costs for the year:

Capacity Cost per Unit

$28,980,000 Budgeted Fixed Manufacturing Costs
÷ 120,000 Units Annual Production Capacity
= $241.50 Budgeted Capacity Cost per Unit

This key number is called the fixed overhead *burden rate*. It's the cost in addition to, or the burden on top of, the variable manufacturing costs of making the product. Management should carefully evaluate whether this capacity cost per unit is too high; they should benchmark the company's burden rate against the competition.

Exhibit 17.1 reveals that the company actually went over budget on its fixed manufacturing overhead costs and did not make full use of its production capacity, which is not unusual. Dividing actual total fixed overhead costs by actual production output gives $265.35 per unit. So, there are two possible fixed overhead burden rates. Which one should be used? This is one of the basic accounting and management analysis problems of every manufacturing business.

Dividing Manufacturing Cost Between Inventory and Expense

As you see in Exhibit 17.1, the company recorded $62,700,000 in actual total manufacturing costs for the 110,000 units produced during the year. This manufacturing costs total has to be accounted for either as expense in this year or as an expense in a later year. This is a key point to understand. Notice the $62,700,000 actual manufacturing costs total is carried into the income statement. But not all of it is charged to expense this period because the company produced more units than it sold. Part of the year's total manufacturing cost is assigned to the inventory increase.

In this example, $5,700,000 is allocated to the inventory increase, and the $57,000,000 remainder is charged to expense for the year. Cost put into the inventory asset account is not charged to cost of goods sold expense until the products are sold sometime later. Taping your favorite TV program on a VCR to watch later is called *time shifting*. Likewise, charging manufacturing cost to inventory for later expensing can be thought of as cost shifting.

What you see in the income statement in Exhibit 17.1 is the *actual cost, actual output* accounting method, which is the most common method used in practice. The $570.00 actual cost per unit is multiplied by 10,000 units to determine how much of the period's total manufacturing cost to put into the inventory increase; and, the $570.00 actual cost per unit is multiplied by 100,000 units to determine how much to charge to expense for the year. This method appears rather clear cut. However, some argue that the amount put into inventory by this method is too high and that more of the total manufacturing cost should be put into expense for the year.

Instead of the $570.00 actual cost per unit, a good theoretical case can be made to use the $536.50 standard cost per unit (see Exhibit 17.1) to value the inventory increase. The idea is that anything more than this figure is too much. The company should have achieved its budgeted costs and should not allocate any of its idle capacity cost and none of its cost overruns to inventory. It is argued that such wasted costs should not be put into inventory cost.

Following the standard cost approach, the inventory increase would be costed at the $536.50 budgeted cost per unit, not the $570.00 actual cost per unit. Inventory would be recorded at $33.50 less per unit. Thus, $335,000 less would be put into the inventory increase (for the 10,000 units inventory increase) and $335,000 more would be shifted to expense for

the year.* The $335,000 difference is not very material relative to the $5,700,000 inventory increase nor the $28,000,000 gross margin amount under the actual cost, actual output method presented in Exhibit 17.1. Few manufacturers use standard costs to value their inventory, but it's not unheard of either.

It should be pointed out that in certain situations there can be substantial idle capacity or major manufacturing inefficiencies. The impacts of these two problems should be separated out for attention in the management income statement and not buried in the amounts charged to cost of goods sold expense and inventory increase. Such wasted costs would not be reported in a company's external income statement to stockholders, except perhaps in very unusual circumstances.

Accountants are under pressure to come up with profit and balance sheet numbers, and, to get on with their job, they stick with certain methods to crank out the numbers. From the management decision-making and control point of view, however, manufacturing costs and how they are accounted for should be taken with a grain of salt. Managers should keep in mind that alternative accounting methods could have been

---

*The $2,415,000 idle capacity cost (10,000 units of unused capacity × the $241.50 standard fixed cost overhead burden rate) and the $1,270,000 variance over budgeted costs (see Exhibit 17.1) are viewed as *period costs*—not to be charged to inventory. The total of these two is $3,685,000; inventory is 10,000 of the 110,000 units produced, and thus would escape 1/11 of these costs, which is the $335,000 given above.

used instead. In any case, actual manufacturing costs should not be accepted as the "best we can do." Managers should relentlessly scrutinize manufacturing costs and test cost performance against best practices benchmarks.

Product Cost: A Closer Look

Variable Versus Fixed Manufacturing Costs

Let me call your attention in Exhibit 17.1 to product cost per unit—both the $536.50 standard cost per unit and the $570.00 actual cost per unit. Production cost per unit consists of two quite dissimilar parts: (1) *variable* costs and (2) *fixed* overhead costs. Variable costs are those that the company incurs only if units are actually produced. If the company were to manufacture no units (an extreme scenario to be sure), its variable manufacturing costs would be zero.

In contrast, at zero production output, the company would still have to pay for its fixed overhead costs (except depreciation, which is not a cash outlay cost as we know). The business could possibly escape from some of its fixed overhead costs by taking drastic actions: furloughing or terminating production employees and managers; deferring maintenance; breaking leases on buildings and machinery; mothballing equipment or disposing of some of its equipment; and so on. But, over the short run the business is stuck with most of its fixed overhead costs.

Breakeven for Manufacturers

Managers should know their break-even production and sales volume. In this example (data from Exhibit 17.1), the company's actual fixed costs are tallied as follows:

Manufacturing Fixed	
Overhead Costs	$29,188,500
Fixed Operating Expenses	8,235,000
Interest Expense	1,850,000
Total Fixed Costs	$39,273,500

Its contribution profit margin per unit is computed as follows (data from Income Statement in Exhibit 17.1 is divided by 100,000 units sales volume):

Sales Price	$850.000
Manufacturing Variable Costs	304.650
Variable Operating Costs	98.875
Contribution Profit Margin	$446.475

Therefore, the company's break-even production and sales volume is:

$$\$39,273,500 \div \$446.475 \ = \ 87,963 \text{ Units}$$

The company's sales volume is more than its break-even volume, so it made a profit, as you see. But herein lies a problem that the next section explores.

Inventory Increase and Profit "Management"

Knowing the break-even volume, we should be able to double-check the company's reported earnings before income tax by taking the excess over break-even volume and multiplying it by the contribution profit margin per unit, as explained in Chapter 10. The company sold 12,037 units in excess of its breakeven: 100,000 units sold – 87,963 break-even volume = 12,037. So:

$$12{,}037 \text{ Units} \times \$446.475 = \$5{,}374{,}000$$

The company's income statement reports earnings before income tax of $8,027,500, considerably more than the amount just calculated. The reason for the difference brings out an important point that managers should understand.

Notice in the foregoing tally of fixed costs that all of the year's fixed manufacturing overhead costs are included. But as a matter of fact, not all of these costs ended up in expense for the year. Recall that 110,000 units were produced, 100,000 were sold, and 10,000 were added to inventory. The inventory increase is allocated (10,000/110,000), or 1/11 of the total fixed manufacturing overhead costs. In other words, the 10,000 units inventory increase absorbed $265.35 per unit of fixed overhead cost, which is $2,653,500 in total.

Guess what? If we take the amount of fixed overhead cost that is inventoried instead of expensed, we find the additional operating profit, figured as follows: $5,374,000 from above + $2,653,500 fixed overhead cost in inventory increase = $8,027,500 operating earnings reported in income statement.

So, there is a certain "magic" in building up inventory. Its share of the fixed overhead cost escapes being expensed to the year and is passed on to future expense.

If inventory had not been increased and only 100,000 units had been produced, then the 100,000 units sold would have had to absorb all the fixed manufacturing overhead cost for the year and profit (operating earnings before income tax) would have been $2,653,500 lower. If production output had been less than 100,000 units, then some of the beginning inventory cost—including fixed overhead cost from the prior period—would be charged to cost of goods sold expense this year. The company would take a hit for all the fixed overhead cost of this year plus some from last year!

This inventory effect can, but in an ideal world shouldn't, lead to profit manipulation by managers. Suppose you want more profit, that is, more *reported* profit. Simply produce more quantity than actual sales volume and thus increase inventory, so that this year's cost of goods sold expense avoids some of the year's fixed manufacturing overhead costs. For this reason, sophisticated security analysts and other investors keep a sharp eye on any material changes in inventory during the year. They know about the inventory increase profit effect for manufacturers.

Growing businesses need enough production capacity for the sales made during the year and to increase inventory in anticipation of higher sales next year. However, a manufacturer may make too many products. Production output may be much higher than sales volume for the period, and there would be a large increase in inventory—much more than what would be needed for next year. Suppose, for example, that the company had sold only 50,000 units during the year, even though it manufactured 110,000 units. Inventory would increase 60,000 units, more than the sales volume for the year!

Before rushing to a snap judgment, the inventory buildup could be in anticipation of a long strike looming in the near future that would shut down production for many months. Or, perhaps the company predicts serious shortages of raw material parts during the next several months. There could be such legitimate reasons for a large inventory buildup. But assume not.

Assume the sales forecast for next year is not all that encouraging. The large inventory overhang at year-end presents all sorts of problems: Where to store it? Should we reduce sales prices to move the inventory? What amount of fixed manufacturing overhead cost should be included in inventory? Producing *excessive* inventory is a false and illusory use of production capacity.

A good case can be made that no fixed manufacturing overhead costs should be included in *excessive* quantities of inventory; the amount of fixed overhead cost that usually would be allocated to the inventory increase should be charged off as expense to the period. Unless the company were able to slash its fixed overhead costs, which is very difficult to do in the short run, it will have these fixed overhead costs again next year. Probably the company will have to downsize its inventory next year, which means it will have to slash production output next year. Unless it can make substantial cuts in its fixed manufacturing overhead costs, it will have substantial idle capacity next year. It is argued that the company should bite the bullet this year and charge off a good chunk of its overhead cost to expense this year.

As a practical matter, it is very difficult to draw a line between excessive and normal inventory levels. Unless ending inventory was extremely large, the fixed overhead burden rate is included in the unit product cost for all units in ending inventory.*

Manufacturing Costs Versus Operating Expenses

Only *manufacturing* costs are included in the determination of product cost, not the nonmanufacturing operating expenses of making sales and running the business. A "Chinese wall" should be built between manufacturing costs and all other nonmanufacturing costs. Sales and marketing costs (advertising and product promotion) are not manufacturing costs; these are treated as costs of making sales, not making products, and are charged to operating expense.

Research and development costs are not classified as manufacturing cost, even though these costs may lead to new products, or new methods of manufacture, or new compounds of materials, or other technological improvements. The general management and administration costs of the organization, as well as its legal and interest expenses are not viewed as manufacturing costs. The gross margin line in the income statement

---

*One theory is that *no* fixed manufacturing overhead costs should be included in ending inventory, whether normal or abnormal quantities are held in stock. Only variable manufacturing costs would be included in unit product cost. This is called *direct costing*, although more properly it should be called *variable* costing. It is not acceptable for external financial reporting nor for income tax purposes.

(see Exhibit 17.1) is the boundary between manufacturing costs above the line and operating expenses below the line.

Some manufacturers have been known to intentionally misclassify some of their costs: Certain costs have been recorded as marketing or as general and administration expenses that in reality should have been booked as manufacturing costs. These misclassified costs were not included in the calculation of unit product cost and thus would not be charged to inventory increase. The purpose is to maximize costs that are charged off immediately to expense. You might refer to the income statement in Exhibit 17.1 again and notice that any dollar of cost not assigned to the inventory increase is thereby charged to expense. By minimizing taxable income for the year, the business delays payment of income taxes.

The 1986 Tax Reform Act took a special interest in the problem of manufacturing overhead cost classification. The experience of the Internal Revenue Service was that many manufacturers were misclassifying some of their costs. The income tax law now spells out in some detail which costs must be classified as manufacturing overhead costs and therefore *capitalized*. To capitalize means that the cost should first pass through the inventory asset account; in other words, such costs should be included in the calculation of unit product cost.

The following costs should definitely be classified as manufacturing costs: production employee benefits costs; rework, scrap, and spoilage costs; quality control costs; and, routine repairs and maintenance on production machinery and equipment. Of course, depreciation of production machinery and equipment and property taxes on the production plant should be classified as manufacturing overhead costs. It goes without saying that all direct production costs should be classified as manufacturing costs.

In our example company, suppose that $2,200,000 manufacturing fixed overhead costs had been recorded instead to the fixed operating expenses account. In other words, the amount you see in fixed operating expenses is $2,200,000 too high, and the amount you see in the manufacturing overhead fixed costs is $2,200,000 too low. If all units produced had been sold during the year, this misclassification would have no effect on operating profit (before interest and income tax), although the cost of goods sold expense would have been $2,200,000 too low and fixed operating expenses would have been $2,200,000 too high. The $2,200,000 is in the wrong place but profit is correct.

In our example, the company did not sell all the units it produced. Thus, some of the fixed overhead cost total for the year is absorbed in the inventory increase. Due to the misclassification, unit product cost is $20.00 too low: $2,200,000 understated overhead costs ÷ 110,000 units produced = $20.00 per unit. The inventory increase should have been assigned $200,000 additional overhead costs ($20.00 per unit × 10,000 units = $200,000). Thus, $200,000 less would have been assigned to expense for the year. In short, because of the misclassification, operating profit and taxable income (which is the purpose of the misclassification) is understated $200,000, which reduces the company's income tax for the year.

A $200,000 difference in pretax profit is not that material in this example. True, it would reduce income tax, but it would also cause the company's income statement to report the wrong net income for the year. Also, target sales prices may be determined by marking up unit product cost a certain percent.

Thus, managers should be very clear regarding whether all manufacturing overhead costs are included in the calculation of unit product cost. If not, the markup percent should be adjusted, since it would be based on an understated unit product cost. The better course of action is to correctly classify all manufacturing overhead costs in the first place.

Normal Versus Abnormal Idle Capacity

Managers should measure, or at least make the best estimate possible of, the production capacity provided by their fixed manufacturing overhead costs. Capacity is the maximum potential production output for a period of time that is provided by the manufacturing facilities in place and ready for use. Our example company manufactured 110,000 units during the year. The 10,000 gap between actual output and its 120,000 units production capacity is called *idle* capacity. The company had only 8.3% idle capacity, which is pretty good:

> The nation's industrial operating rate was unchanged in January at 82.2% of capacity . . . Manufacturers of durable goods . . . operated at 79.9% of capacity . . . while manufacturers of non-durable goods operated at 86.1% of capacity. Normally, when operating rates get about 85%, economists begin to worry about bottlenecks and rising prices. [(Boulder, Colorado) *Daily Camera*, 19 February 1988, p. 6B.]

The generally accepted accounting rule is that the fixed manufacturing overhead burden rate does not have to be based on production capacity, but can, instead, be based on normal, practical output levels, which generally are in the 75–90% range of capacity. It must be admitted, however, that there is no hard-and-fast rule on this.

The theory is that the actual number of units produced should absorb all fixed manufacturing overhead costs for the year, even though a fraction of the total fixed manufacturing costs were "wasted" because the company did not produce up to its full capacity. In this way, the cost of idle capacity is buried in unit product cost, which would have been lower if the company had produced at its full or maximum capacity and had spread its fixed manufacturing overhead over 120,000 units. In short, some amount of normal idle capacity cost is loaded into the unit product cost because the fixed overhead burden rate included in the product cost per unit is based on an output level less than full capacity.

If, in unusual circumstances, output is substantially less than production capacity, then not all of fixed overhead cost should be loaded into the calculation of product cost per unit. A fraction of the total overhead cost should be removed and recorded as a period cost in the internal profit report. (External income statements seldom report the cost of excessive idle capacity as a separate expense.)

Manufacturing Inefficiencies

Idle capacity is a form of manufacturing inefficiency: the company has too much capacity and too much *fixed* overhead costs given its actual output for the year. The company may also have *variable* manufacturing cost inefficiencies.

Ideally, the manufacturing process has no wasted materials, no wasted labor, no excessive reworking of products that don't pass inspection the first time through, no unnecessary power usage, and so on. The goal is optimum efficiency and maximum productivity for all variable costs of manufacturing. Today the word is TQM, or total quality management as the method to achieve efficiencies and to optimize quality.

Management control reports should clearly highlight productivity ratios for each factor of the production process—each raw material item, each labor step, and each variable cost factor. One key productivity ratio, for instance, is the direct labor hours per unit. Ten to fifteen years ago it took ten hours to make a ton of steel, but today it takes only about four hours; a recent article in the *New York Times* commented that the relatively few workers seen on the production floor of the modern steel plant is truly remarkable.

Unit product cost is based on the premise that the manufacturing process is reasonably efficient, which means that productivity ratios for every cost factor are fairly close to what they should be. Occasionally, things get way out of control, which raises the accounting problem regarding how to deal with gross inefficiencies. Suppose the example company had wasted raw materials during the year to the tune of $3,300,000. The total raw materials cost in Exhibit 17.1 includes this amount of raw materials wastage.

These materials were scrapped and not used in the final products. This waste may have been caused by inexperienced or untrained employees, or, perhaps inferior quality materials that were not up to product quality control standards were used as a cost cutting measure. This problem should have been stopped before it amounted to so much; quicker action should have been taken. In any case, assume the problem persisted and the result was that raw materials costing $3,300,000 had to be thrown away.

The preferred approach is to remove the $3,300,000 from the raw materials cost before the product cost per unit is calculated and to charge the $3,300,000 to expense immediately. However exposing the excess raw materials cost in a management profit report is a touchy issue. Would you want the blame for this waste laid at your doorstep? Production managers may prefer to bury the cost in unit product cost and let it flow against profit in this way, rather than as a naked item in profit reports to top level managers.

Tracing Versus Allocating Manufacturing Costs

We now consider the additional accounting methods and problems of businesses that manufacture many products. Let me stress that the fundamental accounting methods and problems already examined for a one-product business example are no different for the multiproduct manufacturing business. The main problem of the multiproduct business has to do with indirect manufacturing costs that do not "hug" production operations, such as raw materials and direct labor.

Direct manufacturing costs can be, should be, and, in fact, are traced to the specific operations of the production process. In this way they are directly coupled with the particular products being manufactured. Even if the company manufactures just one product, its managers need very detailed information about the quantity and cost of each raw material item and the time and cost of each direct labor operation. If the company manufactures two or more products, it needs this information for every product.

All manufacturers keep very detailed records to accumulate direct materials costs and direct labor costs from the beginning to the end of the production process for every product, which requires an enormous amount of meticulous bookkeeping. The demands are even greater for manufacturers that make many different products. The assembly of automobiles is estimated to require 10,000–15,000 different parts; a brewery takes over 1,000 separate steps to make a barrel of beer. Keeping track of all direct costs of raw materials and labor puts very heavy demands on the company's accounting data processing system.

If the business makes just one product, then all its overhead costs have only one destination. However, for the multiproduct manufacturing company, indirect manufacturing costs have to be *allocated* or *distributed* among many products. For instance, consider a print order for the production of 10,000 copies of a book such as this one. The paper and ink cost (raw materials) can be identified to each production run. Likewise, the time of employees setting up and operating the presses (direct labor) can be identified and matched to the job. However, overhead costs cannot be directly identified with particular press runs.

By their very nature, manufacturing overhead costs cannot be directly connected with any particular batch of products, or work station, or production department, or separate step in the production process. Nevertheless every product manufactured should be charged with its proper share of the manufacturing overhead costs. In theory, these indirect costs should be allocated according to the benefits the products receive from these indirect but necessary support functions in the production process.

Traditionally most manufacturers selected a *common denominator* of production activity to allocate manufacturing overhead costs to different products. Direct labor hours was a popular choice because all products required direct labor, and many of the indirect overhead costs could be interpreted as supporting the time, effort, and effectiveness of labor. Thus, the direct labor hours of each product were used as the common measure across all products on which to base the allocation of both variable and fixed manufacturing costs.

Over the last two to three decades, however, the world of manufacturing has changed drastically. Today direct labor in many industries is only 20% to 25% or even less of total manufacturing cost. Direct labor has become a very questionable basis on which to allocate overhead costs. Direct materials often are 50% or more of total product cost. Some measure of materials, such as weight or size, might be a better common denominator.

Two or more overhead burden rates could be used for allocating manufacturing overhead costs. Indeed, the separation between variable and fixed manufacturing overhead costs suggests that this method is better. There is likely to be a variable measure of production work that fits hand in glove with variable overhead costs. For instance, electricity costs of running the production plant could be allocated based on the machine hours required for each product. Indeed, if each machine had its own meter, the kilowatt hours of each machine would be the obvious basis for allocating electricity costs.

Given the many different types of variable overhead costs and the even larger diversity of fixed overhead costs, it is very difficult to develop a logical path of allocation for each overhead cost to individual products. Recently, the approach called *activity-based costing* (ABC) has been receiving a lot of press, because it offers a more rational and more management-useful method for allocating overhead costs. We first examined the ABC method in Chapter 15 in discussing sales mix analysis. We now look at ABC for manufacturing overhead cost allocation.

The key step in the ABC method is to identify the distinct, separate activities and functions that support the production process. The costs for each of these basic activities are accumulated in a separate overhead cost pool. Burden rates are computed for each of these cost pools based on the measure of activity of the functions provided by the cost pool. In this way, the cost of the activity is allocated to individual products according to how much of the activity each product uses. For instance, the manufacture of many products starts with engineering design and development of product specifications. Following the ABC approach, the company would identify the engineering department as a separate function and accumulate the costs of this activity into one separate pool. The company would measure how much of the engineering department's time and effort is required for each product and allocate the cost of the department on this basis.

Traditional cost accounting methods threw the engineering department's cost in with many other service department costs, including such diverse departments as purchasing, plant security, plant maintenance, and so on. A very broad-based common denominator, for example, direct labor hours, was used to allocate the conglomerate pool of overhead costs among the company's individual products. ABC methods certainly appear to be more accurate compared with traditional methods that were based on such gross measures as direct labor hours. The traditional approach, developed before the widespread use of computers, favored a simplistic and practical method of using one general overhead burden rate as a broad brush across all products.

Some management accounting theorists argue that traditional overhead cost allocation methods led to misleading unit product costs.* It's a little too early, in my opinion, to say whether traditional cost accounting allocation methods have been all that misleading. There has been a fairly enthusiastic initial reception to the ABC method, but time will tell. Everyone wants to believe that there is a better method of allocation—one that is more "realistic" and more "relevant." As pointed out in Chapter 15, even with computers it is not practical to have too many separate activities, each with its own cost pool and basis of allocation.

No matter which basis and method is used to allocate manufacturing overhead costs, managers should be aware that all allocation methods are arbitrary—it's just a matter of degree. Some products are favored and others penalized no matter which allocation method is used. Managers should take manu-

---

*See, for example, H. Thomas Johnson and Robert S. Kaplan, *Relevance Lost: The Rise and Fall of Management Accounting* (Harvard Business School Press, Boston, 1987).

facturing overhead cost included in product cost with a large grain of salt. One product can be made to look less or more profitable merely by changing the method of allocating overhead costs.

Standard Cost System

Many manufacturing businesses have adopted a *standard cost system*. Perhaps the term *system* here is too suggestive and overreaching. What is meant is that certain procedures are adopted by the business to establish performance benchmarks; then actual costs are compared with these standards to identify deviations. This variance information is used by managers to carry out their control function.

Quantity and price standards for raw materials, direct labor, and variable overhead costs are established to serve as yardsticks of performance, and variances from the standards are reported. In Exhibit 17.1, we see that for all four basic manufacturing costs (raw materials, direct labor, variable overhead, and fixed overhead), the company had variances. This situation is not unusual.

The main question confronting managers is twofold: Do the variances reflect standards that need adjustment, or do the variances reflect manufacturing operations that need adjustment? Usually the answer is some of both. Managers also have to discriminate between significant variances that should be looked into versus those that do not deserve management time and attention. Some variances are due mainly to random fluctuations that even out over time, whereas other variances are symptomatic of serious production problems that need immediate attention.

Standard cost systems have clear advantages, but many manufacturers do not use any formal standard cost system. For one thing it takes a fair amount of time and cost to develop and to update standards. If the standards are not correct and up to date, these yardsticks can cause more harm than good. Nevertheless, actual costs should be compared against benchmarks of performance. If nothing else, current costs should be compared against past performance. Many trade associations collect and publish industry cost averages, which are very helpful benchmarks of comparison.

Summary

Given the complexity of most manufacturing processes and the multitude of costs that go into the manufacture of most products, managers need a lot of detailed information about production costs. It's easy to get lost in the forest of details and thus fail to see the trees. Managers should keep an eye on the larger picture and focus on certain basic analysis issues and fundamental accounting problems, without getting lost in the welter of manufacturing details.

Manufacturers find that budgeting and standard cost systems are helpful for planning production operations and for keeping control over production processes. Accordingly, the main example in the chapter includes budgeted sales and production output volumes, as well as budgeted manufacturing costs based on standard costs established for each of the four basic manufacturing costs—raw materials, direct labor, variable overhead, and fixed overhead. Variances between actual and budgeted costs are vital signals to managers to improve production operations or to revise and update standard costs.

The manufacturing example company in this chapter provides a comprehensive frame of reference that demonstrates the fundamental manufacturing accounting methods and problems that managers should have a very good grip on. Managers not only should be informed users of this information; managers should confer with the accountants in deciding the best ways to handle several questions that must be answered to measure product cost per unit and how to report manufacturing costs in the internal income statement.

Product cost per unit is the value basis for the inventory increase during the period; the remainder of total manufacturing costs are charged to expense. The determination of product cost directly affects the profit measurement for the period. The chapter also discusses certain bothersome problems: excessive idle production capacity; misclassification of manufacturing costs; production inefficiencies resulting in significant wasted manufacturing costs; excessive production output and inventory buildup; and the allocation of indirect manufacturing overhead costs. Managers should remain alert for these problems, which can have a material impact on the company's success.

18

BUDGETING LONG-TERM CAPITAL INVESTMENTS

Business Long-Term Investments

As you most likely know, businesses make investments in many kinds of long-term operating assets—land and buildings, machinery and equipment, furniture, fixtures, tools, computers and data processing hardware, vehicles, and so on. A business may also make investments in intangible assets—patents and copyrights, customer lists, computer software, and so on. The new assets may replace old assets that have worn out, or may be additions in kind to expand the business, or may be ventures into new technology and ways of doing business. How do business managers make these very critical decisions in the life of the business?

It goes without saying that in deciding whether to make capital investments in long-term operating assets, managers should determine whether the new assets are really needed and how they will be used in the business operations. Of course, in selecting between two or more assets and vendors, managers should carefully compare the alternatives. This book is not about purchasing and procurement; the concern here is the *capital investment* aspects of the decision.

Chapter 7 looks at the business entity as an investment enterprise, or user of capital. The business is viewed as an investment project that requires a portfolio of operating assets and liabilities. The entity must raise the total capital needed for the investment in its net operating assets. Capital has a cost: interest is paid on debt capital, and net income has to be earned on equity capital. Chapter 7 explains the basic measures for evaluating and assessing the investment performance of a business, in particular the return on assets (ROA) and the return on equity (ROE).

In making long-term capital investment decisions, managers should look at how the new assets blend into the present mix of operating assets. The long-term capital investments of a business are just one part, although an important part to be sure, of its overall profit strategy and comprehensive budgeting process. This approach to the business as a whole is an *integrative* one; managers focus primarily on how well all assets work together in achieving the fundamental financial goals of the business.

There are also some very useful analysis tools to help managers make decisions on individual, specific long-term capital investments. These techniques apply the cost of capital requirements of the business to particular investments—to test whether investing in the long-term assets passes muster from the cost of capital point of view. These techniques allow managers to focus on individual capital investment decisions. These capital investment analysis tools are explained in this chapter and Chapter 19.

Capital Investment Example

Suppose a company is considering buying new, state-of-the-art electronic cash registers that read bar coded information on most products the business sells. The main purpose is to automate the marking of sales prices on products. The company would avoid the labor cost of marking initial sales prices and sales price changes on its products, which takes many hours each time products are stocked and when prices are changed. Also, the new registers would provide better control over the prices rung up at the point of sale. In the past, the company's cashiers sometimes punched in wrong prices, either by error or intentionally for their friends.

The investment in the new cash registers would generate future labor cost savings. If the new cash registers were used, the company's future annual cash outlays for wages and fringe benefits would decrease. Avoiding a cash outlay is as good as a cash inflow; both increase the cash balance. The cost of the new cash registers—net of the trade-in allowances on the old cash registers, and including the cost of installing the new cash registers—would be $500,000 and would be paid immediately. The company would tap its general fund of cash to make the investment in the cash registers. It would not use direct financing for the investment (such as asking the vendor to lend the company a large fraction of the purchase price).

The manager decides to adopt a five-year planning horizon for this capital investment. In other words, the manager limits the recognition of cost savings to five years, even though there may be benefits beyond this time. Labor time savings and wage rates are difficult to project beyond a five-year period and many other factors can change. At the end of five years the cash registers are forecast to have no residual value, which probably is very conservative.

The future annual labor cost savings have been estimated based on how many work hours would be saved. Of course, these estimates could turn out to be wrong, but there isn't much choice because some forecast must be made. The labor cost savings are estimated to be $165,000 per year for five years. (The annual cost savings could vary year to year.) The labor cost savings would occur throughout the year, but for convenience of analysis, we assume that the cost savings occur at each year-end. In other words, we assume that the company's cash balance would be this much higher at year-end due to the labor cost savings.

The total *cash returns* from the capital investment would be $825,000 ($165,000 annual labor cost savings × 5 years = $825,000), which is $325,000 more than the $500,000 initial capital investment. In other words, the company's operating earnings (profit before interest and income tax) would increase by $325,000 over the five years after deducting the cost of the assets. From the capital investment point of view, the key question is: Are these future returns (cost savings) adequate to meet the company's cost of capital?

This question leads us back to the company's capitalization structure, which is summarized as follows:

Capitalization Structure and
Cost of Capital Assumptions
- 2 to 3 debt to equity mix
- 9.0% annual interest rate on debt
- 34% income tax rate
- 15.0% annual ROE objective

These assumptions conform closely with the example company used throughout the book. At the end of the next budgeted year, its debt is $2,000,000 and its total owners' equity is $2,847,151 (from Exhibit 8.2), which is close to the 2 to 3 debt to equity ratio adopted here. The interest rate is a little higher, but the income tax rate and ROE target rate are the same as used before.

There may be other incentives to invest in the cash registers. The company may anticipate that there will be increasing difficulties in hiring qualified employees. The new cash registers provide better control over ringing up correct sales prices and would enable the company to collect marketing data on a real-time basis, which it cannot do at present. These may be very important reasons for buying the cash registers. However, attention here focuses on the financial aspects of the decision.

Analysis of the Investment

Exhibit 18.1 presents an analysis of the investment in the new cash registers. Please do not be put off by the exhibit; it may seem complex but it really isn't. The basic approach is to start with the cost savings each year and then "make demands" on these cash returns. There are four demands: (1) interest on debt capital, (2) income tax, (3) ROE (return on equity), and (4) recovery of the cost of the assets. The first three are fixed demands. The fourth is a "free floater"; it can follow any pattern from year to year but its sum over the five years must add up to $500,000.

We will walk down the first year in some detail; the other four years are repeats of the first year. The first claim on the annual cost savings is $18,000 in interest: $200,000 debt at start

of year × 9.0% interest rate = $18,000. Second, income tax is deducted. The company's taxable income is higher because of the labor cost savings.

Income tax each year depends on which depreciation method is used for tax purposes. As you can see in Exhibit 18.1, the straight-line method is assumed, which is $100,000 per year for five years with a zero salvage value. (The accelerated depreciation method could be used instead.) Notice in Exhibit 18.1 that interest expense for the year is deducted to determine taxable income.

Third, the earnings on equity capital used during the year are taken out based on the established ROE objective of 15% per year. ROE for the first year is $45,000: $300,000 equity capital at start of year × 15.0% ROE = $45,000. We don't know whether the forecast cash returns from the investment are enough to actually achieve this ROE goal. What we are doing is using the ROE benchmark rate to see whether the predicted cash returns are enough to earn at least a 15% annual ROE.

The fourth and final "demand" on each year's cash return is for *capital recovery*. Capital recovery is the residual amount remaining after deducting interest, income tax, and the ROE amount for the year. For year one, capital recovery is $86,020 (see Exhibit 18.1). This amount of cash is recycled back to the "central bank" of the company. It is not reinvested in additional cash registers; the company has all the cash registers it needs.

Capital recovered is not rolled over or reinvested in new cash registers. At the end of this investment's life, there is no more capital invested in this particular investment. In the first year, the company liquidates $86,020 of its investment; this

EXHIBIT 18.1   ANALYSIS OF CASH REGISTERS CAPITAL INVESTMENT

	Year One	Year Two	Year Three	Year Four	Year Five	Five Year Totals
Cash Returns						
Forecast Labor Cost Savings	$165,000	$165,000	$165,000	$165,000	$165,000	$825,000
Distribution of Cash Returns						
Interest (@ 9% annual interest rate)	$ 18,000	$ 14,903	$ 11,454	$ 7,613	$ 3,335	$ 55,305
Income Tax (see below)	15,980	17,033	18,206	19,512	20,966	$ 91,696
ROE (@ 15% annual ROE rate)	45,000	37,258	28,636	19,032	8,336	
Capital Recovery	86,020	95,806	106,704	118,843	132,363	$539,736
Capital Balances at Start of Year						
Debt (2/5 of Total Capital)	$200,000	$165,592	$127,270	$ 84,588	$ 37,051	
Equity (3/5 of Total Capital)	300,000	248,388	190,905	126,882	55,576	
Total Capital Invested in Assets	$500,000	$413,980	$318,174	$211,470	$ 92,627	

Total capital recovery is more than entry cost, or the initial capital invested. Thus, the amount taken out each year for ROE is too low.

	Year One	Year Two	Year Three	Year Four	Year Five	Five Year Totals
Income Tax Computation						
Operating Profit Increase	$165,000	$165,000	$165,000	$165,000	$165,000	$825,000
Depreciation Expense (straight-line)	100,000	100,000	100,000	100,000	100,000	$500,000
Interest Expense (see above)	18,000	14,903	11,454	7,613	3,335	$ 55,305
Taxable Income	$ 47,000	$ 50,097	$ 53,546	$ 57,387	$ 61,665	
Income Tax @ 34% (entered above)	$ 15,980	$ 17,033	$ 18,206	$ 19,512	$ 20,966	$ 91,696

These are audit totals, to check that total cash returns equal total revenue for income tax, total depreciation equals cost of assets, total interest deductions equals total interest on debt, and so on.

much capital that was invested in the assets is recovered and is no longer tied-up in this particular project.

Therefore, the amount of capital invested during the second year is reduced by $86,020: $500,000 initial capital – $86,020 capital recovery = $413,980 capital balance at start of year two. The analysis of a single capital investment does not follow where the capital recovery "goes." This amount of capital leaves this project (the cash registers investment). The company may put this money into another investment, or may increase its cash balance, or may reduce its debt, or may pay a higher cash dividend.

From year to year this investment "sizes down." Thus, the annual amounts of interest and ROE earnings decrease year to year, because the total capital invested decreases from year to year. However, you might notice that the income tax increases year to year because the annual interest expense deduction decreases.

Are the future cash returns enough to yield an annual 15% ROE? The answer is found in the total capital recovery over the life of the investment, which is summarized as follows (data from Exhibit 18.1):

Capital Recovery from Investment

Year One	$ 86,020
Year Two	95,806
Year Three	106,704
Year Four	118,843
Year Five	132,363
Total Capital Recovery	$539,736
Less Initial Capital Invested	500,000
Excess Capital Recovery	$ 39,736

Total capital recovery is $39,736 more than the initial capital invested. This excess is not really capital recovery; it constitutes additional earnings over and above the annual earnings on equity already included in the exhibit based on the 15% ROE rate. In other words, the actual ROE rate is higher than the 15% used in Exhibit 18.1. The cash registers investment is attractive from the cost of capital point of view because the company would earn a rate higher than its 15% ROE hurdle rate.

What is the precise ROE rate for this investment? This rate can be solved for because we can change the ROE rate so that the total capital recovery is exactly $500,000.* However, is this really the most important question? The forecast of labor cost savings may turn out to be too high. Perhaps the more relevant question to ask is: What is the minimal annual labor cost savings that would earn 15% ROE on the investment? Managers should ask for the minimum annual labor cost savings that would justify the capital investment from the cost of capital viewpoint.

Determining Returns to Earn Target ROE

The analysis template shown in Exhibit 18.1 for the cash registers capital investment example is the printout from my personal computer spreadsheet program. One reason for using a spreadsheet is to do calculations quickly and surely. Another reason is

---

*Exhibit A1 in the Appendix presents the solution; the annual ROE rate is 18.0632%.

that any of the factors in the analysis can be easily changed to test impacts of different assumptions. I changed the cash returns to find the amount of annual labor cost savings that yields exactly an annual 15% ROE to make total capital recovery exactly equal to $500,000. Other factors were held constant; only the annual labor cost savings amount was changed.

Finding the precise answer requires a trial and error process that is repeated until the exact amount of future cash returns is found that makes total capital recovery $500,000. This may seem to be time consuming, but it's really not. Only a few trials, or passes were required to zero in on the exact answer. From Exhibit 18.1, we already know that $165,000 is too high, so a first guess might be $150,000. This would be too low. After a few tries we find the exact amount. Exhibit 18.2 presents the answer; annual labor cost savings of $155,405 for five years would yield a 15% ROE.

As you can see, the total capital recovery is exactly $500,000. The annual ROE rate is 15%, the goal established by the company. The manager must now decide whether the company could realistically achieve $155,405 annual labor cost savings. This is one of the hardest parts of the decision-making process, but at least the manager knows that if the annual labor cost savings were this much or more, then the investment would turn out to be a good decision from the cost of capital point of view.

As previously mentioned, any of the factors in the analysis can be changed to test how sensitive the results would be to the change. For instance, we could go back and use accelerated depreciation for income tax, or, we could assume more labor cost savings in the early years and less in the later years,* or, we could change the debt to equity ratio, and so on. This is a major reason for using spreadsheets.

Notice in Exhibit 18.2 is that the annual depreciation tax deduction amounts are *not* the same as the annual capital recovery amounts. For instance, the first year's depreciation tax deduction is $100,000 (using the straight-line method), but the first year capital recovery is $79,687. Both total depreciation and total capital recovery are $500,000 for the five years combined. But the two amounts differ from year to year. This disparity is typical in capital investment analysis and is not any problem when using the spreadsheet tool. As we shall see, the difference between the two is more of a nuisance in using the mathematical tools discussed in Chapter 19.

Lease Versus Buy

Business managers are often faced with the lease versus buy choice. Almost any long-term operating asset (trucks, equipment, machinery, computers, telephone systems, and so on) can be leased either directly from the manufacturer or indirectly through a third-party leasing specialist. The cash registers probably could be leased instead of purchased. Managers generally are interested in leasing, especially if the business is short of cash.

---

*Exhibit A2 in the Appendix presents a scenario in which the labor cost savings increase year to year; ROE is held at exactly 15% in this example.

EXHIBIT 18.2   RETURNS REQUIRED TO EARN EXACT 15% ROE

	Year One	Year Two	Year Three	Year Four	Year Five	Five Year Totals
Cash Returns						
Minimum Labor Cost Savings Required	$155,405	$155,405	$155,405	$155,405	$155,405	$777,024 ◄
Distribution of Cash Returns						
Interest (@ 9% annual interest rate)	$ 18,000	$ 15,131	$ 11,936	$ 8,378	$ 4,414	$ 57,859 ◄
Income Tax (see below)	12,718	13,693	14,779	15,989	17,337	$ 74,516 ◄
ROE (@15% annual ROE rate)	45,000	37,828	29,840	20,944	11,036	
Capital Recovery	79,687	88,752	98,849	110,094	122,618	$500,000
Capital Balances at Start of Year						
Debt (2/5 of Total Capital)	$200,000	$168,125	$132,624	$ 93,085	$ 49,047	
Equity (3/5 of Total Capital)	300,000	252,188	198,936	139,627	73,571	
Total Capital Invested in Assets	$500,000	$420,313	$331,561	$232,712	$122,618	

Total capital recovery is exactly equal to the entry cost, or the initial capital invested. Thus, the amount taken out each year for ROE net income is just right. The annual ROE is precisely 15%

Income Tax Computation						
Operating Profit Increase	$155,405	$155,405	$155,405	$155,405	$155,405	$777,024 ◄
Depreciation Expense (straight-line)	100,000	100,000	100,000	100,000	100,000	$500,000 ◄
Interest Expense (see above)	18,000	15,131	11,936	8,378	4,414	$ 57,859 ◄
Taxable Income	$ 37,405	$ 40,273	$ 43,469	$ 47,027	$ 50,991	
Income Tax @ 34% (entered above)	$ 12,718	$ 13,693	$ 14,779	$ 15,989	$ 17,337	$ 74,516 ◄

These are audit totals, to check that total cash returns equal total revenue for income tax, total depreciation equals cost of assets, total interest deductions equals total interest on debt, and so on.

Perhaps the lessor has a lower cost of capital, in which case the business would be better off leasing rather than investing its own capital in the assets.

Suppose this company could have leased the cash registers instead of buying them, and assume the lessor had offered an annual rent of $155,405 for five years, which is precisely the minimum annual labor cost savings necessary to earn 15% ROE (see Exhibit 18.2). Generally, the lessee bears all costs of possession and use of the assets as if it had bought them outright. For example, the company would pay the fire and theft insurance on the assets whether they are owned or leased. By leasing the cash registers, the company would reduce its annual labor costs by $155,405 but would pay annual lease rent of the same amount. From the financial point of view leasing versus buying is a standoff.

Leases involve certain other considerations beyond just the financial aspects. For one thing, the company may prefer not to assume the economic risks of owning the cash registers. In a fast-changing technological environment, the business may be unwilling to assume the risks of buying cash registers that may be obsolete in two or three years. Thus, the company may shop around for a two- or three-year lease.

To illustrate the lease versus buy analysis consider the following new example. Suppose the company has just installed new production machinery and equipment in its plant to expand its annual output capacity. These assets have just been installed and are ready for use. The contract price for the machinery and equipment and their installation is $575,000.

The contractor that built and installed the machinery and equipment has offered to lease everything to the company for five years at $214,248 total annual rents. At the end of the lease, the company would have the option to purchase the assets for $35,000. The company estimates that in five years from now the assets will have a fair market value that is considerably more than this $35,000 purchase price. If the company buys the assets, it would depreciate them over five years for income tax purposes. Is the lease attractive given the company's cost of capital?

The spreadsheet analysis tool used for the cash registers capital investment example earlier in the chapter is equally useful for the lease versus buy decision. The basic idea is that by investing $575,000 today the company could avoid the lease payments. The lease payments are equivalent to the labor cost savings in the cash registers example.

Exhibit 18.3 presents the analysis of the lease. For convenience of presentation, the lease rents are put on an annual basis; without paying the lease rents the company's cash balance would be this much higher at the end of each year. Also, notice that the $35,000 purchase option price at the end of the lease would be avoided by purchasing the assets, and therefore, is shown as a future return on the investment.

The analysis in Exhibit 18.3 shows that the lease rents would yield a 24% ROE, which is much higher than the company's 15% ROE benchmark. Thus, leasing is not a good decision. The company would be better off purchasing the assets, relative to the leasing alternative. The ROE based on the lease rents avoided is 24% which is much higher than its ROE goal. Putting it another way, the lessor (the contractor who made and installed the machinery and equipment) would earn a 24% ROE if it had the same capitalization structure as the com-

EXHIBIT 18.3   LEASE VERSUS BUY ANALYSIS

	Year One	Year Two	Year Three	Year Four	Year Five	Five Year Totals
Cash Returns						
Lease Rents Avoided	$214,248	$214,248	$214,248	$214,248	$214,248	$1,071,241
Purchase Cost Avoided					$ 35,000	35,000
						$1,106,241
Distribution of Cash Returns						
Interest (@ 9% annual interest rate)	$ 20,700	$ 17,674	$ 14,141	$ 10,016	$ 5,198	$ 67,729
Income Tax (see below)	26,706	27,735	28,936	30,339	43,877	$ 157,594
ROE (@ 24% annual ROE rate)	82,800	70,698	56,566	40,063	20,791	
Capital Recovery	84,042	98,141	114,605	133,831	144,382	$ 575,000
Capital Balances at Start of Year						
Debt (2/5 of Total Capital)	$230,000	$196,383	$157,127	$111,285	$ 57,753	
Equity (3/5 of Total Capital)	345,000	294,575	235,691	166,928	86,629	
Total Capital Invested in Assets	$575,000	$490,958	$392,818	$278,213	$144,382	

> Total capital recovery is exactly equal to the entry cost, or the initial capital invested. Thus, the amount taken out each year for ROE net income is just right and ROE is 24%.

	Year One	Year Two	Year Three	Year Four	Year Five	Five Year Totals
Income Tax Computation						
Operating Profit Increase	$214,248	$214,248	$214,248	$214,248	$249,248	$1,106,241
Depreciation Expense (straight-line)	115,000	115,000	115,000	115,000	115,000	$ 575,000
Interest Expense (see above)	20,700	17,674	14,141	10,016	5,198	$ 67,729
Taxable Income	$ 78,548	$ 81,574	$ 85,107	$ 89,232	$129,050	
Income Tax @ 34% (entered above)	$ 26,706	$ 27,735	$ 28,936	$ 30,339	$ 43,877	$ 157,594

These are audit totals, to check that total cash returns equal total revenue for income tax, total depreciation equals cost of assets, total interest deductions equals total interest on debt, and so on.

pany. Of course, the lessor may have a different debt to equity mix, and its interest rate and ROE goal may be different, as well as its income tax situation.

A Last Comment on "Capital Budgeting"

In theory, a business should assemble all its possible investment opportunities, compare them all, and rank order them according to their return on investment rates, in particular ROE. The business should select the one with the highest ROE first, and so on. In allocating scarce capital among competing investment opportunities, ROE is the key criterion. According to this view of the world, the job of the business manager is to ration scarce capital among competing investment alternatives.

From the point of view of rationing scarce capital resources, you can see why the general topic of capital investment analysis is sometimes called *capital budgeting*. The term "budgeting" here is used more in its allocation or apportionment sense, not in the overall sense of business management planning, and goal setting. I have not used the term *capital budgeting*. This chapter focuses on the techniques of analysis for capital investment analysis.

We have not examined the comparative analysis of two or more capital investments when there is not enough capital available to pursue all the investments that promise a ROE higher than the company's hurdle rate. The comparative analysis of competing investment alternatives is beyond the scope of this book. Corporate finance books cover this topic in some depth.

Summary

Business managers make many long-term capital investment decisions. Their analysis hinges on the cost of capital requirements of the business, which is determined by the company's mix of debt and equity capital, the cost of each, and the income tax situation of the business. The cost of equity capital is not a contractual rate like interest. The ROE goal and objective of the business must be determined by top management.

Given the benchmark ROE goal of the business, the manager should put the projected future returns from an investment to the cost of capital test. Alternatively, starting with the entry cost of the investment, the manager can determine how much the future returns would have to be to satisfy the ROE goal of the business. Then the manager has to judge whether these future returns can be actually achieved.

This chapter explains in a practical and straightforward manner how to apply the cost of capital imperatives of a business to capital investment decisions. A computer spreadsheet program is an excellent tool of analysis. The versatility of computer spreadsheet programs today makes them very powerful.

Analysis is important, to be sure. But we should not get carried away with it. More important is the ability of managers to find good capital investment opportunities and blend them into the overall strategic plan of the business.

Appendix: Supplemental Exhibits for Chapter 18

EXHIBIT A1   EXACT ROE FOR CASH REGISTERS CAPITAL INVESTMENT

	Year One	Year Two	Year Three	Year Four	Year Five	Five Year Totals
Cash Returns						
Forecast Labor Cost Savings	$165,000	$165,000	$165,000	$165,000	$165,000	$825,000
Distribution of Cash Returns						
Interest (@ 9% annual interest rate)	$ 18,000	$ 15,234	$ 12,103	$ 8,558	$ 4,544	$ 58,438
Income Tax (see below)	15,980	16,920	17,985	19,190	20,555	$ 90,631
ROE (@ 18.0632% annual ROE rate)	54,190	45,863	36,436	25,763	13,680	
Capital Recovery	76,830	86,983	98,477	111,489	126,221	$500,000

This is the rate solved for in this exhibit.

	Year One	Year Two	Year Three	Year Four	Year Five	Five Year Totals
Capital Balances at Start of Year						
Debt (2/5 of Total Capital)	$200,000	$169,268	$134,475	$ 95,084	$ 50,488	
Equity (3/5 of Total Capital)	300,000	253,902	201,712	142,626	75,733	
Total Capital Invested in Assets	$500,000	$423,170	$336,187	$237,710	$126,221	

Total capital recovery exactly equals the entry cost, or the initial capital invested. Thus, the amount taken out each year for net income based on the annual 18.0632% ROE is precisely correct.

	Year One	Year Two	Year Three	Year Four	Year Five	Five Year Totals
Income Tax Computation						
Operating Profit Increase	$165,000	$165,000	$165,000	$165,000	$165,000	$825,000
Depreciation Expense (straight-line)	100,000	100,000	100,000	100,000	100,000	$500,000
Interest Expense (see above)	18,000	15,234	12,103	8,558	4,544	$ 58,438
Taxable Income	$ 47,000	$ 49,766	$ 52,897	$ 56,442	$ 60,456	
Income Tax @ 34% (entered above)	$ 15,980	$ 16,920	$ 17,985	$ 19,190	$ 20,555	$ 90,631

These are audit totals, to check that total cash returns equal total revenue for income tax, total depreciation equals cost of assets, total interest deductions equals total interest on debt, and so on.

EXHIBIT A2 INCREASING YEAR-TO-YEAR RETURNS FOR CASH REGISTERS CAPITAL INVESTMENT

	Year One	Year Two	Year Three	Year Four	Year Five	Five Year Totals
Cash Returns						
Forecast Labor Cost Savings	$135,000	$145,000	$155,000	$165,500	$190,435	$790,935
Distribution of Cash Returns						
Interest (@ 9% annual interest rate)	$ 18,000	$ 15,616	$ 12,723	$ 9,264	$ 5,162	$ 60,765
Income Tax (see below)	5,780	9,991	14,374	19,120	28,993	$ 78,258
ROE (@ 15% annual ROE rate)	45,000	39,040	31,808	23,160	12,904	
Capital Recovery	66,220	80,353	96,094	113,956	143,377	$500,000
Capital Balances at Start of Year						
Debt (2/5 of Total Capital)	$200,000	$173,512	$141,371	$102,933	$ 57,351	
Equity (3/5 of Total Capital)	300,000	260,268	212,056	154,400	86,026	
Total Capital Invested in Assets	$500,000	$433,780	$353,427	$257,333	$143,377	

> Total capital recovery exactly equals the entry cost, or the initial capital invested. Thus, the amount taken out each year for ROE net income based on the annual 15% rate is precisely correct.

Income Tax Computation						
Operating Profit Increase	$135,000	$145,000	$155,000	$165,500	$190,435	$790,935
Depreciation Expense (straight-line)	100,000	100,000	100,000	100,000	100,000	$500,000
Interest Expense (see above)	18,000	15,616	12,723	9,264	5,162	$ 60,765
Taxable Income	$ 17,000	$ 29,384	$ 42,277	$ 56,236	$ 85,273	
Income Tax @ 34% (entered above)	$ 5,780	$ 9,991	$ 14,374	$ 19,120	$ 28,993	$ 78,258

These are audit totals, to check that total cash returns equal total revenue for income tax, total depreciation equals cost of assets, total interest deductions equals total interest on debt, and so on.

19

EVALUATING CAPITAL INVESTMENT RETURNS

Time Value of Money and Cost of Capital

The one pivotal idea behind this and the previous chapter is the *time value of money*. This term does not refer just to money but to *capital* or economic wealth in general. Capital should generate an income, or gain, or benefit, or profit over the time it is used. Karl Marx said that capital is "dead labor" and argued that capital should be publicly owned for the good of everyone. We won't pursue this economic philosophy any further. Quite clearly, in our economic system, capital does have a time value, or rather a time cost, depending on whose shoes you're standing in.

The time value of money is measured by the rate of return, or earnings, or gain on the capital invested. The time cost of money for a business is determined by its *capitalization structure*, which refers to the sources and mix of its capital, the cost of each source, and the income tax rate. The example company in the last chapter has the following capitalization structure:

Capitalization Structure and
Cost of Capital Assumptions

- 2 to 3 debt to equity mix
- 9% annual interest rate on debt
- 34% income tax rate
- 15% annual ROE objective

For a $100,000 block of capital invested in its net operating assets, how much operating earnings should the company make before interest and income tax? This is the idea of the cost of capital–the minimum amount of operating earnings necessary to cover interest on its debt, its income tax, and the return on equity (ROE) goal of the business. Using a $100,000 block of capital makes the calculations easier to follow.

Given its debt to equity ratio, the company's $100,000 capital comes from $40,000 debt and $60,000 equity. The annual interest cost on the debt is $3,600: $40,000 debt × 9% interest rate. The business needs $3,600 operating earnings to pay the interest, but no more than this because interest is deductible for income tax. In other words, the $3,600 operating earnings would be offset with an equal amount of interest deduction, so that the company's taxable income is zero. The cost of equity capital is a different matter.

For $60,000 equity capital, the company needs to earn $9,000 net income: $60,000 equity × 15% ROE = $9,000. To earn $9,000 net income after income tax, the company needs to earn $13,636 operating earnings before income tax: $9,000 ÷ .66. The .66 is the after-tax keep; for every $1.00 of taxable income, the company keeps only 66¢ because the income tax rate is 34%. On $13,636 earnings the income tax is $4,636, which leaves $9,000 net income after tax.

The key difference between interest on debt and net income on equity is that for each $1.00 of operating earnings, the company can pay $1.00 of interest to its debt sources of capital. But for each $1.00 of operating earnings, the company can "pay" only 66¢ of net income to its equity owners. Alternatively, on a before-tax basis, a business needs to earn just $1.00 of operating earnings to cover $1.00 of interest expense. But it needs to earn $1.52 to end up with $1.00 net income, because income tax takes out 52¢.

In total the company needs $17,236 in annual operating earnings on $100,000 capital ($3,600 interest plus $13,636 net income before income tax). The company's annual pretax cost of capital rate is therefore 17.236%: $17,236 ÷ $100,000. The business should strive to meet or exceed this return on assets (ROA) benchmark to justify the capital it is using. We can use this cost of capital rate in the following equation:

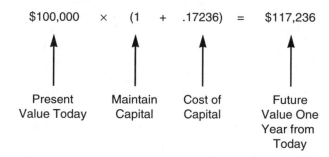

$$\$100,000 \times (1 + .17236) = \$117,236$$

| Present Value Today | Maintain Capital | Cost of Capital | Future Value One Year from Today |

Notice the terms under each factor in the equation. Present value means the amount of capital at the start of the period, and future value means the amount of capital at the end of the period. If the company laid out $100,000 cash at the start of the year and ended up with $117,236 cash at the end of the year, it would earn just enough to pay interest, income tax, and earn net income to make its ROE.

The company must preserve the initial capital invested, which is the 1 inside the parentheses; the amount of initial capital invested has to be maintained. In order to make a profit the entry cost, or initial amount of capital invested, has to be recov-

ered. The 1 plus the cost of capital rate gives 1.17236 which is the ratio between the present value and the future value.

To generalize, we use the following equation:

$$PV \times (1 + r) = FV$$

where

PV = present value, or entry cost of the investment today
r = company's annual cost of capital rate for the period
FV = future value, or terminal value of the investment at the end of the period

The equation goes from left to right; knowing the entry cost (PV) and the cost of capital rate we move across the equal sign to determine the amount of capital needed one year later (FV). I'm sure you see that we can flip PV and FV around. If we know the FV and r (cost of capital rate) we can solve for PV as follows:

$$FV \div (1 + r) = PV$$

Now suppose the business had an investment opportunity that would generate a value of $175,855 one year from today before income tax. What is the PV of this investment? That is, what is the amount the company should be willing to invest today and earn its cost of capital rate? To determine the PV amount, we plug in the numbers and solve the equation as follows:

$$\$175,855 \div (1 + .17236) = \$150,000$$

To check this answer we can prepare the following mini-income statement, keeping in mind that to finance this investment the company would use $60,000 debt ($150,000 × 2/5) and $90,000 equity ($150,000 × 3/5):

Mini-Income Statement to Check Equation Answer

Future Value One Year from Now	$175,855	
Less Present Value Today	150,000	
Operating Earnings from Investment		$25,855
Interest on Debt: $60,000 @ 9% =		5,400
Taxable Income		$20,455
Income Tax @ 34%		6,955
Net Income: $90,000 @ 15% =		$13,500

As you see everything checks out. If the company invested $150,000 it would earn exactly its cost of capital rate. If the company could enter the investment for less than $150,000 it would realize a ROE rate greater than 15%.

You've probably noticed that to this point I have limited the discussion to a one-year investment. The equation for the multiyear case requires more mathematics, which I've wanted to avoid to make sure you understand the basic idea of the cost of capital without getting bogged down in the math. But, you may ask, didn't we analyze a five-year investment for the cash registers example in the last chapter? Yes we did, but we did it with the spreadsheet tool of analysis, not equations.

Spreadsheets Versus Equations

To do the analysis in Chapter 18, I used a popular personal computer spreadsheet program. Spreadsheet programs are very versatile. Different scenarios can be examined quickly and efficiently, which is an enormous advantage. In most practical business capital investment situations, several critical assumptions and forecasts must be made, and the manager is well advised to test the sensitivity of each critical input factor.

Even if you are not a regular spreadsheet user, the logic and layout of the printout is important to understand. With spreadsheets it is easy to present all relevant information—both for the management decision-making analysis phase and for management control follow-through after a decision is made. The year-by-year formats shown in the exhibits in Chapter 18 are good illustrations of this. The columns for each year provide essential benchmark information for monitoring and controlling the actual results of the investment as it plays out year by year. In short, spreadsheets are a very useful tool for analysis and presentation of information.

Another reason for using the spreadsheet approach in the previous chapter is to avoid mathematical-based methods to analyze capital investments. In Chapter 18, not one mathematical equation was presented, and so far in this chapter only one equation has been presented. In my experience, managers are put off by a heavy-handed mathematical approach loaded with arcane equations and unfamiliar symbols.

Before spreadsheets were available, certain mathematical tools and techniques were developed to evaluate the series of cash returns from a capital investment. These techniques have become the touchstone for capital investment analysis. The names of these mathematical equations and techniques have become household words and the terms are used freely in the business and financial world. You should know what the terms mean and how they are applied.

The remainder of this chapter presents a quick tour of the elementary mathematical techniques for capital investment analysis. To the extent possible, an intuitive approach is relied on without going into all the computational equations, which are of little interest to business managers. Basically the techniques are just another way to skin the cat, compared with the spreadsheet approach used in Chapter 18.

Discounted Cash Flow (DCF)

The basic capital investment analysis equation is the following:

$$FV \div (1 + r)^n = PV$$

The terms are the same as before; what's new here is the n factor, the exponent on the $(1 + r)$ factor in the equation. Most capital investments are for more than one period and n is the number of periods. The previous discussion in the chapter is for the $n = 1$ case, that is, for one-period capital investments.

The equation method is used when the future returns from an investment are known or can be predicted fairly accurately. The purpose is to determine the present value of the investment, which is the maximum amount the business should invest today in exchange for the future returns.

The r factor in the equation, as before, is the cost of capital rate. The n and r in the equation must be for the same time interval; in other words, r is the rate for one period of time. For the moment I will be a little vague about the cost of capital rate being used to deliberately postpone the discussion on this point.

For now, our concern is how to get from one period to the next period. Moving from one period to the next involves either *compounding* of capital or *recovery* of capital, both of which are extraordinarily important concepts to understand. To illustrate the compounding and recovery of capital we now shift to a rounded-off cost of capital rate. Don't worry; later we'll return to the company's precise cost of capital rate. The cost of capital rate, or r in the equation, is now set at 18% per year. Keep this rate in mind.

Assume a business has identified a capital investment opportunity that would require a $100,000 entry cost today and that promises two $63,872 future cash returns, the first to be received one year from today and the second two years from today. Two present values can be computed and added to compute the total present value of the investment as follows:

$$\$63,872 \div (1 + .18)^1 = \$\ 54,128$$
$$\$63,872 \div (1 + .18)^2 = \$\ 45,872$$
$$\text{Total Present Value} = \underline{\$100,000}$$

A financial calculator was used to compute the PV of each of the two future returns. As you see, total PV is exactly $100,000, which is the entry cost of the investment. From the cost of capital investment point of view this is a break-even investment opportunity; the business would earn its cost of capital rate, but no more.

Computing present value in the manner just shown is called *discounting* the future cash flow, or the *discounted cash flow*

(DCF) method. The required cost of capital rate is used to discount, or to take out from the future cash returns, the amounts needed to cover the cost of capital requirements on the investment, leaving the capital recovered from the investment. In other words, present value is the amount of capital recovered from the investment after deducting the amount of earnings required to cover the company's cost of capital.

The DCF technique is correct, but it has one serious problem; well, actually two problems I should say—one not so serious and one very serious. The not-so-serious problem concerns how to do these computations. The solution is to use a hand-held business/financial calculator; such calculators are very powerful, relatively cheap, and easy to use. (However, you do have to know which keys to use for entering each factor in the equation.) The second problem is much more serious and has nothing to do with making the computations to determine PV, but rather with the lack of computations and of information from using the DCF technique.

The unfolding of the investment over the two years is not clear from the PV calculation we just did. Rather than opening up the investment for closer inspection, the PV computation closes it down and telescopes the information into one number. The method doesn't reveal important information about the investment over its life. Exhibit 19.1 presents a more complete look at the investment.

Exhibit 19.1 shows that the cash return at the end of year one is divided $18,000 to earnings for cost of capital and $45,872 to capital recovery. The capital recovery aspect of the investment is extremely important to understand. The capital recovery portion of the cash return at the end of the first year reduces the amount of capital invested during the second year.

EXHIBIT 19.1   CAPITAL RECOVERY EXAMPLE

Capital Investment at Start of Year	Year	Cash Return End of Year	Cost of Capital Earnings at 18%	Capital Recovered
→$100,000	1	$63,872	$18,000	$ 45,872
$ 54,128	2	$63,872	$ 9,743	$ 54,128
				$100,000

Only $54,128 is invested during the second year: $100,000 − $45,872 = $54,128. Most business capital investments are self-liquidating over the life of the investment; there is some capital recovery each period, as in this example. Notice that the total capital recovery over the entire life of the investment equals the initial capital invested. This proves that the earnings rate is 18% per year.

Managers should anticipate what to do with the $45,872 capital recovery at the end of the first year. (For that matter, managers should also plan what to do with the net income.) Will the capital be reinvested? In which specific new investment? In particular, will the business be able to reinvest the $45,872 to earn its 18% cost of capital? Maybe not. This concept is called the *reinvestment risk*. To gauge this risk and to budget ahead for the capital recovery flow from the investment, managers need the information presented in Exhibit

19.1 that tracks the earnings and capital recovery year by year. The DCF technique does not generate this information.

The opposite of capital recovery is the *compounding* of capital. We change to a different investment example to illustrate compounding. Suppose at the end of the first year there is no cash return; only one cash return is received at the end of the second year in the amount of $139,240. The present value equation in this case is as follows:

$$\$139,240 \div (1 + .18)^2 = \$100,000$$

The main difference is that there are two periods of waiting to get to the cash return from the investment. However, notice that PV equals the $100,000 entry cost of the investment, as the first example.

The company had $100,000 invested during year one and earned $18,000 for the year, but it did not receive a cash return at the end of the first year. No problem; it is still counted as earnings. Exhibit 19.2 shows how this investment unfolds over the two years.

The $18,000 amount earned but not received for the first year is compounded, which means it is added into the capital investment balance at the start of the second year. For the second year, the 18% cost of capital is based on the higher investment balance–see Exhibit 19.2. The capital recovery column shows a negative amount for year one, which means that the earnings for the year are not available for withdrawal from the investment and therefore have to be reinvested during the second year.

It's as if the company received the $18,000 earnings at the end of the first year but immediately had to turn around and put the money back into the investment to keep it going. In

EXHIBIT 19.2   CAPITAL COMPOUNDING EXAMPLE

Capital Investment at Start of Year	Year	Cash Return at End of Year	Cost of Capital Earnings at 18%	Capital Recovered (Compounded)
$100,000	1	$ 0	$18,000	($ 18,000)
$118,000	2	$139,240	$21,240	$118,000
				$100,000

comparing Exhibits 19.1 and 19.2, you can see that capital compounding is the reverse of capital recovery. There is no reinvestment risk in this situation since the 18% rate applies on the amount reinvested.

Compound interest is commonly used to describe the reinvestment of earnings, although the term *interest* is too restrictive. The term actually refers to earnings in general and not just interest income. Compound interest (earnings) can be compared with Retained Earnings in a company's balance sheet, which is its net income earned but not paid out as dividends and which has been reinvested in the business.

At this point, you might ask which is the better of the two investments? Both earn 18% per year, which is another way of saying both have the same $100,000 present value even though the two patterns of future returns are quite different. If you absolutely had to have some cash flow at the end of the first year, then the second investment example is not for you.

The first investment has more reinvestment risk, as mentioned above; the second one locks in the 18% rate over two years. On the other hand, the first one might have lower risk because the capital is recovered sooner; less capital is at risk during the second year. Clearly, there are many factors to consider that go beyond just the number crunching we have done.

Net Present Value (NPV) and Internal Rate of Return (IRR)

Another example for a two-periods, two future cash returns investment is now introduced to demonstrate two other techniques for capital investment analysis. The entry cost today is $100,000 for the investment, as before. The future cash returns are $54,900 at the end of the first year and $81,862 at the end of the second year. Using the 18% cost of capital rate to discount these two future returns we compute PV as follows:

$$\$54,900 \div (1 + .18)^1 = \$\ 46,525$$
$$\$81,862 \div (1 + .18)^2 = \underline{\$\ 58,792}$$
$$\text{Total Present Value}\ = \$105,317$$

As you can see PV is $5,317 more than the entry cost. This excess is called the *net present value* (NPV); it is the additional amount from the investment over and above the initial capital invested. Net present value is negative when the PV is less than the entry cost of the investment. In this case, NPV is positive and represents additional earnings in excess of the 18% cost of

capital rate. The NPV has informational value, but it is not an ideal measure to compare with other investment opportunities.

Instead, the *internal rate of return* (IRR) can be determined for this investment example. The IRR is that precise discount rate that makes PV exactly equal to the $100,000 entry cost. The IRR is a very useful measure of the investment's performance. Given the $100,000 entry cost today and the two future cash returns, the IRR is 22% which, of course, is higher than the 18% discount rate used to compute the PV.

How did I determine that the IRR is 22%? I used my financial calculator. How does the calculator find the IRR? A trial and error process is used to solve for the IRR—whether you do it with a financial calculator or with a spreadsheet for that matter. The trial and error routine (algorithm) is programmed into calculators and spreadsheet programs. Basically, you start with a feasible discount rate and then the rate is adjusted in the right direction until the answer comes out just right. The electronic process is so fast that you think it's just one computation, but it isn't.

Exhibit 19.3 demonstrates that the IRR for the investment is indeed 22%. This rate is correct because the total capital recovered equals the $100,000 entry cost. To sum up briefly: The company would invest $100,000 today to start the investment. One year later it receives an after-tax return of $54,900. From this return, the company takes out, or discounts 22% which for year one is $22,000. The $32,900 remainder is the capital recovery for year one.

The company's capital investment for the second year is reduced by this capital recovery amount at the end of the first year. So, the company would have only $67,100 invested during

EXHIBIT 19.3   IRR EXAMPLE

Capital Investment at Start of Year	Year	Cash Return at End of Year	Internal Rate of Return at 18%	Capital Recovered (Compounded)
➤$100,000	1	$54,900	$22,000	$ 32,900
$67,100	2	$81,862	$14,762	$ 67,100
				$100,000

the second year. For both years combined, the total capital recovered is exactly $100,000, which is the entry cost. Therefore, the 22% annual rate of earnings (the IRR) is correct.

Businesses should favor investments with higher IRRs in preference to investments with lower IRRs, and should not accept any investment that has an IRR less than the company's hurdle rate, which is its cost of capital rate. Put another way, a business should not accept an investment that has a negative net present value. At least this is the theory.

Capital investment decisions are very complex and involve many nonquantitative or qualitative factors that are difficult to capture in the analysis. A company may go ahead with an investment that has a low IRR because of political pressures or to accomplish social objectives beyond the profit motive. For instance, the company may make a capital investment even if the numbers don't justify the decision in order to forestall competitors from entering its market. A company may make

capital investments to upgrade, automate, or expand because they may languish and eventually die if they don't.

The After-Tax Cost of Capital Rate

To be frank, I have skirted one issue so far in this chapter (although not in Chapter 18)—the impact of income tax. Exhibits 18.1 and 18.2 include the income tax calculation for each year. Income tax is one of the four take-outs from annual cash returns. Spreadsheet programs made it feasible to handle income tax this way.

The traditional equation-based techniques for evaluating capital investments were developed long before personal computer spreadsheet programs became popular. These techniques had to come up with some way to deal with the income tax factor, and they did. I don't think it's all that easy to understand, but the method has become the conventional technique for dealing with the income tax factor. You will encounter this approach and it's important to know it.

Instead of the before-tax cost of capital rate, the traditional methods use an after-tax cost of capital rate. Returning to the example introduced earlier in the chapter, the company's after-tax cost of capital rate is computed as follows:

After-Tax Cost of Capital Rate

Source of Capital	Weight		After-Tax Cost of Capital Rate		
Debt:	2/5	×	(9%)(1 - 34%)	=	2.376%
Equity:	3/5	×	15%	=	9.000%
After-tax cost of capital				=	11.376%

If we compute the before-tax cost of capital rate in this manner, it would be as follows:

Before-Tax Cost of Capital Rate

Source of Capital	Weight	Before-Tax Cost of Capital Rate	
Debt:	2/5 ×	9%	= 3.600%
Equity:	3/5 ×	(15%)/(1 − 34%)	= 13.636%
Before-tax cost of capital			= 17.236%

We know that this before-tax rate is correct. We already tested it in one example earlier in the chapter. To be doubly sure, however, let's test it here on another example.

Suppose the company could invest $100,000 today and one year later it could cash-out the investment for $117,236 before income tax and interest (and of course before net income). Notice that the $100,000 present value is multiplied by (1 + .17236) to determine the $117,236 future value. The following mini-income statement is presented in the same manner as before:

Mini-Income Statement to Check
17.236% Pretax Cost of Capital Rate

Future Value One Year from Now	$117,236	
Less Present Value Today	100,000	
Operating Earnings from Investment		$17,236
Interest on Debt: $40,000 @ 9% =		3,600
Taxable Income		$13,636
Income Tax @ 34%		4,636
Net Income: $60,000 @ 15% =		$ 9,000

Interest is paid on debt, income tax is taken out, and net income equals 15% of owners' equity. Thus, the pre-tax cost of capital rate is correct.

Now, suppose we were to do the following: The gross return is $117,236. If all of this income were taxable, then the after-tax return would be $77,376, after taking out 34% for income tax. But wait a minute; isn't the $100,000 entry cost of the investment deductible? Yes, of course it is. As such, we have to recognize the income tax benefit of this deduction: $100,000 deductible cost × 34% = $34,000. The after-tax return of $77,376 added with the $34,000 tax benefit gives a total of $111,376.

Take a second look at this amount. Notice that it's (1 + .11376) times the $100,000 PV of the investment. The after-tax cost of capital rate is .11376, or 11.376%. If we take the $111,376 FV and compute its PV based on the company's after-tax cost of capital rate we get the following:

$$\$111,376 \div (1 + .11376) = \$100,000$$

As you see, the present value of the investment is $100,000 using the after-tax cost of capital discount rate, thus, this rate is correct. To be more precise, the after-tax cost of capital rate is the correct discount rate to use if, and only if, the after-tax returns on the investment are calculated as just explained.

This method of analysis may not seem like a very good way to compute the present value of an investment. However, this method in fact is a practical way of discounting a series of future before-tax cash returns from an investment. It may not be very obvious, but it works rather neatly. One can handle a fairly large number of future before-tax returns from an investment with no more than a hand-held financial calculator.

Although the method works well, it has one rather unfortunate side effect. Please refer back to the calculation of the after-tax cost of capital rate on page 213. In particular, notice that the 9% interest rate is multiplied by (1 – 34% income tax rate) to put it on an after-tax basis: 9% × (1 – 34%) = 5.94%. This after-tax interest rate is then multiplied by the debt weight of the company's total capitalization.

The danger is that managers and investors tend to think that the "real" cost of interest is the 5.94% after-tax rate instead of the 9% before-tax rate. This is a very misleading way to look at the cost of interest. As explained many times before, the cost of interest to a business is how much operating earnings it has to earn on its debt to pay the interest. Clearly, the business has to earn 9% operating earnings on the amount of its debt capital; earning only 5.94% would not be enough.

A good example to demonstrate how the after-tax cost of capital rate is used is the one discussed in the previous chapter—the investment in the new cash registers. Recall that the entry cost of the investment is $500,000 and the minimal required annual labor cost savings (the annual cash returns on the investment) are $155,405 (see Exhibit 18.2). Remember that the company's after-tax cost of capital rate is 11.376%. Two steps are required by the after-tax cost of capital discount rate method.

STEP ONE

The before-tax cash returns from the investment are taxed at 34%. This step ignores the depreciation deduction, which is taken into account in the second step. Interest is also deductible, so this step also overstates income tax, but this is adjusted for by putting the interest rate on the after-tax basis.

Year	Before-Tax Returns	Less Tax @ 34%	After-Tax Returns
1	$155,405	$52,838	$102,567
2	$155,405	$52,838	$102,567
3	$155,405	$52,838	$102,567
4	$155,405	$52,838	$102,567
5	$155,405	$52,838	$102,567
Present Value @ 11.376% Discount Rate			$375,519*

This step provides only part of the total answer; income tax is overstated because the depreciation deduction has not yet been considered, which is done in the second step.

*You can solve for this amount on a financial calculator by entering N = 5, PMT = $102,567, INT = 11.376%, and then pushing the PV key. Make sure that the calculation is set for end-of-period payments and that the ending value (FV) is set equal to $-0-. The FV key is used to enter the terminal value of the investment. Computer spreadsheet programs include the PV, as well as many other financial functions.

STEP TWO

The present value of the depreciation so-called tax savings is computed. In this example, the straight-line depreciation method is used, so the company deducts $100,000 depreciation each year, which reduces taxable income and thus income tax $34,000 each year: $100,000 × 34% tax rate = $34,000.

Year	Depreciation	Tax Savings @ 34%
1	$100,000	$ 34,000
2	$100,000	$ 34,000
3	$100,000	$ 34,000
4	$100,000	$ 34,000
5	$100,000	$ 34,000
Present Value @ 11.376% Discount Rate		$124,481

Adding together the two present values gives $500,000: $375,519 + $124,481 = $500,000. The $500,000 present value exactly equals the entry cost of the investment. In other words, the company would earn exactly its cost of capital, which is also shown in Exhibit 18.2.

If the company could buy the cash registers for less than $500,000, it would make a higher ROE (assuming the interest rate remains the same). One advantage of the spreadsheet method is that the ROE can be solved for, which is much more difficult by the traditional DCF method. As you have probably surmised, I favor the spreadsheet approach because it offers more versatility and more information for capital investment analysis. The spreadsheet approach is also more intuitive and straightforward, both of which are very important features.

Regarding Cost of Capital Parameters

A few brief comments are offered here on the cost of capital parameters. Most discourses on business capital investment analysis assume a constant mix or ratio of debt and equity, and the cost of each source of capital, as well as the income tax rate, is held constant. Before spreadsheets came along, there were very practical reasons for this, usually to avoid using more than one cost of capital rate in the analysis. Today these constraints are no longer necessary.

If the situation calls for it, the manager should change the ratio of debt and equity from one period to the next or change the interest rate and/or ROE rate from period to period. In other words, each period could be assigned its own cost of capital rate. Sometimes this is necessary in the analysis. For instance, a capital investment may be of a *direct financing* variety, in which a specific loan is secured that is tied to this one, and only one, investment.

One example of direct financing is when a business leases its products instead of selling them. The assets being leased may be used as collateral for borrowing on the assets leased out. The business commits to a definite payoff schedule on the loan. The mix of debt and equity capital invested in the lease will differ period to period in this case. Furthermore, the interest rate on the lease loan, as well as the ROE goal for the lease investment, may be quite different as compared with the company's main line of business.

Summary

The time value of money, or to be more precise, the time cost of money, bears down heavily on business entities who are users of capital. A business should carefully evaluate every capital investment being considered to test whether the investment promises to yield operating earnings that can cover its cost of capital.

This chapter presents a succinct survey of basic mathematical techniques for analyzing business capital investments. The broad generic name for this equation based set of tools is *discounted cash flow* (DCF). A series of future cash returns is discounted to calculate the present value (PV) or the net present value (NPV) of the investment. Alternatively, the internal rate of return (IRR) that the future returns would yield is determined and the IRR is compared against the company's cost of capital rate.

If I had to go with one or the other, I certainly would choose spreadsheets for analyzing capital investments over the DCF equation-based methods. Spreadsheets are more versatile, easier to follow, and make it easy to display all information relevant to management decision making and control, which is more than you can say about the DCF methods.

INDEX

Statement of financial condition, *see* Balance sheet
Stockholders' equity, *see* Owners' equity
Sunk costs, 131–132

Tax accounting, 12
Time value of money, 206

Total quality management (TQM), 110, 148, 186
Tracy, John A., 89 *fn.*
Tracy, Tage, 40
Trade credit, 30, 118; *see also* Accounts payable
Trade-offs, 128, 155–156, 170–171, 174

Trading on the equity, *see* Financial leverage

Variable expenses, *see* Sales-revenue-driven expenses; Sales-volume-driven expenses